Forbidden Orphanage

OUTSIDE THE FORBIDDEN CITY

Becky Cerling Powers

FLARE BOOKS

Forbidden Orphanage

OUTSIDE THE FORBIDDEN CITY

Becky Cerling Powers

FLARE BOOKS

Flare Books, El Paso, Texas

Forbidden Orphanage Outside the Forbidden City

Published by Flare Books
www.catalystpress.org

FIRST EDITION

ISBN 9781963511260

Library of Congress Control Number: 2025936336
Library of Congress subject headings:
Richards, Laura, 1893-1981
Orphans – China – 20th Century
China – History – 20th Century
Missionaries, medical – China – Biography

Interior design by Vicki Trego Hill of El Paso, Texas

Cover design and illustration by Karen Vermeulen,
https://www.karenvermeulen.com

FRONTISPIECE: Laura May Richards, b. February 25, 1893, d. April 22, 1981. This is probably the portrait taken for Laura's 1911 high school graduation at age 18 in the small farming community of Sidney, Ohio.

Original group of five orphan baby girls. Left to right, Lydia (nicknamed Foreign Doll), Charity, Rachel, Rose Mary, and Sarah.

Contents

TO THE CHILDREN *of Canaan Home Orphanage*
and their families

Author's Note

Forbidden Orphanage Outside the Forbidden City is a nonfiction work based on old letters, published accounts, eyewitness interviews, and historical research. Detailed information about sources is provided in Endnotes published at **www.beckypowers.com**. Chinese names are written in traditional Chinese fashion, surname first. Names have also been changed to protect individuals and/or their family members who still live in the People's Republic of China, with a few exceptions such as easily identifiable people like Nieh Shou Guang and Wang Ming Dao.

The modern names for Chinese cities mentioned in the text are as follows: Paotingfu is modern day Baoding, Peking is Beijing, Tientsin is Tianjin, and Shuntefu is Xingtai. I chose to use the place names as Laura used them rather than modern names, with one exception. From 1928 to 1949, Peking was called Peiping. I use the name Peking throughout to avoid confusion.

Foreword

LAURA MAY RICHARDS was my grandmother. She raised my mother and aunt as two of her adopted daughters in the Canaan Home orphanage in China. My mother came into the orphanage when she was eight years old, right after her father prematurely died in 1939. That was two years after the Japanese invaded Beijing and began occupying China. My mom called Laura "Mama."

After Pearl Harbor Day in December 1941, Laura's volunteer staff had to leave because, if Chinese people helped an American in occupied China, Japanese soldiers might kill them or their families. There were over one hundred children in the orphanage. Many were babies or toddlers. Some had severe disabilities. Without the volunteer helpers, the children had to do the work chores. When the children's socks or clothes got holes, my mom and older kids would mend the clothes and socks with Laura.

The Japanese soldiers confiscated the farmers' harvests, causing a famine. Many people died, and the orphanage often ran out of food. The children would pray, and then someone would send money or bring food. Because of Laura's leadership, dedication, faith, and incredibly hard work, all the children survived.

I grew up hearing stories about Laura and the orphanage not only from my mom, but also from my aunt (another Canaan Home child) and from all the orphans who came to visit them. I really badly wanted to know the whole story about the orphans. Laura and Canaan Home stories became part of my life.

My mom took English classes and learned some English at Canaan Home. When I was growing up, she taught me some English. I decided I wanted to learn the English language, so I studied very hard. Eventually I was able to start working for General Electric, an American company in Beijing. I met an American gentleman through the work, who became my husband later, and I came to America to live.

One day I got a phone call from Ruth, a friend of my mom's, who used to be a Sunday School teacher for Canaan Home. Ruth came to the States because her mother was an American. She told me that Laura's relative, an American woman, was writing the story of the Canaan Home orphanage. Through her, I connected with Becky Cerling Powers. We started talking on the phone, and I told Becky that I would like to translate her book free of charge into Chinese, although I was very naive, for I had never translated a book before. For twenty six days, I couldn't get the first chapter translated, even though I felt that I could recite the entire chapter. But after I struggled twenty six days, suddenly the Chinese translations came out of me like a flood. Other people may use their skills or education to translate books, but I used my heart. I relived Laura's life during the translation work.

Translating the story built up my faith in God, helping me in my marriage and in raising my son and my two stepchildren.

One day Becky and I had a sharp argument about publishing certain details in the book. It made me stop my translation work. Ruth told Becky to go to China with me and visit the former orphans in China. Becky went with me and visited my mom and the orphans in Beijing. Our reunion was such a precious time!

Laura Richards saved the lives of my mother, my aunt, and around 200 other orphans. Without Laura Richards, neither my brother nor I nor my cousins would even exist. Our children would not exist either. And neither would many, many other people, for three to four generations. Not only did Laura Richards save many children's lives, she also truly brought us hope.

I was honored to receive a Hall of Fame award on behalf of Laura exactly 100 years after Laura graduated from from her Sydney, Ohio high school. When I stood on her school platform, I knew my God is faithful and mighty, who always works out everything for the people who love Him! I love God, I love Laura. Even though I did not have a chance to meet Laura in person, we are all connected through the love of God!

Laura is my hero forever! She was ordinary, but she lived an extraordinary life and impacted many souls. That's the reason today, I am a soul winner, I wanted to carry Laura's baton and continue to bring the love of God, HIS salvation to people everywhere I go.

—Sherry Lucas

Sherry Lucas, retired Subsea Engineering Quality Assurance Leader for a global company in Houston

Sherry Lucas uses a pseudonym to protect relatives inside China and to avoid political backlash while traveling.

Prologue

In later years, Laura said it was the beggar women of Paotingfu who set her feet on the pathway that led to the founding of Canaan Home and all the adventures and stories that followed. But Laura Richards was a woman of action, not words. All that she did, she accomplished quietly, without fanfare, and often without keeping records.

Had it not been for Laura's friend Florence Logan, hardly any of the story of Canaan Home would have been recorded. True, Laura did write several detailed letters about the first children she rescued from 1929 to 1936. After that, though, she became too busy to write. Since Florence felt that the story of Canaan Home should be told while it was happening, she occasionally squeezed time out of her own busy schedule to record unfolding events. Fortunately Laura wrote a few memoirs several years before she died as well, finally breaking her long silence about the Chinese Communists' attempts to take over Canaan Home. In addition, after Laura's death, two of her grown Canaan Home children wrote their own long memoirs. Their recollections filled in details of the middle of the story, which Florence had been unable to record while she was imprisoned by the Japanese and then repatriated to the U.S. during World War II.

In this way, most of the following story was recorded in detail except for the beginning—the account of how Laura left Paotingfu and the Presbyterian Mission. Laura wrote only briefly about her encounters with the Paotingfu beggars and her decision to leave the Presbyterian Mission to begin Canaan Home. So it was left to the author to research the background of Canaan Home's beginning through various written histories as well as personal interviews with friends who knew Laura during her stay in Paotingfu.

It may have begun like this....

1

The Beggar Women of Paotingfu

Paotingfu, 1925

IT WAS THE SPRING OF 1925 after the harvests had failed, and crowds of villagers—normally self-sufficient farmers and craftsmen—trekked into Paotingfu daily from the countryside, seeking food. Beggars flowed like tears upon the face of the earth, trailing along the road that led from the wall of the city to the railroad station. They pooled in a broad puddle of misery before the Temple of the Fire God, where Jesus followers from the Presbyterian Church had set up a soup kitchen for the hungry.

Nearby, above the great carved gate of the Presbyterian Mission compound, huge painted Chinese characters proclaimed the words "Good News Park." Had these illiterate villager-beggars been able to read the symbols, they would have judged the sign accurate. The Jesus followers who lived in this compound provided good news in times of trouble—a refuge to which they could flee when the warlords were battling, and food to fill their bellies when famine struck. Besides that, the foreign missionaries provided medical care at two hospitals located on the compound, strictly segregated by sex in accordance with Chinese custom. All the nurses and doctors in the women's hospital were female; all those in the men's hospital were male. Both hospitals provided training for Chinese youth to become nurses and doctors.

Many educated Chinese, however, saw the "Good News Park" sign differently. To them, the presence of the sign on that particular gate represented bad news—the humiliating news that glorious China, father of culture, had grown so weak that Westerners could thumb their noses at Chinese sovereignty. The "unequal treaties" that China had been forced to sign gave foreigners living on this compound immunity to Chinese law. Behind these walls Westerners could practice their foreign medicine, preach their foreign doctrines, and teach their foreign ideas to Chinese children, all beyond the control of the Chinese government. Mission schools in particular infuriated Chinese political sloganeers. Why were the schools in this Presbyterian Mission compound run by foreigners? Chinese should be in charge of educating Chinese youth.

Miss Laura May Richards, superintendent of nurses at the women's hospital, knew nothing about this when she applied to the Presbyterian Board of Missions to go to China. She had arrived four years before, dreaming dreams...that her hands would bring life to people's bodies through her work as a nurse...that her words would bring life to people's souls. It had been a painful shock to find out that politically aware Chinese regarded her as an enemy of their people.

She had arrived in 1921—twenty-eight years old, the quiet daughter of an Ohio farmer, a petite woman with light brown hair and eyes, slightly prominent teeth and a wide mouth, made for smiling. After a year of language school, the Presbyterian Mission assigned her to serve as superintendent of nurses at Hodge Memorial Hospital for Women in Paotingfu. There her primary duty was to direct a school for nurses, which placed her squarely in the category of politically resented foreigner, teaching Western ideas to Chinese youth. But China was short on Western-trained nurses and doctors. She set to work preparing young Chinese women to become competent medical professionals.

One of her nursing students was threading her way through the crowds of beggars massed at the entrance to the soup kitchen near the mission gate. Miss Lin had spent the night visiting her family in the city, and she was dressed in her off-duty attire—cloth shoes and a wadded gown and pajamas to ward off the chill of early spring. She exchanged polite greetings with the gatekeeper seated before the ornate, turreted gate of the Presbyterian mission compound.

"Incline your eyes toward that woman by the wall," he suggested respectfully. He jerked his chin in the direction of a listless beggar squatting a dozen yards away. A begging bowl and pointed stave lay at her feet, and she shivered in a blue summer gown.

Miss Lin walked over, noting with concern the young peasant's dull hair, skinny arms, and great, bulging stomach. "Honored lady, I am Miss Lin, a student nurse from the mission hospital for women," she introduced herself. "Is something troubling you?"

Slowly the woman lifted her head. She appeared dazed. "My time has come," she mumbled. She tried to rise and started to topple.

"Ai ya!" Miss Lin exclaimed, stooping to help her. "You must come inside to the hospital to deliver this child. Allow me to assist you."

She led the beggar through the mission gate.

"Her name is Autumn Leaf," Miss Lin told Laura when the pair arrived, "and her bag of waters has already broken. We can save her and the baby, can't we?"

Laura smiled, then turned to look directly into the beggar woman's weeping eyes. "Jesus cares what happens to you and your baby," she said, "and so do we. We will pray hard and do everything we can to give you a safe delivery."

Laura was unsure how hopeful she could be. Autumn Leaf was young, only a teenager, it looked like, and most likely this was her first baby. She was thin, pale, probably anemic—definitely malnourished. That meant potential complications for both mother and baby.

Laura and Miss Lin led Autumn Leaf to a room to be examined by Dr. Maud A. Mackey, director of the women's hospital. Dr. Mackey was a round, motherly little woman who reminded Laura of a fur-lined boot—as soft and comforting as she was tough and practical.

The doctor asked Autumn Leaf if she had eaten that day. She said no, but she had been eating millet porridge for the last few days at the soup kitchen. That, at least, was good news. The young peasant sobbed throughout her interview with Dr. Mackey, which surprised Laura. It was normal for American women in labor to moan and complain, cry loudly and make demands. But Chinese women were normally stoical, tearless, undemanding, and silent until their baby's head popped out. Then they let out a good scream and delivered their child into the world.

Dr. Mackey examined Autumn Leaf. "She is nearly ready," the round little doctor announced.

Ten minutes later Dr. Mackey said the baby's head was crowning. Suddenly Autumn Leaf screeched, and, like a tiny dancer in slow motion ballet, the beggar woman's baby came forth. The head emerged first, next the shoulders rotated gracefully one after the other into Dr. Mackey's waiting hands, and last of all, the miniature torso twisted free.

"It's a girl," the doctor announced.

The baby was undersized and ashy gray—limp, silent, and far too pale beneath her creamy coating of vernix. Dr. Mackey handed the little one to Laura. Vigorously she rubbed the tiny form all over with a clean cloth. The newborn remained limp.

In her peripheral vision, Laura could see Dr. Mackey in a red splattered lab coat, reaching inside the mother's birth canal for bits of retained placenta. The beggar woman was hemorrhaging. Mother and baby both were in trouble.

Miss Lin handed Laura a blanket she had warmed by the portable stove, and Laura wrapped the child in it, continuing to rub her. She flicked the soles of the tiny feet with her fingers, trying to startle the baby into crying.

"The cup!" she ordered Miss Lin. "And bring another clean cloth!"

Laura placed her lips over the baby's nub of a nose and sucked gently. She breathed in the fresh scent of vernix and spat a soft mucous plug into the cup that Miss Lin held ready at her shoulder. Several times she sucked and spat. Runny mucous began dribbling from the baby's nose and mouth, and Miss Lin wiped it away with the cloth.

Then, at long last, the baby shrieked, and her tiny hands, feet, face, and whole body flushed pink. Laura exhaled a sigh of relief, then looked up to see what was happening with the mother.

Dr. Mackey was massaging the beggar's belly energetically. She was still in trouble.

The little one wailed in spurts, catching her breath and gasping in gulps of air between her cries. "Now-now-now," Laura murmured, rocking her gently. When the child's wailing quieted to fretting, Laura coached Miss Lin through the task of cutting and tying the umbilical cord. They swaddled the little girl tightly in a fresh blanket.

"Bring the baby!" Dr. Mackey said.

Laura stepped over to Autumn Leaf. "You need to nurse your baby to help the bleeding stop," she explained.

Feebly, the young mother pushed her child away. "Leave us alone and let us die," she said.

"We can't do that," Dr. Mackey said. "You and your baby are precious in the eyes of God."

"We are worthless," Autumn Leaf said. "In the eyes of my mother-in-law, we are worthless." She yelped in pain from the uterine massage and tried to push Dr. Mackey's hands away. "If I bring my daughter home, her grandmother will kill her."

The baby started to howl, as if she understood the words. Laura tried again to ease her to the young mother's breast. Once again the woman turned away. Miss Lin coaxed, "You and your daughter may stay a while with us at the hospital and become strong. The heart of your mother-in-law may change. There is hope for her life."

"No!" Autumn Leaf said fiercely, and gave another little cry of pain. It was not clear whether she was objecting to Miss Lin's statement or the pain of the contraction brought on by Dr. Mackey's uterine massage. The young woman took a couple of deep breaths, then burst out, "We are doomed. We are baby sparrows whose nest has fallen into a snake pit. We are cursed."

"Jesus can change a curse into a blessing," Miss Lin said.

Dr. Mackey was keeping up the womb massage; baby was keeping up the din. "Let your child nurse," Laura pleaded. "It will quiet her. And you will feel better."

Autumn Leaf sighed, and ceased resisting. Her daughter gave one last wail and began to suckle. "We are cursed," the young mother said again. "My mother-in-law will kill her. *Mei yo fa tse.* It can't be helped."

And then, surrounded by a sympathetic audience, her strength rallied and her story poured out.

Autumn Leaf and her husband were newly wed peasant farmers who lived with the husband's parents according to Chinese custom. During the previous summer, one of the warlords sent his soldiers to their village to kidnap the men and force them to fight in a battle with guns. The soldiers captured her husband and her father-in-law, but left behind her husband's ten-year-old brother. Then the crops failed. When the family ran out of food, they begged from the neighbors. When the neighbors began turning them away, they left their village and hiked to the city. Autumn Leaf lost her relatives in the crowds when her labor started, but they were probably somewhere nearby, staying close to the soup kitchen.

"My mother-in-law has one son still to keep alive," Autumn Leaf explained. "She will say we can't afford to raise a girl who will just marry and take care of somebody else's ancestors. Anyway, even if she let my daughter live—even if my husband escaped from the warlord's soldiers and told his mother not to kill her—what would happen the next time famine strikes? My father sold my 11-year-old sister to a brothel three weeks ago so that he could feed my brothers. She was my baby sister, my precious jewel. When she was born, Mama was so weak that my father gave in to her and pretended not to see when I hid my sister behind the bag of millet. Mama gave me money to buy a little opium so she would sleep and not cry and no one would notice her. I saved her life—for what? In brothels, little girls die soon. It is better for my baby to die now than to end her life like my flower."

The brief story took the last of her energy. Her eyes closed, and Laura propped the baby firmly against her breast with a pillow. Laura wanted to weep.

By the time Autumn Leaf's story had ended, the crisis had also ended. The young mother fell asleep. The strong smell of birth permeated the room—a distinctive aroma mingling the rich odors of blood and sweat with the clean scents of vernix, amniotic fluid, and betadine disinfectant. A wonderful smell, Laura always thought—the fragrance of babies coming to life.

For a few last seconds Laura feasted her eyes on the sight of sleeping mother, nursing child. She could almost feel the bond between them pulse and strengthen. She allowed herself to feel briefly triumphant, to rest a moment in the sense of a job well done. They had saved Autumn Leaf and her baby. She and Miss Lin and Dr. Mackey had saved the precious lives of mother and child....

But for what? The beggar woman's question demanded an answer. *Saved them for what?*

It was Saturday and, theoretically, her day off, which meant it was the day she checked in briefly to see how everything was going, and then left if the nurses were carrying on well without her. Now that Autumn Leaf and her baby were safe and stabilized, she could leave. So Laura walked to the nurses' residence and changed from her uniform into her usual Western attire.

She sat at her desk and tried to read her Bible, tried to pray. But somehow she could not focus her mind. She kept hearing the beggar woman's voice: *"My mother-in-law will kill her....*Mei yo fa tse....*It can't be helped.... We are like baby sparrows who have fallen into a snake pit."*

Laura pictured a steep-sided pit, with snakes of all markings and sizes, drooping lazily in bushes and sunning themselves on rocks. Then a nest of young sparrows tipped into the hole, and the pit became alive with sinuous bodies slithering toward the little birds with plain purpose. The fledglings hopped pitifully.

Laura shivered. She pushed away from her desk, and before long found herself walking thoughtfully through the mission gate to the street outside the compound. The crowd was much thinner toward the right, in the direction of the railroad station.

The train was late of course. No one expected trains to run on schedule any more. The question was, would civilians be allowed to board? Or had the train been commandeered by one of the rival warlords to transport his army to yet another battle?

As she neared the station, she could see a crowd of Chinese in roomy gowns and handmade cloth shoes waiting hopefully. Then an engine chugged up to the Paotingfu railroad station, billowing grime into the dry

North China sky. It was mid-afternoon by now, and she knew that some of these people had been waiting calmly since early morning, hoping for a train to come, hoping they would be permitted to board.

This time they would. The train was packed tight with civilians. Several passengers extricated themselves from the pungent mass inside and struggled out the doors. Then the waiting crowd moved forward and tried to wedge itself inside. When the doors would take no more, gowned figures began hoisting themselves up the greasy sides of the train, poking their bodies and parcels into the open windows. And when the windows would take no more, the figures climbed higher still, settling themselves and their bundles in the soot on the train roof.

The engineer tooted again, and Laura watched the train chug away north to Peking—north through the clashing of the warlords' armies, north through the overtaxed farm plots of the peasants, north through the destitute villages, impoverished by famine, injustice, and greed...north through the world of Autumn Leaf.

All of China seemed to be overrun by predator snakes, swallowing up the weak and fighting each other for the spoils. Chinese efforts to overthrow the emperor and establish a strong central government had succeeded only in overthrowing the emperor. The country had disintegrated into a chaotic struggle for power between dozens of rival warlords and even greater numbers of bandit gangs, all grasping for power and trying to squeeze wealth from the local people.

A faint toot from the departing train nudged Laura out of her reverie. She noticed a tangle of beggar women and children closing in on the passengers who had disembarked. *"K'e lien!"* they wailed, holding out their begging sacks for gifts of food or money. "*K'e lien!* Have pity!"

She rehearsed what she would say to these people when they begged alms. In language school she had learned the specialized medical vocabulary required for training nurses and working in a hospital. Gospel preaching demanded a different vocabulary.

The beggars noticed her and hurried over, herding children and wailing *"K'e lien! K'e lien!* Have pity!"

"My pity can never do enough to help you," Laura said, and she began doling out bits of money into the women's outstretched hands. "You need to pray to Jesus. He will help you."

Two bony little girls about eight or nine years old stood directly in front of her, gawking—so awed they forgot to hold out their hands for alms. Both girls had babies tied to their backs, and they were dressed, like their elders, in the familiar blue cotton gowns of Chinese peasants. Laura felt conspicuous and foreign in her sensible leather shoes and Western style dress, with its fitted, buttoned bodice and full skirts falling to her ankles. She supposed that her round, hazel eyes and brown hair made her conspicuous, too.

"Pray to Jesus," she repeated doggedly. "Depend on him instead of other people to meet your needs."

The group stared at her blankly, and Laura felt uneasy. "God is able to take care of your needs," she tried again. "We receive his blessings when we depend entirely on his son, Jesus."

The women bowed politely and began moving away, trailing children. "How pale her face is," a grandmother with bound feet remarked to her neighbor.

"Yes, like a ghost," her companion replied.

"Do you think the skin underneath her gown is as white?" the older woman asked.

Laura laughed, but she felt like a pricked balloon.

She turned to walk back to the mission, thinking as she walked about the two gawking girls who had been too shy to beg. How much longer would their mothers feel they could afford to share the family's food with a worthless daughter? They were too young to be sold to a brothel. What would happen to them?

Laura walked back to the compound, hearing again the voice of Autumn Leaf. "My mother-in-law will kill her. *Mei yo fa tse.* It can't be helped."

"Mei yo fa tse." It was one of the first idiomatic phrases she had learned in language school. One heard it all the time in China. *"Mei yo fa tse."*

That was what her family back in the United States believed, too: "It can't be helped. It's futile to try. You can't do anything with people like the Chinese."

Her family had argued with her about coming here. They said they could not understand her. Why would she waste her life...her education, her talents, and her prospects for marriage and a normal life...why would she waste herself on this backward people, who fertilized their farm plots with human excrement and drowned their baby girls in rivers like unwanted kittens?

But God had called her, hadn't he? Surely he had called her to come here to China to do the work of Christ—to bring wholeness, to save lives.

As Laura passed through the ornate, turreted gate of the Presbyterian mission compound, she had an odd feeling that she was passing from one world into another, that she was moving from a North Chinese street—from the world of Autumn Leaf—to...to what? This world behind the compound walls was not America, although the compound did look distinctly American. That was probably because...she looked about at the familiar landscape with fresh eyes...that was probably because all the buildings were American-style architecture.

The imposing three-story men's hospital of gray brick looked like a dozen hospitals she had seen in the U.S. Then there was Martyrs Memorial Church nestled between the men's and women's hospitals and named after the missionaries and their children who had been killed in Paotingfu 26 years before during the Boxer Rebellion. Martyrs Memorial Church could easily be mistaken for a well-attended Presbyterian church anywhere in America. Her relatives would feel at home attending a Presbyterian church that looked like that. The modest lines of the women's hospital came next into view, and behind that lay a simple residence hall where family members of patients at the two hospitals could stay.

The compound was a kind of American garrison within the land of North China. Inside it, Laura could save the life of a baby girl. Beyond it, she could not. Outside the compound, out in the world of Autumn Leaf where the train was traveling now, out there she was powerless.

But God was not powerless in that world.

Beyond the residence for patients' families sat the Ladies' House, where Laura lived with the other nurses. Her troubled eyes traveled over the outline of this, her home in China—an unpretentious gray brick building with a wooden, second-story porch attached in front and an outhouse tacked to the back. It was the roof over her head, provided by the Presbyterian Board of Missions who paid her monthly salary.

The beggar women she had spoken with today had no roof, no salary, no means of any kind.

She decided not to go back to her room at the Ladies' House just yet. Some of her students would probably see her and want to talk, and she did not feel like facing their enthusiasm and chit chat now.

A pungent whiff of goat manure guided her to the goat yard. Here was a place to sort out her thoughts. In the far corner of the pen, a large Swiss nanny munched steadily on hay in a feeding trough. Two kids guzzled milk from her bulging bag. Laura leaned on the fence, and a half dozen goats of varying sizes trotted over curiously. She rubbed their rough, furry heads, and tried to ignore the odor of goat's breath.

The goats belonged to her colleague Dr. Mackey and several of the missionary families on the compound. Dr. Mackey had started this herd several years ago when one of the missionaries became sick and needed milk to recover. Since dairy products were not part of the Chinese diet, Dr. Mackey bought a pair of Swiss goats, in Peking most likely, and started developing her own milk supply. Then the missionary families with children started raising goats, too. When the families took a vacation, they brought their goats along for milk.

How alien our missionary life must seem to those beggar women I spoke with today, she thought. *Milk, goats, vacations....*

Laura pulled up a patch of weeds and started feeding the long green strands to the herd.A parade of memories from the past drifted through her mind: the solemn cadence of a congregation singing hymns at her mother's funeral when she was nine years old; waking at 4 a.m. on wash days as a young teenager so she could do all the family laundry for her invalid stepmother before leaving for school; learning to walk again after she caught diphtheria in nursing school; coping with the blood, the vomit, the endless muck in that terrible barracks in France where she and Orpha Gould had nursed soldiers during the Great War....

All her life, Jesus had been with her. Yet her need had never been as desperate as the need of these beggar women and their children. *You have never been as poor as they,* she thought.

And you have never been as poor as Jesus, either. The thought dropped with a shock into her mind from somewhere beyond herself, the idea so brightly defined that it was almost an audible voice.

Jesus had been poor—dirt poor, as they said back home in Ohio. He had been born on the floor of a stable that smelled as bad as that goat shed over there. And his mother had had no place to put him down to sleep except a manger—just like that feeding trough where the mother goat was gobbling hay.

It was quiet here. The twins pulled at mama goat's bag, and the other goats stretched out their necks for Laura to scratch their ears. Absentmindedly, she pulled her arm away from one of the goats, who had started to nibble at the sleeve. *Am I willing to follow Jesus in poverty?*

She had told the beggar women the truth today, if only they could receive it. If they followed Jesus, became his hands, his feet, worked to bring in his kingdom....God would answer their prayers and provide.

But where could she find Chinese words to explain such a wonder? She was not like her good friend Florence Logan, who was also with the Presbyterian mission and preached in the countryside. Words poured right out of Florence, and the words always made sense. Florence trained as a journalist before becoming a missionary, so she wrote well, too. She was articulate in English, fluent in Chinese. Besides that, she was a vivacious, extroverted brunette whom everyone noticed and heeded. Laura, in contrast, was too ordinary looking and reserved to attract attention. And the truth was, she preferred it that way. She had always been shy, always hated the limelight. She felt she expressed herself hesitantly even in her native tongue. And in Chinese...well, she had no special gift for the language. Her students struggled to understand her thick accent, her strange pronunciations, her misplaced tones.

She communicated with them by example. They watched the way she took care of people in the hospital, and they learned proper nursing techniques by seeing them demonstrated, patiently, over and over again.

The air felt cold. Laura noticed that the shadows from buildings and trees were lengthening, connecting, spreading darkness over the grounds of the compound. She glanced at her watch. It was time to check on Autumn Leaf and her baby.

She didn't know what would happen to Autumn Leaf. Most likely the beggar woman would stay at the hospital until she became strong enough and the weather became warm enough for her to journey home. Somehow the nurses would find a way to give her some seed for a new crop, and she would blend into the tide of peasant beggars returning to their villages to start again. Laura knew that when that happened, it was unlikely she would see Autumn Leaf again. That was the way things happened here.

But Laura knew she would not soon forget Autumn Leaf and the other beggar women she had met today. Meeting them was changing her. She could not put it into words yet, but she could feel it. Somehow, something in her way of life would have to change as well.

Meantime, her first responsibility was to her nursing students. She could not leave them. In just one year the mission would be sending her back to America for a year-long furlough to see her family and renew ties with the church at home. She had a lot of teaching to do to prepare her staff to manage the nursing school and hospital work while she was gone.

Laura Richards, age 22, in 1915, when she graduated as a registered nurse from Minneapolis General Hospital. "In my probation year," Laura recalled, "I was given the work of cleaning up the diphtheria rooms after they were fumigated. Here I developed diphtheria. For three months I was kept in a dark room as the disease affected my eyesight. I was slightly paralyzed for a while and had to learn to walk again."

The Furlough

From Laura's testimony,
written about 1957 for Go, Ye Fellowship:

Upon arriving at my destination in China, I was not so joyful when I found that my Biblical training was inadequate. In early childhood my mother had taught me to pray, and my own daily reading was all the knowledge that I had of the Book. However, in the nurses' training school to which I had been assigned, I bravely taught Daniel and Revelation, with the help of a good textbook.

Four and a half years soon passed, and it was time for the only furlough I ever had. On this furlough in 1926-1928 (there were two years on account of unrest in China), I had the privilege of studying in the Biblical Seminary in New York. It was during these two years of study there, that I decided to trust the Lord only for my support.

I wrote to my colleagues and friends in China concerning my belief in what the Lord would have me do, but they earnestly asked me to return to the work which I had done before. I returned to the field still under the Presbyterian Board.

1985 interview with Laura's cousin,
Laura Jane Eberhardt Cerling,
who was seven years old the fall of 1928:

I remember that Laura visited us on her furlough. She gave me a book of old fairy tales that her friend Lois Lenski had rewritten and illustrated. The book had a special meaning to me because Laura had given it to me. Also, I thought that it was special that a girl Laura had played with and gone to school with, grew up and wrote a book and illustrated it.

Laura had a missionary friend with her, and I can still visualize the group as they sat around our round oak table that evening. The adults sat a long time talking after dinner. I got off my chair and listened under the table. Laura's friend told about their experiences being in an earthquake in someplace beginning with a P. She said a great crack opened and swallowed houses and people. I thought,* That must be a story she made up. It can't really be true.

1985 interview with Laura's brother, Harold Richards, commenting on his attempts to persuade Laura first not to go, and then not to return to China:

She just had notions and convictions, and that's the way she did things. She was real determined.

**Author's note:* Laura's memoirs mention that she and her seminary classmates toured Egypt and Palestine during an earthquake.

2

Leaving Paotingfu

Paotingfu, 1928

FLORENCE LOGAN wheeled her bicycle through the Presbyterian mission compound, past the Ladies' House where her friend Laura Richards lived, to the little gray brick house that she shared with Dr. Mackey. It was a crisp October evening, and fallen leaves crunched under her bicycle tires. She felt chilled after several days camping out on a preaching trip into the countryside with a team of Chinese evangelists. So, after she unloaded her camping gear from the bike, she headed straight for the kitchen to make a pot of hot tea.

To her delight, she saw a pot already steaming on the table. But then she noticed something wrong. Dr. Mackey was seated at the table, with her back to Florence. The little doctor's elbows were on the table, supporting her head in her hands, and her compact figure was hunched. The doctor must have heard her come through the door, though, because she straightened, turned, and smiled.

"Welcome home, Florence!" she said. "Please join me for tea."

"That I will," Florence said cheerfully. She fetched a teacup from the cupboard and sat down directly across from her house mate. "You look down, Doc," she said. "You look like you've lost your best friend."

"Well, I haven't lost my friend," the doctor said, "but I *have* lost my nursing director. Laura Richards has decided not to return to the women's hospital."

"What!" Florence exclaimed. "Richie is not being driven out by the propagandists, I hope! Surely Richie of all the people on this mission compound cannot be having trouble with students!" Everyone had always said that Laura's rapport with her students was extraordinary, especially in light of the touchy, anti-foreign climate in China.

"It isn't that. Her students love her as much as ever," Dr. Mackey said. "But as soon as she returned from furlough, she took a tour of the hospital and heard a full report from the nursing staff about what happened the two years she was gone. You know, we never expected her to be gone as long as she was, but with all our riots and wars here.... Well, anyway, after she finished the tour and heard the report, she said the nurses don't need her anymore. She said that if she came back, she would be intruding."

"Intruding!" Florence said. "You must feel terrible. You and Richie are a perfect team."

"It is a hard blow indeed," Dr. Mackey admitted. "I will miss working with her."

I wonder if there is something else behind this that Richie isn't talking about, Florence thought.

She invited Laura to tea the next day. She knew it didn't do to push Richie, so after her friend settled down to tea in the kitchen, Florence chatted about other things until Laura brought up the subject herself.

"Perhaps Dr. Mackey has told you that I have decided not to return to the women's hospital," Laura said.

"She did," Florence said, "and you could have knocked me over with a licorice stick. I'm dying to know why."

Laura smiled her wide smile. "They no longer need me," she said. "I would be intruding."

Florence removed her glasses and stared in an expression of dramatic disbelief. "Now, Richie, how could *you* be intruding? They adore you!"

"I know they love me. I love them, too," Laura said, "but their situation has changed since we left on furlough over two years ago."

That was certainly true. A lot had happened in Paotingfu from 1926 to 1928 while Florence and Laura were in the United States on their first missionary furlough. Their leave of absence had originally been scheduled for only one year, but the Presbyterian Mission had extended the time until it seemed safer to send them back. Riots against foreigners in China had intensified, and the North Chinese warlords had fought fiercely. So the two friends had been away more than two years.

By the time the mission finally decided to let them return, China had a new leader, General Chiang Kai Shek. When they left the country in 1926, the general had been in control of part of South China. While they were gone, he swept northward through China, wiping out weak warlords and forcing strong ones to admit his supremacy and unite with him by treaty.

But why should these events have caused Richie to leave the women's hospital? Florence wondered.

"When I left on furlough," Laura said, "the medical staff hoped that the nurses at the hospital could manage for one year without a missionary nurse in charge. None of us guessed they would have to run the hospital for a much longer time. For over two years, they have carried on through riots, epidemics, battles, and bandit invasions. Yet they have maintained high professional standards through it all."

Laura took a couple sips of tea. Florence waited, chewing a cookie.

"Besides, you know that nationalistic feelings are running high now," Laura went on. "There is great anger against foreigners, and that affects the nurses."

So, maybe the propaganda was behind this after all, Florence thought.

General Chiang Kai Shek gained popular support and demoralized his enemies by using a propaganda corps to assist his Kuomintang soldiers. Their slogans aroused hatred not only against local warlords but against foreigners. "Down with imperialism!" was particularly effective. The general's promise to repeal the hated "unequal treaties" hit a deep, responsive chord. Among other things, those treaties gave immunity from Chinese law to foreigners like them, living on missionary compounds like theirs. Mission schools in particular infuriated Chinese political sloganeers. They insisted that mission schools should not be able to teach foreign ideas to Chinese youth beyond the control of the Chinese government. It was a matter of Chinese sovereignty.

"People say Chinese schools should be run by Chinese," Laura said. "Now circumstances have forced these Chinese nurses into running the nursing school and performing all the nursing functions at the hospital for two full years. Since they have proved themselves, it would be intruding for me to take over again."

When Richie put it that way, it did seem sensible. Florence wrinkled her forehead. "But are they also spiritually ready to take over?"

"They have matured spiritually while I was away," Laura said. "The responsibility will continue to challenge their faith, but that will be good. They will have to learn to trust entirely in God. Florence, it is time for the nursing program at the women's hospital to become fully Chinese."

Florence could make no argument. In fact, Laura's reasoning dove-tailed with her own beliefs and policies. She encouraged the rural churches where she preached to become self-supporting and self-propagating. She wanted Chinese Christians to become fully responsible for their own churches.

Laura reached over and patted Florence's hand. "Don't worry, Florence, God will help the nurses," she said, "and they will be highly motivated as well. I believe that now they will work harder even than before, to prove that my faith in them is well placed."

No wonder they love her, Florence thought. *Richie is a real peach—soft and sweet, with a tough kernel.*

Aloud she said, "Well, they'll never get another baby's nurse as good as you, Richie. The doctors say you do miracles with the babies."

"I *will* miss working with the babies," Laura admitted.

"What do you plan to do now?"

"I am still trying to decide," Laura said. "Dr. Sun has invited me to go with her and a medical team into the countryside." Dr. Sun was another of Laura's colleagues, a Chinese female medical doctor who worked at the women's hospital.

"I am hoping," she added, "that God will show me my next step on this trip."

• • •

The air was crisp with the bite of approaching winter as the medical team bicycled from village to village that fall. Frost furred the harvested fields and feathered the weeds along the pathways in the mornings; then it melted into dew and evaporated in the warmth of mid-day. Village women raked the season's fallen leaves into their cooking fires, and the fires crackled and snapped like mule drivers' whips. The smell of burning leaves mingled with the penetrating odor of dung, both animal and human, spread carefully out to dry for fertilizer.

One day the team passed a ditch where they told Laura that they had found a dead baby the previous winter. It had been a girl, of course. She had been left outside to freeze.

In the villages, street-cleaning boys hung about the streets and gathered up droppings from foraging pigs or passing donkeys and mules to help fertilize their family fields. They were usually eight or nine years old, and their heads were shaved bare—a popular hairstyle which was easy to maintain and discouraged lice. Laura liked to watch them compete with each other to see who could rake up the most dung. Nothing delighted these children more than the sight of a mule stopped dead in his tracks, with his tail lifted.

"They haven't much of a future," Laura remarked to Dr. Sun.

"But more of a future than many," the doctor said, jerking her chin in the direction of a ragged urchin filching pears from a fruit stall.

Laura nodded. She was seeing scores of children with far less future than the street-cleaning boys—children begging and stealing in the markets, shivering in the morning frost with their feet bare and their bony limbs exposed through the tatters of a summer gown. Some were merely hungry. Others showed clear signs of malnutrition and disease, with bleeding sores spreading over their bodies, chronic diarrhea, and pus creeping from their ears and eyes and the tooth sockets of their swollen gums.

"I would like to help children like these and baby girls like the one you found in the ditch," Laura said. "Maybe I could take in a few orphans."

"It is forbidden by the mission," Dr. Sun reminded her.

Laura was silent. Starting an orphanage was a popular idea with idealistic young missionaries, but the Presbyterian Mission had a firm policy forbidding it.

Orphanages were easy to start, hard to sustain. What would the mission do if some zealous young worker started a home for children and than became sick or too emotionally worn out to carry it on? Once begun, an orphanage could not be abandoned. The mission could potentially be left with a heartbreaking responsibility and no one to manage it. China's need was so overwhelming that the board was forced to make some hard decisions about mission priorities. This was one.

Dr. Sun was right. If Laura wanted to take in orphans, she could not do it as a Presbyterian missionary.

Orphans, orphans, Laura thought as she bicycled between villages. She was half orphan herself. Her own mother had died when she was nine years old, and Laura had never stopped missing her. Never.

Snatches of her childhood visited her memory as she pedaled, and she saw her little girl self rummaging through nearly empty cupboards in a silent farmhouse, trying to fumble together a meal for herself and her little brother Harold. How vulnerable they had been, how small and alone. Fortunately, Mother had taught her how to pray when she was still quite small, and her childish faith in Jesus had held her head above the waves when she felt she would drown in the pain of missing her mother.

These children are even more alone than I was, Laura told herself.

A new thought dropped into her mind. *Why can't I trust God for some little ones' support as well as my own?*

She realized that the Holy Spirit was speaking to her.

The question echoed inside her all the way back to Paotingfu, where she shut herself up in her room. She kept her Bible on the bedside table for reference and retreated to prayer and fasting.

Starting an orphanage on faith clearly lined up with the Bible's emphasis on taking care of orphans and looking to God for sustenance. And the work fit well with her training, her temperament, and her gifts. Yet leaving the Presbyterian mission and relying on God alone for her support was a drastic move—too drastic to take out of wishful thinking.

Living by faith alone had become a familiar concept to her through her acquaintance with missionaries from the China Inland Mission. Over 60 years before, in 1865, Hudson Taylor had founded that nondenominational mission society on the belief that Christians who prayed could rely on God to take care of them even if they lived in remote areas of a foreign country without personal resources. On that premise, CIM's workers opened interior China to Protestant missions. Presbyterians were in Paotingfu only because CIM pioneers paved the way.

Clearly CIM had proved, she thought, that God could provide for missionaries who lived and worked among the poor in China's rural hinterlands without a regular mission salary. CIM's missionaries never borrowed money or asked for contributions. They merely reported what was happening in their ministries to their supporters back home. Plainly God took care of them, sometimes providing through supporters' contributions and sometimes providing in other ways—ordinary ways, coincidental ways, dramatic ways.

On the other hand, one Christian's obedience to God could be another Christian's presumption. All the missionaries knew people who called themselves faith workers, but who then begged help from other missionaries. At best they were a nuisance. At worst they dragged down the health and resources of other Christians.

How could she let God be God and avoid slipping into the trap of taking over situations under duress? She needed clear guidelines to ensure that she relied strictly on God and not on people. She needed reassurance, too, that she was not presuming on God's goodness by taking in helpless children with no promise of support from a church. She felt like a pioneer contemplating a dangerous journey into an unknown wilderness.

One day it occurred to her that she could look for answers in the sitting room library. The biography of Praying Hyde in India had given her inspiration and guidance on prayer in the past. Perhaps the library contained another book that would help her.

She searched the bookshelves. *The Life of Trust,* by George Mueller caught her eye, and she carried it back to her bedroom. As she read it, her hesitations fell away. Yes, the journey into the wilderness was dangerous, but here was an explorer who had not only traveled through the territory, but had blazed a trail and drawn a map. Here was her reassurance, here were her guidelines.

She began to lay plans. And now that she had made up her mind, she felt she wanted to talk it all over with Florence. Her friend always asked good questions, and she was a sympathetic listener. Surely Florence would understand and support her.

So as soon as Florence returned from her preaching journey in the countryside, Laura made a visit to Florence for tea and private conversation.

Florence was eager to hear all about her trip and future plans. Laura described the villages the medical team had visited, the clinics they had held, and the multitude of castaway children she had seen. Florence understood her friend's feelings. She knew all about the overwhelming conditions in the villages.

"You sound as if you have come to some sort of a decision, Richie," Florence said finally.

"Yes, I have," Laura said. "I have decided to leave the mission and start trusting God only for my support in China."

Florence nearly dropped her teacup. A miniature waterfall of steaming green sloshed over the rim and burned her hand. Florence set her cup down quickly. "Leave the mission?" she asked. "I can understand your decision not to return to the hospital again, but why do you think you should leave the mission?" She began sopping up the spilled tea with a napkin. "There's plenty of other work with us that you could do."

"I should like to take in orphans," Laura explained, "but I cannot start an orphanage as a Presbyterian missionary. Also, I believe God wants me to live among the poor. If I give up the regular salary the mission pays me, I will become poor like the people in the countryside. Then they will be able to see for themselves how God takes care of people who are completely dependent on Jesus."

"Are you sure that's really necessary?" Florence asked.

"Not for every Christian, no," Laura said. "God calls different ones to different places and different tasks. But for me…for me, I think it is necessary." She paused.

"You see," she began, and Florence saw her hesitate, "you see, Florence, people are willing to follow Jesus in many things, but not many are willing to follow Him in His poverty."

"And you intend to do just that," Florence said. It was a statement, not a question.

Laura said nothing. Florence studied her teacup, and quietness stretched between them like a taut kite string. Florence felt dubious and uncertain of what to say. She had seen a number of manipulators who pasted the label "faith in God" over their scheming. Richie was not like that. Richie was one of the most genuine people Florence knew, but still…doubts swarmed through her mind, doubts that it seemed cruel to put into words. Richie was 35 years old. Was this really the Holy Spirit's prompting? Or was her friend being tempted to manipulate God into fulfilling a mid-life spinster's yearning for children of her own? And then, there was a financial consideration. The Presbyterian mission had paid Laura's salary during her two-year furlough and then her passage to China because they expected her to provide them with another five years service in North China. Was it right for her to resign in light of the Presbyterians' financial investment in her?

Besides all that, the idea just sounded so idealistic and impractical. Florence knew what conditions were in the villages. She wondered if Richie really understood what it would be like to live in places like that, or to eat the kind of food that poor Chinese ate day after day. And then to try to feed and clothe children without regular support? The children Richie would be taking in would not be healthy either. They would be malnourished. They would have diseases and handicaps and other serious medical conditions. How would Richie manage to care for such children in poverty conditions, without regular support? Could this really be a genuine call from God?

Florence had a way with words, but it was failing her. She felt powerless in the face of her friend's determination. Finally she spoke. "I do sympathize. I know you want to follow Jesus completely." She lifted her gaze from her china cup and looked straight into the eyes of her friend. "But please don't do anything rash, Richie. You need to be absolutely sure you have God's guidance before you do something this drastic."

Richie would know that she was trying to discourage her. "Be sure you have God's guidance…be sure you have heard the voice of God…." These were code phrases in missionary circles. They were intended to be a nice way of saying, "I disagree. I don't think you should do this."

The subject changed. They finished their tea, and Laura walked back to the Ladies' House. Florence made another pot of tea and sat in her kitchen, sipping from her cup and staring at the wall. She knew that people tended to overlook Richie because she was so quiet. Yet those who had an opportunity to get close to her—those she lived with, those she took care of, those who worked alongside her—they all loved her for her gentle ways and her practical good sense. Florence sympathized with the orphanage idea, but she was still doubtful. She hoped Richie wasn't making a mistake.

Laura walked back to her room. She felt disappointed but not discouraged by her friend's response. She still felt buoyed by the memory of discovering George Mueller's biography in the sitting room library. On the one hand, she felt she had failed to describe the vision of the orphanage so that Florence could see it and understand it. And she had obviously failed to enlist her friend's wholehearted encouragement. On the other hand, that failure could not dampen the excitement she still felt from having read the account of a man who had founded five orphanages in Bristol, England during the mid-1800s and had supported several thousand orphans over a period of 60 years, all through prayer.

For the rest of the year, through the Christmas season, Laura made trips into the villages with an evangelism team. Between trips, she reread George Mueller's book, taking careful notes on his teachings about prayer and the life of faith. Then in early January, she boarded an express train for Peking to resign from the mission. Florence was in the villages preaching, so she was unavailable to see Laura off.

It was a bitterly cold day, much like the winter days she had known growing up in Ohio, except that here in North China there was less snow. Looking at her reflection in the train window, she saw a trim Caucasian woman, with a calm, ordinary face, dressed in a long wool coat with a fur collar. Once she started the orphanage, she would have to pack away these Western winter clothes and wear a padded winter gown like a Chinese woman, with a long *ta ao* over-garment covering her gown to ward off winter's bite.

She gazed out the window at the bleak landscape and recalled the merry times she and Florence had enjoyed in Peking less than four months earlier, coming back from furlough. Although they had stayed a full week in the capitol city waiting for an express train, there had not been enough meal times to go around to all the friends who had wanted to entertain them. Now she would be seeing those friends again, and they would be curious to know why she had returned.

She felt a little breathless from pushing down the excitement that kept wanting to bubble forth from her outwardly calm exterior. She was looking forward to finding out how God would support her venture. She shrank from the prospect, though, of explaining her decision to resign to the director of the mission in Peking. She hoped he would understand.

Laura Richards in China, receiving mail delivery from a Chinese postman. This photograph was probably taken between 1923 and 1926 at the Presbyterian mission compound in Paotingfu, where Laura served as superintendent of nurses at Hodge Memorial Hospital for Women. Working alongside Dr. Maud A. Mackey, she oversaw all the nursing work of the hospital and directed a school for female Chinese nursing students.

Laura's Report on Leaving Paotingfu

Laura's letter written from Chao Yang An, June 8, 1931:

My Heavenly Father gave me a very precious work to do in Paotingfu, but my heart was not at rest. There were a number of beggar women who used to ask me for money, and I used to give to them and tell them not to be so dependent upon people, but to put their trust in the Lord. Often I felt that they were thinking how easy it was for me to trust in Him when I had a certain amount of money coming in every month. Often I thought that the Lord was speaking to me about it, and it seemed that I could not do very much good for others until I answered Him. So after more than four years I determined that if it were my Father's will, I should no more have a stated salary but become as poor as those women, and yet to show them and others that, after all, we are not poor while we have our loving Heavenly Father.

3.

Starting Out

Peking, May 1929

AN OLD WOMAN WAS coming to Laura through a howling rainstorm, hobbling on bound and broken feet, her hair plastered slick and gray upon her neck, raindrops or teardrops trickling over her wrinkled cheeks. She halted and bowed low.

"Happy Plum Flower Richards," the woman began, addressing her by her Chinese name. "Will you take my neighbor's baby girl? She is four days old, and her mother died last night."

"If the family is poor, I will take her," Laura said. "Where is this baby?"

"Come," the woman replied, and began hobbling back the way she came.

"You are too ill, Miss Richards," protested a deep voice at Laura's shoulder. She turned to see the specialist who had diagnosed her case at the Peking Union Medical College. Around him stood the entire Presbyterian missionary community of Peking.

"How can you leave us?" one of the ladies demanded, softly but firmly. "You have barely returned to China, and the mission is counting on you."

"Are you sure of this decision, Miss Richards?" the mission director asked. "You must be absolutely certain you have heard the voice of God before you make such an important decision…."

Laura turned from them and saw the woman's bent form hobbling unsteadily forward in the distance.

"You'll drown," warned a chorus of gentle voices behind her.

Laura looked down. Between her and the old woman there now appeared a churning yellow river with waves that rose as high as trees. Lightning split the sky, and thunder echoed the old woman's voice with a deep, rumbly, "Come."

"How exciting," said the prim voice of Miss McCoy, the principal of the School of Gentleness for girls. "Take this with you." And Laura felt her friend thrust something into her right hand. She looked and saw it was a baby bottle filled with milk.

Then Laura sensed the tall, awkward presence of her old friend Orpha Gould, towering beside her. "I'll come help you take care of the baby whenever I can," promised the familiar voice of her friend.

A leftover chunk of lightning remained in the sky, fuzzy and low down, glimmering just above the laboring figure of the hobbling old woman. Laura fixed her gaze upon the light and then stepped onto the surface of the river.

A wave smacked into her right side, and then a second, larger wave swept over her head. It would have knocked her down except that she sensed strong arms holding her upright. She managed to keep her eyes open, fixing her gaze through the water on the bit of light still beckoning dimly. She dared not close her eyes or focus them anywhere else but on that light.

The wave passed on, and Laura continued moving forward, one foot in front of the other, struggling against the storm, and panting with urgency. She must hurry, hurry, hurry. She must reach the baby.

The surface beneath her feet grew rough and firm, and at last she caught up to the old woman. The hobbling form emerged from the straw gate of an outlying village hut. The woman carried a small bundle wrapped in a dirty gray quilt, and she was clearly crying now.

"We are too late," she told Laura. "Her grandmother smothered her with this quilt."

Laura gathered the bundle into her arms and drew back the cover.

She kissed the little one's still features, sat down, and gave herself to grief, crying until her body jerked with sobs and the quilt became wet with her tears.

When she could cry no more, she noticed that the bundle had grown heavier. She looked down. A healthy three-month-old baby blinked up at her, whimpering.

The dream startled her so much that she woke up. With the power of the dream still on her, it took a few minutes for her to recognize her surroundings: the firm mattress beneath her, the ironed muslin sheet pulled to her chin, the light of a late afternoon sun filtering through starched white curtains at the window, the perfume of May flowers drifting through the open casement.

Of course. She was lying in her slip on the bed in the little room the Presbyterians had given her while she stayed in the Peking mission compound. She had been taking her daily nap, as the doctor had ordered. Laura's cheeks felt wet, and she realized she had been crying. She propped herself up on one elbow to take her handkerchief from the bed stand and blow her nose. Then she checked her watch. Two more hours before her dinner invitation with James and Mieps Leynse.

She lay flat again, replaying the dream in her mind. Again she followed the crippled woman through the storm, heard the voice, felt the urgency. In those few brief scenes, the dream had captured the essence of her experiences since arriving in Peking in January.

Nothing had gone smoothly. She felt like her resignation had shocked the entire Presbyterian community in North China and put her in the spotlight, which she normally avoided. She had tried hard to present her case diplomatically. People still interpreted her decision as a criticism of Presbyterian mission policy. To be fair, she had to say that the Peking missionaries were basically kind. But they were skeptically noncommittal, which hurt, because many of them were dear friends. It made her feel uncomfortable to be living here on the mission compound.

Few of the people she knew in the U.S. had sympathized either. The Women's Auxiliary from the church in New York, who had taken responsibility for her support in China, withdrew all financial contributions. Most of her friends and family in Sidney, Ohio were as shocked with her as the Peking missionaries. How could she give up her salary? It made no sense to them. Only a handful of people in America stood by her in her decision—her old high school teacher in Sidney, for one, and her old high school friend Lois Lenski, for another. So, unlike Hudson Taylor, founder of the China Inland Mission, she had little backing at home.

Then there was the passage money issue. Some missionaries thought she should reimburse the Presbyterian mission for her passage to China because she was resigning so soon after they had paid that expense for her. But her salary was insufficient to cover that cost, and she was cutting herself off from her salary anyway.

To top it all, as soon as she arrived in Peking, she began suffering heart problems like those she had suffered during her battle with diphtheria as a student nurse. The symptoms were so severe that doctors at Douw Hospital, the Presbyterian medical center in Peking, finally referred her case to a specialist at the prestigious Peking Union Medical College of the Rockefeller Foundation. The specialist told her that her mission would have to send her back to the United States for treatment. His pronouncement presented her with yet another dilemma. She must either remain with the mission and return home, or she must resign from the mission and remain in China, in weakness and pain.

As in the dream, the calling voice won out. She chose to stay. She had offered her resignation in February, and the Presbyterian Board of Foreign Missions had accepted. They were still unhappy, but there was little they could say. Obviously they were going to lose her as a worker one way or another. Her resignation inside China saved them the cost of her return passage, and all talk of reimbursement faded.

The only encouraging part of her experience since coming to Peking had been the wholehearted support given her by Orpha Gould and Miss Bessie McCoy. Orpha Gould was a nurse at Douw Hospital in Peking. Laura had known Orpha ever since they both served in the U.S. Army as Red Cross nurses during the Great War in Europe. Miss McCoy was the China-born principal of the mission's school for girls. She had attended classes at the Biblical Seminary in New York with Laura during their last furlough. Miss McCoy donated money for some of the orphanage's startup costs and located a small compound for Laura to rent near Miss McCoy's own summer place in Chao Yang An (Turned to the Sun), a rural village in the Western Hills about a dozen miles from Peking. Laura planned to move there in two weeks and pay the first rent installment on arrival.

Laura puzzled over the scenes in the dream that involved the crashing sea and the baby. She was unsure what it all meant exactly, but she sensed it was a warning—one final warning before she left for Chao Yang An—to give her a glimpse of what lay ahead, and to see if she was still willing to go through with the adventure.

"And I am willing, dear Father," she prayed. "All these weeks I have asked You to lead me on the path that most glorifies You. Jesus suffered and died for me. If I must also walk a very rugged path to make Your goodness clearly known, so let it be. I am willing."

At the time of her resignation, the mission director told her she could continue to stay in this room on the mission compound to convalesce. She spent the spring months resting, praying, planning, and making short trips into the countryside. Today James and Mieps Leynse had sent her a dinner invitation, with a request to come tell them more about her plans. Perhaps they would be willing to help.

She threw back the sheet and dressed thoughtfully for dinner.

A temple gong droned in the distance as she ambled through the mission grounds to the Leynse home. The air was fresh, and a riot of reds and yellows, blues and whites, lavenders and pinks bloomed in the gardens along her way. She paused several paces away from the Leynses' freshly scrubbed doorstep to admire the wrought iron picture that James Leynse had designed for his family's front door. A large bird was quenching its thirst in a stream bordered by a stand of leafy bamboo and shaded by a blossoming peach tree. The scene was sandwiched between two wire screens and created an impression that the door stood open.

The Leynses' oriental callers understood the message of welcome that this picture implied, James had told her once on an earlier visit. After admiring it, Chinese visitors usually walked straight into the house unannounced. Laura, however, being a Westerner, looked around for the door knocker and gave it a clack.

Inside, another riot of fresh blooms greeted her. James and Mieps loved flowers, and the local flower man kept every sunny spot in their large house blooming brightly. The Leynses loved beauty in other forms, too. Exquisite paintings, finely crafted furniture, jade and ivory carvings, and porcelain lamps and bowls and vases caught Laura's eye in every downstairs room.

James had been an artist before becoming a missionary. Both he and his wife were heirs of wealthy, upper-class Dutch families, each with independent means. They used their wealth to help the poor and to surround themselves with beauty and elegance. She had often heard James quote the prophet Isaiah to describe his missionary calling as bringing "beauty for ashes." He said that he and Mieps wanted to use the decor of their home to symbolize that calling.

Laura chatted with the Leynses' school-aged boys in the sitting room, and then the family ushered her into the dining room, where a well-trained servant seated her at a table covered in starchy, white tablecloth and elaborately set with silver. Laura spread a fine linen napkin on her lap and looked around, enjoying the elegance of the Leynses' aristocratic Dutch heritage, reproduced half a world away from Holland here in this spacious formal dining room.

It seems a strange setting, she mused, *for trying to describe a calling to follow Christ in poverty.*

Yet the family appeared sympathetic when she described the work she was beginning in the Western Hills. James often traveled through the poor villages of that region with teams of Chinese evangelists. He taught Bible classes to new converts in Chao Yang An, and he had rescued several young country girls from being sold into brothels, placing them in the mission's school in Peking. Mieps worked with women and girls in Peking. They both recognized the need for an orphanage, they said.

"How do you plan to support this work, Miss Richards?" James asked.

"I hope that the Chinese people will begin to participate in it, and support it, and see it as their own ministry," Laura said. "That was part of the reason why I cut my formal ties with the American church."

"Have any shown a willingness to join you yet?" Mieps asked, as a Chinese servant deftly removed the family's soup bowls.

"A Christian couple named the Sus have agreed to move to Chao Yang An with me," Laura said, "and a young woman from Paotingfu has offered to come as well, at least for a time. Miss Chang is recovering from tuberculosis. She wants to teach me Chinese while she stays with me in Chao Yang An, building back her health."

"A good arrangement!" James pronounced with approval. "Miss Chang will receive the best nursing care in North China, and you will receive the services of a full-time language instructor."

Laura needed the language instructor as much as she needed money, workers, moral support, and better health. Her move to the countryside required a whole new vocabulary.

During the main course, Laura described her intention of living just like the poor Chinese—eating their food, wearing their clothing, and working alongside them as an equal partner. She would call her orphanage Canaan Home, she said, and she would take in homeless orphans, asking no pay and making no appeals for contributions. "I will have to learn to wait on God constantly and look only to Him for my needs," Laura told them.

They listened so warmly that she was tempted to say more—tempted to give them a few more details about her needs, to tell them that she was nearly penniless, that as soon as she paid her first quarter's rent, she had little more than enough money to pay a carter to move her donated furniture out to Chao Yang An.

But she gave herself a pinch and held her tongue. She must discipline herself to keep her promise to the Lord. The Leynses were obviously interested and sympathetic, but they had asked no direct questions about the state of her finances.

The dinner conversation turned to the political situation, which was still uncertain. Chiang Kai Shek was concentrating his attention first on wiping out his former ally, the Chinese Communist Party, and then on trying to control the warlords who had pledged him their allegiance under duress during his successful northern expedition. He had his hands full trying to strengthen and solidify his hold on the nation, but he appeared to be bringing Peking under control. At least the countryside where Laura intended to begin Canaan Home seemed to be stabilizing.

The Leynse's servant removed the family's dinner plates and served dessert: Peking Dust, an elaborate concoction of chestnuts ground up fine as dust and placed inside a ring of grapes, crab apples, oranges, and nuts, all glazed together with melted sugar and topped with whipped cream.

Rich and sweet—just like this evening with these friends, Laura thought. She strolled back to her room in the dusky coolness of the May evening, relishing her memory of the evening. The Leynses had given no promise of support, but she sensed she had forged a strong tie with the family that night.

Two weeks later, with only enough cash in her pocket to pay the carter when she arrived, Laura was prepared to set out for Chao Yang An with the Sus and Miss Chang. Just as they were leaving, a note arrived from James Leynse with money enclosed.

"I just now received this money in a letter today from a group of working girls in Holland," he wrote. "They promised to continue sending money for the support of one little orphan, and as you know, we ourselves have no work for orphans. So the Lord must have touched their hearts at this time to give to your work opening in the Western Hills."

Laura sat still with the note and the money curled in her hand. She felt light, as if an invisible burden had suddenly been removed from her back and shoulders. All her muscles relaxed, and she realized how alone and anxious she had been feeling.

"Thank You, Father," she said. "Thank You that You love and care for little children, and thank You for showing me in this way that You want me to move forward."

Wayside shrines, stones of healing, and ancient trees festooned with cloth prayer streamers greeted her along the road to her new home. Each dusty shrine contained an idol and an altar, with a paper sing-song doll to please the male gods, and a piece of shiny paper placed upon it to represent money. A hundred different gods were represented in the shrines she passed, a god for every worry of mankind: the goddess of birth, the goddess of scarlet fever, the lady of good sight, the god of the road, the god of travelers, the goddess of small pox, the water god—

The villagers believed that if they took proper care of their ancestors, their ancestors would be able to protect them from evil spirits and help them gain the blessings of the gods. They were unable to imagine the One God of the Christians, a God so different from the gods they served: a God so near they could get His full attention in a moment, a God so wise that He could not be tricked, a God so powerful that He needed nothing and so could not be bribed or controlled. The Christian God of care and love and insistent holiness....How ever could they come to believe her words about Him?

The cartman's springless wagon jerked toward the outlying mud huts and straw gates of Chao Yang An, and she began hearing the roar of market day in the village. Soon their way became crowded with peddlers swinging baskets on shoulder poles and cart men yelling curses at their mules. Beggars pierced the din with their cries of "*K'e lien! K'e lien!* Have pity!"

Makeshift stalls clogged the street, narrowing it to a crooked lane. Pigs scurried and squealed among the stalls, foraging for spilled grain. A young father with a baby tucked in the front of his jacket strolled past a brass beater hammering on a copper wash bowl. A trio of women stopped at a stall to finger fragile toys constructed of paper, straw, and feathers. A medicine man hawked rhubarb and arsenic, toad skins and tiger bones. Two boys lifted strips of blue cotton from a steaming indigo vat, while an ancient idol-maker squatted in the dust, molding the god of grasshoppers in clay.

These were her new neighbors—and, she hoped, her new friends. Perhaps, God willing, a few might even become new partners.

A tall brick pawnshop loomed above the crowds, the shops, the makeshift stalls, and the low-lying dwellings of the village. It was a formidable place, built like a feudal stronghold, with many small windows piercing its massive walls, and heaps of stones piled on its roof to throw down on the heads of attackers—a fortification indeed, for times of trouble in Chao Yang An.

But the old fortress could not protect the villagers against the enemy that devastated their homes and fields that summer of 1929, as their crops withered in the fields, while the sky remained serenely blue, and everywhere the water springs dried up. The fortress could only protect the villagers from bandits and soldiers. It wielded no power against a siege from their ancient enemy, drought.

Laura had to buy Canaan Home's water supply from a neighbor who trundled it in tubs on a creaky wheelbarrow through the alleys of Chao Yang An. At every dwelling needing water, he filled two wooden pails from the water tubs and carried them into the house with each pail dangling from a chain on the end of a pole balanced across his shoulders. All the water for drinking, cooking, laundry, and bathing was delivered in this way from the water seller.

As the hot days of summer passed and the drought deepened, the water seller steadily increased the price of the water supply. Miss Chang and the Sus protested in eloquent Mandarin, but it did no good. The water seller's shrewd eyes gleamed, and he held his ground.

"We must ask our Heavenly Father to give us water some other way," Laura told her Chinese colleagues. "I believe it is wrong to pay such an exorbitant price."

So they prayed about the problem, and then the rains began at last, very late in the season. The family collected rain in barrels until the rains stopped.

While this was going on, Orpha Gould and the other medical staff at Douw Hospital sent Canaan Home its first orphan. Apple Blossom was an attractive eight-year-old girl whose mother, a lame beggar from a nearby village, had sold her daughter as a slave to a woman from Peking. One day, the slave owner's daughter stabbed Apple Blossom in the wrist with a pair of scissors, severing her wrist artery. After several weeks in the hospital, the little girl recovered, but no one ever came back to claim her. So the hospital sent her to Laura.

One day after the rains stopped, when the family's water supply was diminishing in the rain barrels, Laura took a walk with a meandering Apple Blossom. "My feet are getting wet," the child complained. Laura checked and found that the girl had stumbled into a boggy patch of weeds alongside the road. When Laura explored the little bog, she discovered a flowing spring.

"How did she find that spring?" the villagers asked the Sus in astonishment. "There has never been one in that place before."

The villagers were curious about Laura. They were not used to seeing a foreigner wearing a common peasant's gown. They greeted her politely in the market, using her Chinese name Rui Lemei, which sounded to their ears like her American name spoken Chinese style, surname first: Richards Laura May. It meant Happy Plum Flower Richards. Laura knew they asked a lot of questions about her behind her back. Some poor local Christians began coming to visit and to ask Laura for medical advice and care.

It was just as well that finding the spring enabled Canaan Home to eliminate the expense of buying water. Although the gift from the Dutch working girls was enough to keep Apple Blossom well supplied with a healthy, varied diet, the rest of the family eked out their food supply on pennies, subsisting mainly on cornbread, salted vegetables, and cooked millet—the food of the poorest Chinese. Neither Laura nor her co-workers were used to the unrelenting sameness of their coarse diet, but Laura felt they must adjust if they were truly going to identify with the poor.

There were other disciplines for Laura besides developing a tolerance for the new diet. It was hard for her to keep up daily language lessons with Apple Blossom's frequent interruptions, and hard to maintain an ordered routine with Apple Blossom steadily resisting her efforts.

Some days Laura thought wearily that a better name for the little girl would be Thistle Blossom. She was wild and stubborn as the thistles Laura had once rooted out of her stepmother's garden. Apple Blossom had lived most of her life on the streets fighting, lying, begging, stealing, and worse. Her mouth was as foul as a mule driver's, and no mule could surpass her in obstinacy. She disliked the family's healthy regimen of regular mealtimes and bedtimes, and she balked when Laura tried to teach her simple chores. Usually Laura had to stand over her to get her to complete even a simple task like washing her hands before meals.

Traditionally, Laura was told, orphans are either grateful or rebellious. Apple Blossom was rebellious.

In early September, while Florence Logan was on a trip north to Peking, she made a special trip out to Chao Yang An to visit Laura. Florence gave Laura all the news from the folks in Paotingfu, asked a lot of questions (as usual), and took Laura's love back with her to Dr. Mackey and Dr. Sun, her nursing students, and the rest of the staff at the women's hospital. She said they were all eager to hear how Laura's new venture was faring. Laura soaked herself in Florence's familiar breezy cheerfulness. She felt refreshed when her friend left, and found it easier to be good-humored with Apple Blossom's irritations.

The harvest that autumn of 1929 was meager, the forerunner to famine. Then the bitter cold of a North China winter settled in. Miss Chang returned to her family in Paotingfu, and the Sus decided not to continue with the work.

It was a hard blow.

Laura wanted Canaan Home to be fully Chinese, to be a ministry that Chinese Christians viewed and participated in as their own. She had hoped that Miss Chang would decide to stay and, with the Sus, help her lay the foundation of a thoroughly Chinese orphanage. But it was not to be, and Chao Yang An seemed lonely without them.

She was grateful, though, that they had helped her become settled in the village and introduced her to some local Christians and other neighbors. They had also shared the daily work with her when she had arrived in such weakness. Laura still felt fragile, but at least now she could manage the routine tasks of building fires, cooking, washing and hanging out laundry, cleaning house, and carrying water from the spring for herself and Apple Blossom.

The new spring that Laura had discovered continued to produce abundantly that winter, even when most other springs dried, until January 1, 1930. When Laura came to draw water that day, she found the spring frozen solid.

Fortunately, the water seller's eyes no longer gleamed shrewdly as before when she stopped him on her way home to bargain for water delivery. He readily agreed to a reasonable rate. Perhaps the neighbors had told him what her God had done for her when he tried to cheat her during the drought.

In any case, Laura was soon relieved to have her water delivered again. Not long after the spring froze over, she took in her first baby. After that she had no time for making trips to draw water.

One freezing morning in January, a local village woman came to Laura's door and handed her a small bundle wrapped in a tattered rag. "It's a boy," she said. "Will you take him?"

"A boy!" Laura exclaimed. "The family must be desperate to be giving away a boy! Please come in and tell me the story."

Laura took the baby and ushered the woman into the kitchen. The bundle in her arms felt airy and light. When she peeked inside the wrapping, the wizened face of a miniature old man peered at her listlessly.

He was a twin, the woman explained. His brother was the stronger one, so his parents were keeping that one at home, hoping to save one son for themselves. They were starving in the famine, and his mother had had to go out to beg for food before the babies were born. Now she and her husband were sick, too weak to get up from bed.

Laura gave her visitor a message to take to the dairy to order milk, and the village woman departed. She kissed the downy softness of the baby's tiny head, and a great tenderness welled up inside her. "I will call you Joshua," she told the baby.

Her health was still poor. She had no one to help her with this new responsibility. And Joshua needed round-the-clock care to survive. He was feeble and sickly, and he weighed only three pounds. There could be no skimping on fuel costs now. She would have to keep him warm. He would need milk, too, for formula. In Paotingfu it had been almost impossible to get milk unless you owned your own goat, but here in the Peking area there were private dairies that catered to the many diplomats and other foreigners living in the capital city. So she could buy him milk, although she did not know how much it would cost. This would be her next big test for trusting her Heavenly Father to supply what was needed for the work He had called her to do.

She stood near the stove to keep Joshua warm and began to pray, thanking God for taking care of her and Apple Blossom thus far through the winter and asking Him for the provisions and the strength she needed to take care of Joshua.

Laura Richards, undated photograph, probably taken during her 1926 to 1928 missionary furlough. Laura's colleagues in China and her family back in the U.S. were nonplused when she decided to resign from the Presbyterian Mission and found Canaan Home in 1929 at the age of 36.

Perceptions

December 10, 1988 interview with Laura's cousin,
Laura Jane Eberhardt Cerling,
discussing her parents' response to the news
of Laura's resignation from the Presbyterian Mission.
Laura Jane was seven years old when her cousin resigned:

I knew that they thought Laura was a very special person. They really liked her. But to go off like that, leaving your country and your family, they couldn't understand why she would want to do that. It was ingrained in me that you did everything you could yourself, but if you had to ask for help, it was your family that you went to. If you wanted to help somebody, you should do it in the United States where your family was close by. China was so far from Laura's family that if anything happened to her, she wouldn't have any chance of anyone helping her.

They thought of the Presbyterian Mission in the same terms as my father working for Hotpoint. She wouldn't get as much money, but at least she had an employer who paid her. They couldn't understand why she would cut those ties, especially when she was cutting all the ties off to home.

It was a very brave thing for her to do.

Fragment of a letter that Laura wrote from Chao Yang An,
with the date "June 20, 1930?" penciled in:

When I resigned, I wrote to these people explaining why I had left the Presbyterian Board and telling them that I could not accept a stated salary. Now I had felt that they would not understand the step that I was taking, and this was true with the exception of one or two.

I believed that I should indeed be thrown wholly upon my Heavenly Father. Should I not be in safe hands if in His loving care? I asked Him to especially cleanse me so that I could be wholly used in His service and to help me to ever keep my eyes fixed upon Him. There were some very wonderful answers to prayer, and there have been times also when the Enemy would have torn the very foundations from under our feet if he had had the power to do so.

4.

The First Babies

Chao Yang An, 1930

THE BITTER GRIP OF WINTER loosened, and the air softened. Then the daily dust storms of early spring whipped through the village, dimming the sun and filling the air with choking, yellow grime. Laura had to cover her face with a scarf whenever she needed to go out into the yard even for a few minutes so she could see and breathe.

Then one fine spring day, after the worst of the windy weather had passed, three neatly dressed Chinese women riding in rickshaws bumped to a halt in front of Laura's gate. "Have you eaten?" they greeted her politely.

"Dr. Sun!" Laura exclaimed. "Miss Lin and Miss Wu! What a surprise! What brings you here all the way from Paotingfu?" She was so glad to see them, she could hardly talk through the smiles that kept stretching across her face. The two young women were her graduate nurses, and Dr. Sun was the doctor who had invited her to join the medical team traveling through the Paotingfu countryside. They had made the long trip out to Chao Yang An to see her while they were in Peking.

Laura invited her guests to come through the inner courtyard to the kitchen. Under a tree in the packed dirt of the inner courtyard squatted two little girls, nine and seven years old, filling a wooden boat with fine yellow powder blown in from the recent windstorms. Laura introduced them as Apple Blossom and Precious Jade. Precious Jade had come a couple months before. Her mother had died, her father was a soldier away from home most of the time, and her aunt could no longer care for her.

Inside the kitchen, a pot of diapers was boiling furiously on an open Chinese burner. Two fragile-looking babies lay in a crib, keeping warm nearby. "This is Joshua," Laura said, picking up a tightly bundled mite with a thin red face and wispy black hair. She kissed his forehead and eased him gently into Dr. Sun's outstretched arms.

"Snow Flake is asleep, so I'll leave her in the crib," she said, indicating the other baby. Snow Flake's mother had trudged many miles from the mountains beyond the Western Hills to bring her to Laura. The mountain mother was seriously malnourished. Since she had no milk, she had fed her daughter flour water, and the baby had grave digestive problems. "Please keep her," the woman had begged. "If she stays with us, she will die." Her husband was a rickshaw man, she said, and they were so poor that they had to give away their seven-year-old son.

"All the other babies are taking naps," Laura said.

"Ai ya!" exclaimed the doctor. "You have more? How many children do you have?"

"Seven altogether," Laura said. "Besides the ones you have seen there are three others—Peace, Sarah, and Charity."

She told each child's story. Peace was three days old when someone found her and brought her to Laura one evening. She had been put out in the cold to freeze during the day, and it had taken Laura all night to revive her. Four-week-old Sarah's mother sent her because the child's father had gone insane. Charity's family gave her to Laura when she was one month old because they were afraid of her. She was born on New Year's Day, which was considered bad luck. Six days after she was born, her 24-year-old brother died in a mine explosion, and all the neighbors started cursing the family because of her.

"The news of so many children astonishes our ears," said Miss Wu. "The Leynses thought you had only one or two."

"I've had no time to write anybody," Laura apologized. She poked at the pot of diapers with a paddle, and then began pouring milk into a pan to prepare formula for the 11 a.m. feeding.

"You will need the strength of Samson to care for all these children," Miss Lin said. "Miss Orpha Gould told us she was concerned for your health, living here by yourself. She said that when you journeyed to Chao Yang An from Peking last year, you were pale as a lily and weak as a noodle cooked in water."

"Indeed I was," Laura said, and she told them how she had prayed for strength when Joshua arrived. "For a while I was too busy to notice that my strength was increasing with each new baby that came. And then one day I noticed that all my symptoms had disappeared. My God has healed me."

The nurses thanked God aloud and started helping pour formula into baby bottles. "How is Dr. Mackey?" Laura asked as she worked. "And Dr. Hinkhouse? And Miss Logan?"

She asked after everyone at the mission station in Paotingfu, recalling each by name, and her guests told her all the news at the Paotingfu and Peking mission stations. It was a special help to Laura that they came on laundry day, because the three nurses cheerfully pitched in to lend her a hand with the back-breaking routine. They hauled heavy loads of wash water; hand scrubbed piles of clothing, sheets, and diapers; rinsed everything twice; wrung it all out by hand; lugged the weighty baskets of wet clothes to the courtyard; stooped, straightened, and stooped over and over again to hang the wash on the clothesline, then stretched and bent anew to take it all down when it dried; then they sorted and folded the fresh smelling loads. In between laundry chores, Laura's visitors helped her feed the children, resolve the little girls' quarrels, and move the babies' cribs into the courtyard for sunshine and fresh air.

Through it all, Laura entertained them with stories of answered prayer. She had many to tell.

One day, she said, she ran out of vegetables, and there was no one she could send to the market to buy any. After three days passed without vegetables, she began praying specifically that God would send the vegetables if she and the little girls needed them for good health. She started building the fire for dinner while she prayed. As soon as she got it going, she heard a knock at the gate. It was a man selling vegetables. Although she had lived in Chao Yang An nearly a year, it was the first time a vegetable seller had ever come to her door.

Then there was the time she ran out of cold cream. One of the babies needed it for a bad diaper rash, and Laura also needed it for her hands. In the wind and cold, her hands grew rough, which made it hard to keep them properly clean.

She searched her trunk, hoping to find a tube of cold cream there, but all she could find was two tubes labeled toothpaste. She brought them both out and prayed for cold cream. That night when she squeezed toothpaste on her toothbrush, it turned out to be cold cream.

"*Ai ya!*" the nurses chorused. "Truly?"

"Yes," Laura said. "It tasted awful."

And then there were the stories of gifts from unexpected sources, which came just when needed.

She told them about the money the Dutch working girls had sent just as she was setting out for Chao Yang An and described the warm woolen clothes they had knit and mailed at Christmas time. A poor cook who worked at the nearby tubercular hospital gave her a gift of vegetables one day, and another time he left her 40 Chinese cents. Several other poor Christians in Chao Yang An had become interested in Canaan Home as well, and they gave what they could. Sometimes they came for a day to help her with the work, and sometimes they made clothes or shoes for her and the children. These people were among the poorest of the poor, and their generosity dumbfounded her. A widow with an income of only five Chinese dollars a month, for example, once gave her one Chinese dollar.

Laura knew these Christians denied themselves necessities to help her and the children. So although she prayed before gifts came in, she prayed just as much when they were in her hand. It was a grave responsibility to use the gifts of such sacrifice.

"These gifts come of people's own free will," Laura explained. "I never speak to anyone about giving. If they come to me and ask questions about the orphanage, I answer their questions, but that is all. I do not want to speak to people about giving. I hope that people will give because God has truly touched their hearts."

She kept a strict accounting of it all. If someone asked her to use a gift for any particular purpose, she used it for that and nothing else. Sometimes people gave her money or supplies "for the children"; sometimes they gave her money or supplies for her own use; and sometimes they made no special designation. Laura kept the children's supplies separate from her own. She ate none of the food and used none of the supplies designated for them.

When she received money for her own use, she set aside a tithe. Once when a Chinese Christian who had a home for lame and blind children came to visit, she gave him five dollars for his orphans. The very next week he came back with a sack of flour and seven dollars for her orphans!

The shadows of late afternoon lengthened in the courtyard, and Laura's visitors helped her move the babies' cribs indoors. It was time for her friends from Paotingfu to return to Peking.

Laura deposited a sleeping baby gently into the child's crib just before walking her friends to the gate. Her hand bumped into something hard on the crib mattress, and she discovered several bills wadded tightly into a hard lump, lying in the crib.

"Miss Lin!" she exclaimed. "You must have dropped your rickshaw fare into the baby's bed!"

She handed the money to the nurse, who took it and excused herself to go into Laura's room to put on her knitted cap. Then the four women walked to the gate to make their farewell bows.

"It is a glad face I will be lifting to Heaven on our return to Peking," Dr. Sun said. "You have refreshed our spirits and filled our hearts with gratitude to God." Then the visitors' rickshaws jounced away in a swirl of yellow dust.

Around midnight, Laura found Miss Lin's lump of money again. This time it was placed beside the babies' bottles. Laura opened it: seven dollars. A second lump of money, five dollars this time, awaited her on her pillow when she lay down for the night.

• • •

Spring passed in a heavy press of duties. Laura often had to get by on only three or four hours of sleep, with only one or two meals because she was too busy to eat. Miss Lin was right. She needed the strength of Samson.

One night when she was washing up the bottles after the babies' 11 p.m. feeding, a wave of weakness crumpled her legs. She sat down quickly, trying to think what could be wrong. Dimly, the reason dawned. She had had only three hours of sleep the night before, and then she had been so busy all day that she had forgotten to eat. No wonder she felt faint. She reheated a bit of porridge from supper and sat down to the table with a bowlful. Then she fainted in earnest. When she came to, it was midnight, and she was face down in cold, spilled mush.

Not many days later, in June, a Chinese mother came to Laura's door. "My baby is dying," she whispered hesitantly. "Can you help her?"

"Bring your daughter to me, and I will do what I can," Laura promised.

The woman returned with a shrunken six-month-old baby, and Laura's heart sank when she saw the child. *A few days at best,* her experienced eyes told her, *but that is all. This little one is nearly dead, and only an outright miracle can save her.*

"Our Heavenly Father's will be done," she told the mother. "If your daughter lives, it can only be because He has healed her. If she dies, I will send for you."

The mother bowed politely and trudged away, and Laura seated herself in a chair with the baby lying in her arms like a limp rag doll. She wanted to cry. How could she summon the strength to take care of this little one? The three healthiest babies were sleeping through the night now, but Joshua and Snow Flake still required both a late-night and an early-morning feeding. Now this new baby would require constant attention around the clock. Apple Blossom and Precious Jade were old enough to be a real help to her, but Apple Blossom was uncooperative. She incited Precious Jade into all sorts of naughtiness.

"Send me help, Lord!" Laura cried. "Send me help so the children will not suffer!"

Her days and nights blurred together, and her body cried out for one uninterrupted night's sleep. For three days she carried on, until she grew too exhausted to form words to her prayers any more. She just pointed an inarticulate cry for help in God's direction. On the third day she heard someone knocking at her gate. Wearily she approached it, hoping dumbly that her caller was not another worried Chinese mother.

It was not. Instead an American woman—a stranger—stood waiting, holding in her hand a letter of introduction from a mutual friend. "I think God wants me to stay here and help you instead of taking my summer vacation," she said.

So Laura had a helper on hand when six-month-old Joshua died a few days later, and also when Peace passed serenely away in her sleep near the end of June after four days of diarrhea. "Cholera infantum," the doctor said.

Her former student Miss Lin offered to stay and help her in July and August. Laura accepted gratefully. In addition to all her other chores, grief was such hard work. She wept for her babies. Joshua had never grown strong. She had known he might not live. But Peace had recovered from her ordeal in the freezing ditch and seemed to be doing well. Laura had had high hopes for Peace.

The sick baby whom Laura had thought would live only a few days lingered on for nearly a month. When she finally died, Laura prepared a little box for her coffin and dressed her in the nicest clothing she had. Then she sent for the baby's mother.

The woman carefully inspected every centimeter of her daughter's body, running her hands delicately over the cool skin, touching the tiny fingers and toes, lifting the baby's eyelids with a gentle finger. She seemed especially concerned about her baby's eyes and chest. Finally she said, "Now I know that the foreign devils do not take out a baby's eyes or cut out its heart for medicine. I am assured of that."

Laura was speechless. Was this what the villagers were saying about her? How desperate this mother must have been to bring her child to Laura's door! No wonder she had waited until her baby was so far gone that there was no hope for her life. It was too bad the little one had died, but at least this mother knew now that Laura had not mutilated her baby. She would tell the neighbors, and word would get around.

Perhaps the woman's story gave one of the village fathers courage to bring his 22-day-old daughter to Laura when he discovered his baby lying in a ditch late in August. His wife, insane for over a year, had thrown the baby there several hours before. It was a hot day, and the little one was horribly sunburned.

Laura named the child Susanna. Whenever a child came to Canaan Home without a name, Laura gave him or her a name from the Bible, as well as a Chinese name that sounded, if possible, like the Biblical name. Laura thanked God that no foraging pigs or dogs had discovered the baby before her father found her.

A few days after Susanna came, a thick skin peeled off her face like a mask, leaving a soft, fair little face. She recovered quickly from her ordeal, and in a few weeks she was smiling and crowing. But her happy spirit scarcely penetrated Laura's grief that fall, when nine-month-old Snow Flake died.

Snow Flake had always been frail. She had never grown strong. Yet her death knocked Laura staggering. She felt abandoned, as bereft as the day her mother had died.

Over half the babies she had taken in had died. Over half! Was this what lay ahead for her? Pouring her life out day and night, strengthening the bond of love with every touch, every meal she missed, every hour of sleep she sacrificed—all this, only to watch her babies fade and die? How could she bear it?

"Is this truly Your will for me, Father?" Laura cried. "Or am I doing something wrong? What do You want? Have I heard You rightly?"

The two women who were helping her had to leave at the end of summer, but Laura was not entirely alone in her grief. News of the little orphanage had begun to spread among poor Chinese Christians in the area. More and more of them began to help.

During the fall of 1930, Christians from the Presbyterian Church in Peking journeyed to Chao Yang An to sweep and clean the courtyard, wash and mend clothing, and mold coal balls, the poor man's fuel, out of coal dust, soil, and water. The Chinese Methodist minister came and papered Laura's kitchen windows for winter. The cook from the tubercular hospital papered the windows in the children's room. Women from the Presbyterian Women's Society in Peking sewed clothes for the children. Other Christians visited the home and left a dollar here and a dollar there. A minister from the tubercular hospital paid a woman to work for Laura as a cook for six weeks. These visitors prayed with Laura, too, and they told her that they prayed for her earnestly through the week.

They comforted her more than they knew. She cherished their prayers, their gifts, the tears she saw gathering in their eyes when they spoke to her about the children.

One morning in October she read three lines from a poem by Hugh Macmillan, which she found in *Streams in the Desert*:

> Amidst my list of blessings infinite
> Stands this the foremost, that my heart has bled:
> For all I bless Thee, most for the severe.

Severe blessings, Laura thought. *That is what God has given me, severe blessings....*

She glanced up at the kitchen window, a traditional Chinese paper window composed of many square panels set in an eight foot square frame, which the Chinese pastor had covered tightly with tough, translucent rice paper to let in the light. The sight of his handiwork reminded her of the words she had spoken at the Leynses' dinner table: *I hope that the Chinese people will begin to participate in this work, and support it, and see it as their own ministry.*

It was happening, although not in the way she had expected.

God had allowed her situation to become so impossible that the poorest of the poor Chinese Christians identified with her. Their situation was impossible, too. She had become so poor that even their pennies could help, so overburdened that even their humble efforts made a difference. Her trials caught their attention. They saw that Canaan Home was not a typical Westerners' ministry with support money coming in regularly from wealthy foreign churches. Canaan Home was a place that needed them, a place where their meager contributions were valuable.

And God had answered another prayer, too. She had asked Him to show her how to depend completely on Jesus, like a branch depending on the vine. Then she had become so isolated and so overwhelmed with work that she had had neither time nor opportunity to hint or beg for help. Jesus had been the only one available to her when she needed anything, so she had developed the habit of turning first to Him in everything. Prayer had become instinctive, her automatic response in any circumstance.

The babies' deaths must be severe blessings, too.

She had wanted to rescue these babies and raise them up to become faithful servants in the kingdom of God. Instead He had allowed her to give them comfort as they died, expressing the love of their Heavenly Father to "the least of these"—these tiny representatives of the most helpless class of all the people in China. God was wiser than she. She had learned that in her head. Now she was learning it with her heart. Her Heavenly Father knew what was best for her, for her babies, for His kingdom in this world. She would just have to trust her little ones to His wise love.

If she was going to follow Christ in poverty and in service, she would have to follow Him in suffering as well.

Severe blessings....

She had a feeling that the severest blessings were yet to be.

Report from Chao Yang An

Excerpt—a letter from Laura Richards, written in Chao Yang An, November 12, 1930:

Oh, such searchings of heart and crying to the Lord that I might know more fully what His will for me was and is.

The Lord has been good to us indeed. Many times He has stretched forth His hand to help us in times of need. One day the Chinese minister from the Methodist Church [Peking] came out for a visit. He returned home and told his wife about the children here and later she came, too. Upon leaving she left a dollar to be used for this work. Later I heard that she had been earnestly praying for God's work here. Then one day word came that this minister and his wife had found a woman who would cook for us and also do other work.

After being here six weeks and having had severe attacks of dysentery, she went to the Hospital in [Peking] for treatment. This again left me alone with the children. But again I called upon our Heavenly Father who had anticipated the need and had started a 17-year-old girl on her way to us two days before from Shanting Province so that she arrived the next day after Mrs. Huang left. She had come to be with her husband in the Hospital, but her husband had left many months before for another place of work so that there was no place for her to stay, and a brother-in-law brought her here, asking if we could make room for her. She has come just in time to finish the Winter sewing.

On the back of this photograph, Laura wrote "The two little girls standing by the crib came when they were a few days old, [Sarah] and [Charity]. When I left China they were taller than I. The two inside the crib are twins [Rachel] and [Rose Mary]." Sarah came to Canaan Home because her father was insane. Rachel and Rose Mary came because their mother died and their father was homeless. Charity came because her superstitious family was afraid of her. She was born on New Year's Day, which was considered unlucky, so her family blamed her when her 24-year-old brother died six days after her birth. A few weeks after she arrived at Canaan Home, her mother died as well.

5.

Old Billy

Chao Yang An, 1932

LAURA STEPPED from the children's bedroom door into the courtyard, wrinkling her nose. The courtyard stunk.

"Baaaaa!" A rangy billy goat lying tied to a tree shook his beard and scolded. "BLAAAAAA-Baaah! BLAAAAAA-Baaah!" He heaved himself to his feet and jerked angrily at his rope.

"Patience, patience, Old Billy," Laura said. "I just put the children to bed. I'll go pull weeds for your supper next."

Old Billy glared at her as if he wished that he could curse her in a language she understood.

Laura started for the gate and then swerved suddenly into the kitchen, remembering that she needed to bring string to tie up her bundle of weeds. To her surprise, there stood Apple Blossom in her pajamas, poking a hole in the rice paper window.

"Why aren't you in bed?" Laura asked.

"I needed to use the outhouse," Apple Blossom said.

"The kitchen is not the outhouse," Laura said, "and besides, you used the outhouse ten minutes ago, just before I put you to bed."

"I didn't want to go to bed," Apple Blossom said.

"You must go to bed anyway," Laura said, taking the 11-year-old's hand. "Bedtime is bedtime."

Apple Blossom whipped her hand from Laura's and burst into a torrent of complaint. "I hate this place! I hate your rules! I was free as a magpie when my mother and I begged in the market. You have turned me into a mule in the market, tied with a rope and burdened by a heavy load. My mother never ordered me to cook porridge for a herd of worthless baby girls. I did what I pleased. My mother never told me when to eat my meals. I took whatever I desired when the eyes of the shopkeeper were unwary. My mother never told me when to sleep. I slept whenever I wanted, wherever I chose—in the ditches and the doorsteps. I did what I pleased and nobody told me what to do."

"But Apple Blossom, darling," Laura said, "don't you remember how hungry you were after the locusts came, and how you trembled and shook in your rags in the cold? Don't you remember how your mother wept when she sold you for money to buy food and a winter gown and a blanket?"

Apple Blossom clapped her hands over her ears.

Laura regarded her sadly. Would she ever get through to this child?

"Come to bed," she said.

Sullenly, Apple Blossom allowed herself to be led back to the bedroom. Old Billy bleated angrily as they passed.

"Worthless goat!" Apple Blossom muttered. "He makes my bedroom stink like dung. Why don't you sell him and buy us some cake? We never eat cake."

"Old Billy is God's gift to us," Laura said firmly, "and we must thank our Heavenly Father for him. I asked God to help us start our own goat herd for the babies' milk, and then the missionaries sent us Old Billy. The milk from the dairy is too expensive."

Most of their money went to the dairy, it seemed, but the milk was poor quality. The children did not seem to thrive on it. Canaan Home really needed a different milk supply, and she hoped Old Billy would become the key to helping them solve that problem.

They also needed rent money. She had rented this court in Chao Yang

An for almost three full years now, and soon, on June 1, the rent for the first quarter of the coming year was due. Every week or so for the past month, the caretaker had showed up and asked if she wanted to lease the place for another year. And every time he had asked, she had said she didn't know.

Laura settled Apple Blossom in bed, and then located her two teenage helpers, Azure Cloud and Sweet Water Pond. They had volunteered to assist her for a few weeks. She warned them to be watchful of Apple Blossom, and then she headed for the gate.

Old Mr. Han let her out. He was another volunteer, an elderly gentleman who had come to help at the orphanage seven or eight months ago. When she went out every night to pull weeds for Old Billy, the two teenagers took care of the children while Mr. Han kept the gate.

Laura hurried to the outskirts of the village and started tearing up handfuls of weeds growing alongside the path. *I wonder if Billy will approve of what I bring him this time,* she thought, doubtfully eyeing the growing pile of wild grass and weeds. Billy was fussy.

Whatever his opinion might be, though, the weeds did him good. When he first arrived in Chao Yang An, he had wobbled through the gate and collapsed under the tree in a smelly heap of limp goat hide. The friend who arranged to have him donated to Canaan Home told Laura that Billy was sick most of the time, and that his owners did not know how to care for him.

My weeds seemed to have cured him, Laura thought. After two months on her weed diet, he had grown so healthy, he was getting hard to handle.

A gentle breeze lifted the wisps of hair clinging wetly to Laura's neck and forehead. She stood still and savored the coolness lapping her skin. The wind licked softly at the beads of sweat on her arms and face. Several yards down the path, an old lady was yanking weeds, too. She waved companionably at Laura. In the Western Hills beyond Peking, only the poorest of the poor pulled weeds to feed their livestock.

"Happy Plum Flower Richards, are you pulling grass again for that old billy goat?" asked a voice at her elbow. The speaker was laughing at her.

"Good evening, Mrs. Lu," Laura said, recognizing a neighbor. Mrs. Lu had started bringing her relatives to Laura when they were sick, and one day when the Canaan Home family had run out of food, Mrs. Lu had unknowingly saved the day by showing up at the gate with a thank-you basket of sweet potatoes.

"Why are you keeping that worthless old billy goat?" the village woman persisted. "He can't be of any use to you!"

"You just wait and see!" Laura said cheerfully, loading up her weeds for the trek home through the village. "One of these days, he'll be useful enough. You just wait and see!"

She really believed it.

For months Laura had been praying about the family's milk supply. Then, soon after she began asking God about the possibility of starting a small goat herd, Old Billy had come. So she thought God must be intending to start a herd with him. All she needed now was some pasture and a nanny goat.

And some more rope, she added to herself, as she neared home. The resounding crashes she heard coming from inside the courtyard told her that Billy was loose again.

A full moon gleamed brightly in the darkening sky, and old Mr. Han stood waiting for her at the gate, grasping a frayed leather strap in one hand and the poker from the stove in the other. Beside him fidgeted the teenagers Azure Cloud and Sweet Water Pond. Mr. Han was too old to chase billy goats, and the girls were too scared.

Laura dumped her load of weeds just inside the gate, caught up the strap and poker, and headed for the goat, who was hurtling between the buildings and the walls, gleefully kicking out chunks of brick with his hooves. He paused and stared at the strap in Laura's hand, then skipped over as if to take a closer look.

"Why do you always get so wild on moonlit nights?" Laura asked him.

His eyes glinted. A two-foot length of chewed up rope dangled beneath his chin, and Laura snatched at it.

But Old Billy was ready for her. Just as her fingers brushed the rope, he bounced vigorously backward and leaped behind the tree. When Laura followed, he romped over to the other side of the courtyard.

She chased him from one end of the yard to the other, over and over, until she was out of breath. When she paused and leaned against the tree to rest, Old Billy cantered leisurely past and started kicking more chunks of brick out of the walls. This place was unusually well built for a Chinese residence, but Old Billy was going to damage it one of these times if he kept getting loose.

Finally Laura managed to prod the goat into a corner with the poker and grab the rope under his chin. Then she led him, bucking and pulling, over to the tree, where she tied him to a branch with the leather strap.

Sweet Water Pond plopped the bundle of weeds beside him under the tree. "There's your dinner, Old Billy," Laura said.

He thrust his nose deep into the bundle, sniffed loudly, and turned his back on the whole pile. Then he knelt down next to his wooden water bucket and started nibbling carefully all around its edge. He closed his eyes, rolled a wad of splinters thoughtfully over his tongue, and swallowed. Then he tasted his strap. His lips made little smacking sounds.

Laura felt like she had spent the evening lying in mud puddles, being run over by the local farmers' solid wheel carts. Her legs and arms ached, and she was wet all over with perspiration. She wondered if she smelled as bad as Old Billy.

A bit of weed had worked its way from the neck of her gown to a point just below her right shoulder blade, and she longed to find a private corner where she could contort her body into the proper position to scratch it. Instead, she checked on the children, who were all sleeping soundly, except for Apple Blossom. Apple Blossom had been standing at the bedroom door enjoying the show ever since Old Billy first broke loose. Laura led her back to bed, protesting, and bade Mr. Han and her helpers a courteous good night.

Then she went to the kitchen, located a basin and a bar of soap, slipped her gown over her head, and stepped out of her pajamas. The moon shone so brightly through the window that she left the lamp unlit. Then she soothed away the grimy stickiness on her face and body with a soapy wash rag and rubbed the bit of grass off her back. She was soaping her feet when she began to feel uneasy, as if someone was watching her through the two foot square pane of real glass set in the kitchen's traditional Chinese paper window. She turned. A bearded face peered at her through the glass.

"Not again!" she exclaimed.

Old Billy heaved his shoulders onto the window sill and started butting his horns against the glass. The windowpane rattled, and shreds of rice paper floated onto the kitchen floor.

Hastily, Laura pulled on her gown, knotted two short lengths of rope together, and dashed outside in her bare feet for another 20 minute frolic with Old Billy in the moonlight.

"Why are you so fascinated with that glass window?" she asked him when she finally caught him again and tied him back to the tree. Butting his reflection in the window and kicking the courtyard to bits were Old Billy's two favorite sports. "One of these nights, you're going to break the glass," she scolded.

Old Billy scratched his rump against the tree and sulked.

When her supply of rope was especially frayed and the moon was bright, she was sometimes forced to get up with Billy two or three times in a night. This time, fortunately, he stayed tied up all night and Laura slept soundly.

She awoke early the next morning wondering if the caretaker would come by again during the day to ask whether or not she wanted to lease the place for another year. What she really needed was a different place, a place with pasture for Old Billy. But she knew of no other place she could afford to rent. And anyway, there was no money in sight to pay rent.

It was a familiar situation. Twice in the last three years she had thought she was going to have to move the family for lack of funds to pay the rent, and each time, money to cover the bill had shown up just in time. Now, though, she needed a new place as well as rent money—and besides that, she reminded the Lord, the cupboard was growing bare.

She stepped into the courtyard. *Now I wonder what Apple Blossom is up to this time,* she thought. The girl was standing next to the goat picking at the knot that tied him to the tree. Old Billy had sucked a section of her dress into his mouth and was grazing contentedly on the hem of her gown.

"Apple Blossom!" Laura called. "Are you untying the goat?"

The child started. Then she shrugged and made a rude gesture. When Laura scolded her, she laughed. So Laura set her to work in the kitchen stirring a pot of wheat cereal for the babies' breakfast. There were four of them to feed now: Charity and Sarah were two years old, Rose Mary was one year old, and baby Lydia was eight months old. Rose Mary's twin, Rachel, was at the Peking Union Medical College hospital and should be coming home to the family any day.

Sweet Water Pond stepped into the kitchen. "Honorable Lady Teacher Minister," she said, "Mr. Han sent me to tell you there is a visitor at the gate."

Laura left the teenager in charge of Apple Blossom and the wheat cereal. At the gate an eight-year-old street cleaner jogged up and down, jouncing a large, reeking basket on one arm. "Foreign Lady! Honorable Lady!" he piped. "I have come! *Shih wo*—it is I!"

The child's head was shaved bare in the popular hairstyle of the time for young boys, and three of his baby teeth were missing. He grinned at Laura, showing off the gaps in his smile, and asked politely, "Have you eaten?" Then he indicated a long wooden rake leaning next to the gate. "I have come to sweep away your goat dung," he said.

Laura invited the boy inside, and he raked Old Billy's contributions into his basket, obviously delighted with the size of the pile he was collecting. Then he patted Old Billy's head and ran his hand admiringly over his rough coat.

"He is growing strong," the boy said.

Old Billy snorted. A mighty whiff of goat's breath slapped into the side of Laura's face and fondled her nostrils. "Yes," she agreed, fanning her nose. He was strong all right and in more ways than one.

She rescued the handle of the rake from Old Billy's teeth and escorted the child to her gate. He bowed politely, then turned and ran shouting down the street to another street cleaning boy several courts away.

Laura stood at the gate, watching the two boys compare the contents of their baskets. She thought about her empty purse and dwindling food supply, and then she started to laugh. She didn't have much, but at least she still had enough to share something with people that they really wanted.

She turned back to the kitchen to supervise the children's breakfast and see what the new day would bring. If there was no money, perhaps there would at least be progress. Perhaps this would be the day when she would finally break through to Apple Blossom.

More Stories from Chao Yang An

EXCERPT FROM LAURA'S LETTER
DATED JUNE 8, 1931:

Again I have waited several days before closing this letter. The baby who came in a few days ago died in the hospital of tetanus. In the first place, she was born on the ground floor, as the people were very poor, and at birth she received a wound which resulted in her developing tetanus. She was here two days when suddenly it became difficult for her to swallow. This was in the evening and that night I did not leave her. By morning she was very ill, and I asked a Chinese evangelist to telephone to the hospital to come for her. She died shortly after reaching the hospital.

Pray for us that many of these little ones may be saved for usefulness in the Lord's Kingdom. My heart goes out in great thankfulness to our Heavenly Father for all of the dear friends who have been remembering us in prayer, and also for those whose gifts have made it possible to receive some of these little ones.

EXCERPT FROM RACHEL'S 1989 MEMOIRS,
TRANSLATED FROM CHINESE:

My mother was a very kindly, lovely mother. She was an American, and she was a nurse. Her name was Laura May Richards.

My [birth] family lived in West Mountain Chenzi village. When my mother gave birth to me and my sister, she was very weak. She didn't have anything to eat, so she died. At this time my father began to live a homeless life with me and my sister. He looked everywhere for food to eat. Two months passed in this way, until the third month when I became very seriously ill. My father had no idea what to do. I was near death. At this time there was a Chinese lady who lived near Chuang Hua Ssu and knew a lot about my mother, Miss Richards. She told my father to send us to Canaan Home orphanage. My father didn't want to do that, but if he didn't, we would die. So finally he made his decision and sent us to Canaan Home with this Chinese lady as our sponsor.

It was 1932. Mother saw that I was very seriously ill, and she immediately sent me to the hospital of the Peking Union Medical College. After a period of time, I recovered and Mama got me back.

On the back of this undated photograph, Laura wrote "The first who came when they were only a few days old." Canaan Home began with two older girls and this original group of five orphan baby girls. Left to right, Lydia (nicknamed Foreign Doll), Charity, Rachel, Rose Mary, and Sarah.

6.

Runaway Blossom

Chao Yang An, 1932

IT TURNED OUT TO BE the day Apple Blossom ran away for the first time.

She had been trying everyone's patience all morning. Wherever Apple Blossom went, one of the children started crying. First she deliberately tripped Sarah when the baby toddled over to the breakfast table. Then halfway through the meal, when Laura's back was turned, she snatched Charity's spoon away. Charity tried to take it back, but Apple Blossom held the spoon just out of the toddler's reach. Charity's bowl of porridge inched precariously close to the table edge as she frantically grabbed for her spoon. By the time Laura realized what Apple Blossom was doing, Charity was in tears, and half the little girl's porridge was in her lap. The other half was on the floor along with the broken bowl.

"You are excused from breakfast," Laura told Apple Blossom severely, removing the older girl's bowl of half-eaten porridge from the table. Then she set Apple Blossom to work hanging out laundry in the courtyard with the teenage helper, Sweet Water Pond.

Laura had barely been back in the kitchen five minutes when she heard shouting and screeching outside. She rushed back to the courtyard to find

Apple Blossom and Precious Jade kicking and clawing at each other while Sweet Water Pond stood helplessly by, shouting, "Cease!" The basket of clean wet laundry had been overturned and most of it was trampled in the dirt. Laura yanked the two girls apart. Precious Jade's forearm was bleeding freely where Apple Blossom had bitten her, and two bloody scratches formed a pathway from her left eye to her chin.

Laura marched the two children, into the kitchen, ordered Apple Blossom to sit on a stool in the corner, and began gently washing Precious Jade's face and forearm. Unfortunately all she had to disinfect the teeth marks with was rubbing alcohol. While Precious Jade shrieked and squirmed, Sweet Water Pond told her what had happened.

As soon as Laura had turned her back, she said, Apple Blossom had dumped the clean laundry onto the ground, trampled it, and then dashed over to Precious Jade and kicked over the wooden boat she was playing with. Then the fight began.

Laura comforted Precious Jade and calmed her down, then turned to Apple Blossom. Her stool sat empty.

At that moment, old Mr. Han rushed in and announced that Apple Blossom had just dashed out the gate. *Now what do I do?* Laura wondered.

Aloud she asked Azure Cloud, "Will you run into the village after her?"

Azure Cloud set off to find Apple Blossom, and Laura stood at the gate, watching. "You will never tame that child," Mr. Han said at her elbow. He shook his gray head wisely. "She is a wind-tossed leaf. All her days she has snarled and fought and foraged in the streets, wild as a she-wolf. Once they taste that life, you can never domesticate them. One cannot erase the imprint of a seal when the wax has cooled."

"God can draw white cotton from an indigo vat," Laura said, repeating a phrase she had heard once from a Chinese evangelist. "Surely God can tame her."

It was a pleasant day in May. A cool breeze bathed Laura's arms and face and freshened the air with the scent of date blossoms. Birds gossiped in the treetops overhead, and the bellows box of the village smith clapped monotonously in the background.

Down the lane, a holy pilgrim from Mongolia caught her eye. He stood up straight in his filthy gown and lifted both hands high above his head. Then he sank to his knees and fell forward on his face in the yellow dust. His midsection humped up, he inch-wormed his body forward through the dirt, and then he rose again on the spot where his hands rested. After a pause, he lifted both hands above his head once again, sank to his knees, and fell face forward.

Laura watched Azure Cloud pass the man without a word. The teenager knew there was no point in asking the pilgrim if he had seen a little runaway girl. Nobody was allowed to talk to him while he was on his pilgrimage, prostrating his way through the main streets of the villages he passed en route to some holy mountain.

Part way down the street, she saw the teenager stop to question a young street cleaner—the same gap-toothed boy who visited the family to collect Old Billy's droppings. The two youngsters stood talking earnestly, and then the street cleaner jogged into a side alley with Laura's helper following at his heels. He must be leading her to Apple Blossom.

Laura returned to the courtyard and started picking laundry out of the dirt.

After a while the gate creaked open, and then Azure Cloud was standing in the courtyard with Apple Blossom, who was cramming the last of a Chinese pancake into her mouth. "Happy Plum Flower Richards," Azure Cloud announced, "I have found Apple Blossom. She was begging in the market square."

"I was hungry," Apple Blossom said with her mouth full.

"Foolish child, the seven openings of your head are all plugged up," Azure Cloud scolded her. "You will swallow much bitterness from what you beg in the market square. There are wicked men in that place. A mouse does not beg from a hawk."

"I was hungry," Apple Blossom repeated stubbornly. "I had to beg. Mama took away my breakfast."

Laura grasped Apple Blossom's hand firmly in her own and strode to the child's bedroom for a talk and a session with the paddle. She could not let Apple Blossom get away with biting people. Laura was unsure how she should handle the running-away incident.

After the paddling, she turned into her own bedroom for a few quiet minutes to think. She felt drained of energy and wit. What was she to do with Apple Blossom? She had prayed and prayed some more, but the girl's behavior only seemed to grow worse.

The child liked her. She gave Laura gifts of pretty stones she found in the courtyard, and she brought her bouquets of wild flowers whenever she was able to go for a walk in the country. But what a trial she was! She stole from the family's visitors when she could manage it, and she played mean tricks on the babies. Although she was old enough to be a real help, she used her energy and imagination to pick quarrels with Precious Jade instead and to incite the younger girl into all sorts of mischief. Laura had to keep a close watch on her at all times—an impossible task with so many babies to care for.

How could she keep her temper under control on only four hours of sleep with an uncooperative, ungrateful child like Apple Blossom? How could she keep from resenting the extra work and trouble the child created? Every night when Laura knelt for bedtime prayers, she confessed to God her failures that day with Apple Blossom. Precious Jade could be trying, too, but Laura thought Apple Blossom was the major obstacle to reaching the mind and heart of Precious Jade.

So what should she do with Apple Blossom? Give her up? Let her go? Define the child as a hopeless case, as Mr. Han implied?

"*There are wicked men in that place,*" Azure Cloud had said. "*A mouse does not beg from a hawk.*"

Undoubtedly Azure Cloud was referring to the procurers Laura had heard about—men who obtained girls for brothels. These predators traveled throughout the countryside looking for poor widows with lots of children whom they could trick. They said they would give the daughters factory jobs with good salaries so they could send money home to their families, but after the widows let their daughters go with the men into the city, the procurers forced the girls to become prostitutes. They also kidnapped defenseless young girls begging in the market.

Apple Blossom would soon be turning 12, and her flat little girl figure was beginning to swell into womanly curves. She had a pretty round face with dark eyes the shape of apricot kernels and eyebrows like willow leaves. How could Laura toss this tender young mouse in the direction of the hawks?

Yet the child was endangering the family. She was a harmful example to the other children, and it was only a matter of time before she caused a serious accident with one of her malicious pranks.

I will write to my friends in Peking and try to find another place for her, Laura decided with a mingled sense of regret and relief. *Surely there is someone who can be a better teacher for her than I.*

When she finally emerged from her reverie and walked into the courtyard, she discovered a young evangelist named Glorious Aim exchanging courtesies with old Mr. Han at the gate. Glorious Aim and his family lived in a nearby village, and she was pleased to see him today. Perhaps he would know of a Christian home or a Christian ministry suitable for Apple Blossom.

But the news Glorious Aim brought her momentarily swept away her thoughts of finding a new home for the former beggar child.

"I have found a big good place with pasture for your goat," the young evangelist announced. "It is Chuang Hua Ssu, the old Russian mission nine *li* (three miles) from here. Surely you can stay there with the children, for the owner can find no one willing to rent it."

"Why not?" Laura asked.

"A ghost haunts it, the people say," he explained. "The Russian priest who was caretaker for the mission was murdered there. His cook and two other servants beheaded him and stole his money. So now everyone is afraid. No one will stay there past nightfall."

Any form of murder resulted in a haunting, the villagers believed, but a beheading produced an especially violent haunting. In China there was no more dishonorable way to die than to be beheaded. So the ghost hanging about the mission would be lethal, lashing out in blind revenge on anybody who happened by the spot after dark.

Laura heard Old Billy snorting loudly behind them and turned to watch him jerking at the rope tying him to his tree. She laughed. "A haunted temple!" she said. "Just the place for Old Billy!"

A Christian neighbor woman agreed to help Azure Cloud and Sweet Water Pond take care of the Canaan Home children so that Laura and Glorious Aim could hike out to inspect Chuang Hua Ssu.

They left on a glorious spring day. The sky was bright blue, and the sun shone steadily down without a single cloud floating in the heavens to lessen the warmth of its rays. Laura enjoyed the sensation of striding along at an even pace, unhampered by clattering buckets or the scratchy loads of Old Billy's dinner weeds. Overloaded carts with blue hoods and solid wooden wheels met them on the road, squeaking and groaning. A camel train swayed past them en route to Peking, kicking up dust and assaulting their noses with the odor of sweaty beasts and freshly laid camel dung.

Glorious Aim and Laura headed away from the city, deeper into the hills, and Laura wondered uneasily whether or not this trek might prove to be too far. Most of Canaan Home's provisions came from the few visitors who journeyed to the little village of Chao Yang An all the way from Peking. Would anybody travel as far as this old mission to come visit them?

They turned off the main road onto a hilly dirt path which led them between small, carefully tended farm plots to first one and then another Chinese village. The people they met were friendly. "Where are you going?" they asked Glorious Aim and Laura again and again as the two trudged by. A couple of old grandparents laughingly asked Laura if she would like to give them her blue cotton gown. It was the same fabric and same design as their own clothes, but it was conspicuous to them today because they had never seen a foreigner wearing common Chinese work dress before.

Laura had lived nine years in China now, but she still marveled at how densely the countryside was populated and how tiny the farm holdings were. There were no meadows with large herds of grazing sheep or cows like the farmlands of Ohio where she had grown up. Here, land was too precious to be wasted on pasture. The land it would take to pasture one cow was enough for a farmer to grow food for his entire family.

Their way grew more rugged as the pair journeyed, and then the farm plots ended. Glorious Aim pointed to a group of buildings in a walled enclosure high on one of the hills they were approaching. "There it is," he said. "The people here call it the Russian Retreat Place."

A clear spring flowed at the foot of the hill. "So much water!" Laura exclaimed in delight. "This spring will supply all the water we could possibly need summer and winter, and at no extra cost."

"And so clear!" Glorious Aim agreed. He dipped his cupped hands into it and tasted. "*Ting hao!* Excellent! Almost as sweet as the emperor's water from the Jade Fountain."

Many stone steps led from the spring up to the old mission gate. Laura counted 75 of them as she climbed. The buildings within the enclosure were in ruins, and one of the main ones was burnt nearly to the ground. "That must be the one that burned down during the old priest's last birthday party," said Glorious Aim. "The caretaker told me one of the buildings caught fire when the fireplace became too hot. Perhaps the owner will rebuild it if you come here. There is enough space in these other buildings for you and the children."

He was right. Enough usable building space remained in the other buildings to provide the family room to manage for now. If they could find a way to make repairs, there would also be room to expand when more children came.

In the back court Laura discovered a majestic pine tree of impressive girth which Glorious Aim said was nearly 100 years old. Beyond the ancient pine lay the remains of an old, neglected orchard. Some of the trees still bore fruit. With loving care, perhaps they might provide a good harvest again one day.

Most important, there was plenty of pasture for a herd of goats. And besides, the natural beauty of the area lifted her spirits. Here she could soak her soul in the glory of God's good creation. "It is wonderful," she said.

"But I didn't realize how isolated it is," Glorious Aim said as they trekked back to Chao Yang An. "Your nearest neighbors are so far away, and it will take much trouble and labor for people to come visit you with their gifts for the children."

Laura was silent a moment. The Russian Retreat Place was certainly isolated. The loneliness of the place made her feel a little vulnerable. For one thing, isolated places attracted bandits. And, as Glorious Aim said, the remoteness of the old mission would make it difficult for visitors to come with news and supplies and help.

"Our Heavenly Father has many ways of making adjustments," Laura said. "It's true He usually supplies our needs through the people who visit us, but not always."

She began telling him some of her stories of God's provision. Once the year before when the family ran completely out of food and money, a letter had come from South America containing a dollar bill. Laura had never heard of the people before nor had she ever received mail before from there. With the dollar she was able to buy food that lasted until the next gift arrived. Another time the children's bathing soap was used up to the very tiniest piece. The very day they used the last of it, a large cake of soap came in the mail.

Then there was the time last winter when the family ran out of almost all their supplies at once, including kerosene for the lamp. It seemed impossible to manage without kerosene for even one day because the days were so short, and she needed light to prepare the babies' night and early morning feedings. The family also needed money for the milk bill and the water bill. But on the very night before the two bills were due, the Evangelistic Committee of the Presbyterian mission brought money enough to pay them and buy kerosene. She had been very grateful to have the money to pay the bills, but disappointed because the money arrived too late in the evening to buy kerosene, and they were right to the end of their supply. Late that night she used the last drop of kerosene, and the light went out just as she finished preparing the 11 p.m. bottles. *How am I going to prepare the 3 A.M. feeding?* she had wondered.

"But God made one of His adjustments and supplied His own source of light," Laura said. "A few hours later when I went into the kitchen to prepare the three o'clock feedings, the moon shone so brightly through the window onto the table that I was able to do the work almost as usual.

"So the Lord will provide as necessary if He wants us to live at the

Russian Retreat Place," she ended. "I think it will be an ideal place for the children."

It encouraged her to recall the stories, and it seemed to encourage Glorious Aim to hear them. He asked a lot of questions.

"When does your lease expire at the court in Chao Yang An?"

"June first," Laura said.

"*Ai ya,* that is most unfortunate," the evangelist said slowly. "The caretaker told me that the owner is in South China right now and won't return until after June first."

"Then I will try to make a special arrangement with my landlord about staying a little longer," Laura said.

Outside the village, the two companions stopped to pull weeds for Old Billy. "I hope Apple Blossom didn't run away again today while we were gone," Glorious Aim said, yanking at a stand of wild grass.

Laura had been thinking the same thing, and she told Glorious Aim about her decision to try to find a new home for the girl.

"I will take this request with me to the Christians in Peking when I journey into the city this week," Glorious Aim promised, "but I think it will be difficult to find any better home for her than yours."

Laura and Glorious Aim gathered up their bundles of weeds in silence and headed toward home to the sound of the village women yodeling. They were calling to their pigs to come home from a day of foraging through the streets and stalls of Chao Yang An. Laura was relieved to find Apple Blossom safe in bed. Azure Cloud and Sweet Water Pond had taken turns helping Mr. Han watch the gate to make sure that, for this day at least, Apple Blossom would stay put.

For several weeks, Laura was unsure which way to turn. Was she supposed to remain in Chao Yang An? Or was the family supposed to move to the Russian Retreat Place?

The landlord for the Chao Yang An court agreed to allow Canaan Home to remain there through the month of June, even though Laura could not promise to lease the place for a whole year. There were other people waiting to rent it if she could not stay, he said, but he wanted her to know that he preferred to keep her as the tenant.

Just enough money came by the end of May to pay the June rent plus the bills for milk and water. Otherwise, May and June were slim months. There was enough of the usual foods during that time for the children, but supplies for Laura and old Mr. Han dwindled to nothing but cornmeal and a few apricots. No more money showed up to cover the advance rent payment for July either, and at the end of the month, the caretaker gave Laura ten days notice.

Then at last she heard from the owner of the Russian Retreat Place. He was anxious to find someone willing to occupy and rent the old mission, and he sent his manager to Chao Yang An from Peking to negotiate a rental agreement. "You can have the place on trial for one year," the manager told Laura. "Then, if you have no funds to pay the rent, you won't have to pay."

That decided it. *This must be the way God is going to provide for us,* Laura thought.

Aloud she said, "I appreciate your offer very much, but I think it would be best for us to follow the usual business procedure and pay at set intervals even though we are not paying it in advance."

The owner wanted $300 rent per year, which was twice the amount of rent Laura paid for the place in Chao Yang An. Laura agreed to pay it in three installments during the year at $100 each. Then she began to spend her nights packing.

The orphanage had accumulated more than Laura had realized. Furniture, clothing, bedding, baby equipment, cooking utensils…it was all loaded onto camels, carts, and a few male carriers and sent on ahead. A check for ten dollars arrived just before moving day, so she used that to pay the carters. Old Mr. Han decided not to move with the family to Chuang Hua Ssu, and the two teenagers had gone home a couple weeks before. Glorious Aim showed up to help her with the last stage of the move.

It had been raining off and on all day, and the air was heavy with the aroma of damp earth and wet billy goat. Laura settled the five babies in the middle of a white iron bed and rigged up a canopy over them with oiled sheeting to protect them from the rain. Four carriers stood by, ready to carry the bed and babies, and Laura put up an umbrella over herself and the two big girls.

Glorious Aim stared thoughtfully at Old Billy who was straining angrily on his rope. The evangelist turned to Laura. "You take him," he suggested.

Laura laughed. "Old Billy won't be offended if I decline," she said. "I have pulled a lot of grass for his dinner these last few months and spent some night duty upon him as well. Besides, the babies and the two girls will need my attention on the way."

A fresh shower began just as the carriers picked up the iron bed, but it was time to leave. There was no other way to manage the move. And so the family set out on their three-mile journey, slipping and sliding on the hilly, muddy paths in a little parade: four men carrying an iron bed with five babies upon it, Laura and the two older girls following behind under the umbrella, and Glorious Aim, soaking wet, tugging at an obnoxious old billy goat.

"Where are you going?" people called after them again and again along the way. They attracted lots of attention and arrived just before dark without any accidents.

Laura's Letters Home

Laura's letter written from Chao Yang An, December 6, 1931:

Because of our Lord's unchanging faithfulness and keeping power, and since it is almost three years since He called me to this work, it is my great joy to tell out the living tidings of His great goodness and faithfulness which I know is not for these only, but for all whose trust is in Him. At the beginning of the work, I asked our Heavenly Father to lead us in the path which would most glorify Him. It seemed to me that it would be necessary many times to walk along a very rugged pathway that His all-merciful, all-protecting love might be clearly known.

Someone has said, "He commonly brings His help in our greatest extremity, that His finger may plainly appear in our deliverance."

George Mueller, that great man of faith, tells us to, "Remember, it is the very time for faith to work when sight ceases. The greater the difficulties, the easier for faith; as long as there remains certain natural prospects, faith does not get on even as easily as where natural prospects fail."

Since I have heard of the serious situation at home and in other countries, it has been upon my heart for a number of weeks to write of His marvelous goodness to us, that some who are in need and who are discouraged may call upon Him in the day of trouble for He does surely answer.

1988 interview with Laura's cousin, Laura Jane Eberhardt Cerling, who was ten years old in 1931:

My brother and I used to ask Mother why we didn't go to church. She said, "Oh, that's for rich people!"

Mother got letters from Laura. She would read them and then put them in the top bureau drawer. She had other things like jewelry and rings that she kept there. There was a story about little girls being thrown into the river, unwanted because they were girls. I thought how awful that was and how could that happen? Then they were out of food, and they prayed and food came. Could I believe those stories? Sometimes I would be left alone in the house by myself. Even though I felt guilty, I would get Laura's letters out and read them for myself. I read them over and over. They were always as I remembered Mother reading them aloud.

After I was in bed, I would hear my parents talking at the kitchen table, worrying about finances—how they would pay for this, how they would pay for that. I always prayed when I heard them worrying about whether Father would lose his job. I got ideas about praying from Laura's letters. It always struck me as so impossible. It seemed like magic. She had no food, then she prayed, and the vegetable man came. Her agony, her desperation did not come through for me then.

7.

Tests and Trials

The Russian Retreat Place, 1932

IN THEIR NEW HOME at the Russian Retreat Place, Canaan Home's food supplies continued to shrink. At suppertime on the last day of July 1932, the family ate their last bite of food.

The next morning dawned, sweltering and stuffy with the heat. Laura checked the floor for scorpions before swinging her feet out of bed, then groped under her pillow for a fresh cotton gown. She had learned that if she folded a freshly laundered summer gown while it was still damp and slept with it under her pillow all night, the wrinkles were pressed out by morning so that it looked ironed.

She woke Apple Blossom and Precious Jade for morning devotions. After the Bible lesson she led the two girls into the kitchen. There she showed them that there was not a grain of cereal nor a crumb of food of any kind for breakfast that day. Then she knelt with the girls on the hard brick floor to pray.

"If there is any sinfulness in our hearts," Laura reminded the girls, "we must ask our Heavenly Father's forgiveness. After that we can go to Him for the food we need."

When they opened their eyes, the gate keeper's daughter stood in the kitchen doorway. "We still have no food for breakfast," Laura said to her, rising to her feet, "but we have been praying. Today we will see the goodness of the Lord."

Milk bottles clinked at the window then, and the gate keeper's daughter hurried to pick up the family's milk delivery. Usually the milkman placed the bottles on the windowsill and left. Today, instead, he waited outside and asked if he could speak to the Honorable Lady Teacher Minister. "A man who lives in the city sent you this money," he told Laura, "and someone gave it to me to give to you." Then he handed her ten dollars.

So the gate keeper's daughter ran off to buy flour, cereal, and vegetables in the village a mile away, and the family ate their breakfast that morning at the usual time. Laura never found out who sent the ten dollars.

Along with several gifts of tomatoes from a Christian neighbor, this money kept the family going through most of August. Friends also sent Laura two nanny goats at the end of the month, so the family finally had their own milk supply. When Laura sent word to the dairy that Canaan Home needed no more milk deliveries, they refused the payment she sent for the last two months' milk bill. "It is our gift," they said.

The torrential rains of summer ceased, and the skies cleared to autumn's brilliant blue. A surprising number of visitors took advantage of the beautiful September weather to travel all the way from the city to visit Canaan Home. Friends from Peking arrived one day with gowns and little shoes for the children, and two weeks later, friends from Paotingfu brought a large bundle of warmly padded winter clothing they had sewn by hand for the family. A former nursing student of Laura's left five dollars in one of the children's cabinets, and a missionary friend turned up at the gate one day with a feast of good things to eat. Soon afterwards a group of over 20 students appeared, showered the children with attention and Laura with questions, then presented Canaan Home with a gift of $20. Another day a Chinese architect, who had spent several years in the United States, showed up to view the ruins of the old mission temple and was astonished to find an orphanage in residence. She gave Laura five dollars for the children.

A teacher from a Christian industrial school gave Laura much-needed help, as well, in late August. He brought two young men, Brilliant Wisdom and State Ambition, to stay at the Russian Retreat Place and tend the goats, haul the family's water, and practice their carpentry skills by repairing the family's living quarters.

Florence Logan and Dr. Mackey called on Laura the last day of August. They hired a car in Peking and brought Orpha Gould with them, jolting up the path through the villages to the spring below the mission. Laura invited them into the kitchen so she could boil diapers on the stove and scrub laundry in the tin bathtub while they talked.

"Orpha and Richie are old friends," Florence told Dr. Mackey. "They were in the Red Cross together before they came to China."

"Why, of course!" Dr. Mackey exclaimed. "I believe I've heard your story. Aren't you the nurse who Laura got converted during the Great War?"

"That's right. Laura led me to Jesus during the war," Orpha said, smiling down at Dr. Mackey and Laura. She was a stocky, dark-haired woman who loomed a full head taller than her old friend and the doctor. "If it weren't for Laura Richards, I'd probably be working in Philadelphia instead of Peking."

"You were in France with Laura during the war, too, weren't you?" Florence asked, drawing out the story for Dr. Mackey.

"Yes, we were both at Camp Kerouon," Orpha said, "and I always used to ask to work the same shifts Laura worked. There's nobody like Laura Richards when it comes to getting a big job done. When she cleans up a ward, it's 'Germs Beware!'"

"Then I guess you came to just the right spot for your talents, Richie," Florence said. "I'll bet you have rats in these ruins."

"Not only rats," Laura said. The place was infested with snakes and scorpions, too. She told them her story about walking into the kitchen to make breakfast her first morning there. A snake was coiled on the table, poised to strike. She killed it with the stove poker—and a pile of others since. Scorpions were everywhere. They hid in cracks and crawled into sacks of flour and cereal. One night when a baby started crying, she had jumped out of bed and landed smack on a scorpion with her bare foot. "I spent the rest of the night dancing around with the pain, waving my foot in the air," she said. "I only had alcohol to treat it."

The twins, Rachel and Rose Mary, toddled over, grasped Laura's legs, and peeped at the visitors from behind her skirts. They felt damp, pressed against her legs. "If you'll excuse me," Laura said, "I need to change the babies. But you should look around the place while you're here. I'll ask Brilliant Wisdom to give you a tour."

She introduced them to a tall youth with an intelligent face and shrewd, black eyes who was lugging two buckets of water on a shoulder pole into the kitchen. The young man greeted them courteously and led them off to inspect the compound.

"The place is so remote and far away from everyone!" Laura overheard Florence say as the three visitors passed by the window of the room where she was changing the twins. "It seems like too much work for one person, and what if she gets sick or has an accident? I wish she had a partner."

Laura wished the same. A parade of kind people had stayed to help her a while and then moved on. She thanked God for each one. Yet they came, and they went. None seemed to share her calling. Few grasped the principles of faith on which her work was based. If the orphanage was going to grow much larger, she would need to draw committed workers into the walk of faith God had directed her to follow.

She was busy cutting the family's noon cornbread when her guests trooped in from their tour with Brilliant Wisdom. The visitors helped the children wash their hands for lunch, and settled down at the table in the hallway to say grace with them. They ate lunches they had packed in Peking.

"We can't stay longer to visit," Florence told her after lunch, "but Dr. Mackey and I wanted to be sure to see you while we were up north."

Dr. Mackey shook Laura's hand warmly in parting, her round face radiating the kindly smile Laura remembered well. Orpha and Florence hugged her. They left behind them $15, a sack of flour, and an aura of encouragement she needed.

It was hard to be the only parent. Apple Blossom grew more stubborn every day. Both places Laura asked to consider taking her in had turned down her application when they found out about her character. One school said they would take Precious Jade when Laura thought she was ready for schooling, but not Apple Blossom. Both places said you couldn't change the ways of a beggar child.

Laura refused to believe it. God could change the child, she thought, although she knew that God would not force Himself on her. Apple Blossom would have to cooperate with the process. "Let Your will be done in her life," Laura prayed daily.

By the end of September, Apple Blossom had run away several times. More and more she wanted to talk about the good old days when she and her mother had lived by their wits in the streets and slept at night with nothing but a doorstep for a pillow. To hear her tell the tale, there had been no pain, no hunger, no cold, only adventure, romance, and excitement.

When Laura tried to warn Apple Blossom about the dangers outside the mission walls, Laura could feel the girl's resistance rise up like an invisible wall. *There is a fortress built up inside this child,* Laura thought, *that is as real as the fortified pawnshop of Chao Yang An.* It was a fortress against the truth. Apple Blossom rejected any reality that threatened her wishes.

Brilliant Wisdom and State Ambition resisted Laura, too, but more subtly. They had seemed interested when she first explained to them the way the orphanage operated on faith, praying to God for the family's needs. But when the food supplies dwindled and the two young men had to go without vegetables or some other food for a time, she could sense their skepticism. A couple of times she overheard them worrying aloud to each other that they might have to use their own salaries to buy themselves food. A church in Peking had agreed to pay them each a salary for the work they did for her, but their food was supposed to come from Canaan Home.

They resisted her teaching on sin and repentance and cleansing, too, enduring her explanations with stoic, Chinese calm. Brilliant Wisdom's shrewd dark eyes grew bright with the questions he would probably voice later on to State Ambition, but never to her. She could sense what they were: "Why is she talking to me about sin? I haven't done anything very bad. I'm a Christian. I've been baptized. Isn't that enough?" And State Ambition's short, wiry form bristled with unspoken protests. He had asked God to forgive all his sins, like the missionaries said. Why go to the trouble to face and name them? And anyway, all this talk about sin and repentance and a holy life was not the most important thing. The most important thing—why could not Happy Plum Flower Richards understand this?—the most important thing was the family's stomachs. The family needed a pantry with a good deal more food in it.

The nights grew chilly, and white frost blanketed the mission grounds when the family woke each morning. Mrs. Kao, a Christian neighbor from Chao Yang An, sewed linings into the family's summer gowns for greater warmth. In late October she came for a whole week to do the family's annual winter sewing. Laura set Apple Blossom and Precious Jade to work helping Mrs. Kao pull apart the family's quilted winter clothes, wash the pieces, and sew them all back together. Mrs. Kao also mended some of the summer gowns the family needed to wear as aprons to keep their winter gowns clean, since the quilted garments could be washed only by being taken completely apart.

The first day of the sewing, Apple Blossom sulked and pouted. The second day she flatly refused to do any work at all. When Laura chided her, she turned and deliberately kicked Mrs. Kao in the leg. Laura marched her into the bedroom, paddled her, and told her she must stay in the bedroom for half an hour to think about what she had done and decide how she would word her apology to Mrs. Kao.

Half an hour later she was gone, and a thorough search of the compound produced no sign of her. Laura sent State Ambition into the villages to see if he could find her, but he returned empty-handed. Before long, though, a local policeman tramped up the steps to the mission gate, dragging a defiant Apple Blossom by the hand. She ran away again five minutes later. Again, State Ambition and Brilliant Wisdom searched for her in the villages, without success.

The day passed slowly. The sun slipped behind the hill, taking with it the lingering warmth of mid-day, and the crisp chill of autumn set in quickly. Then the night turned cold, with still no sign of Apple Blossom. Numbly Laura put the children to bed, her mind preoccupied with a flow of troubling questions. Had the child found some place indoors for shelter? What had she managed to find to eat before the night came? Was she hurt or crying or lonely? Had a procurer snatched her? And then the worst question: had Apple Blossom insisted on having her way so persistently and so long that God had finally decided to go ahead and let her have it?

Tears slid over Laura's cheeks in warm, salty trails as she slipped into bed that night. The tears chilled and turned raw with the cold. She slept poorly, and in the morning she hurried to Apple Blossom's bedroom to see if the girl had found her way home in the darkness and slid back into her bed in the night. But Apple Blossom was still gone.

Lydia, age two, was nicknamed Foreign Doll because her eyes and hair were brown instead of black, like the other children.

Reports from the Russian Retreat Place

From Florence Logan's letter dated August 31, 1932:

In the afternoon we again hired the shop car and went out to call on Richie. She has moved to this old Russian mission place which is very remote and far from anyone else. She is all alone with her seven kiddies and no one to help her. Except that a couple of boys who are enrolled in an industrial school are there temporarily. Their teacher is a Christian interested in fixing up the place for Miss Richards and using it as practice work for the boys. The lads milk the goat and carry water for her, too. Otherwise, she does everything herself—all the housekeeping and cooking and everything for her little brood. Both times I have been there she has been on the run every minute. Not a moment to sit and visit. Just a round of changing diapers and feeding babies. Wish she had an associate.

Excerpt from Laura's letter dated January 18, 1934:

I have told you much about what our Lord has done for our material needs, but now about the spiritual. There are some great trials in the work. Two older girls have taken much of my time and patience without much fruit-bearing. But although there seemed to be no change in their own little hearts, still in my own heart God was working a knowledge and sense of my own unworthiness and a greater dependence upon the Lord.

Now I must write about that which I would rather leave unrecorded. My oldest and first little orphan, the little beggar girl, about whom I have before written, left us on October 23.

8.

The Lord's Fast

The Russian Retreat Place, 1932-1935

Mrs. Kao and Precious Jade completed the winter sewing. The family dressed for the cold in warm quilted gowns and pajamas, with cloth shoes from the Christians in Peking and warm woolen socks, stocking caps, scarves, and mittens from the working girls in Holland. Laura folded Apple Blossom's warm clothes away in a cabinet.

Only a few visitors dropped by with gifts during the month of October. During the first half of November, no one came at all. The family's supplies, including coal for the kitchen stove, dipped very low. Laura ate sparingly and prayed for strength to carry on despite her lack.

On November 12, when the two young men saw that Laura's and their food was used up, Brilliant Wisdom asked permission to visit his church family in the city to renew his and State Ambition's supplies. Laura gave permission reluctantly. "But please do not mention any needs except your own," she said. The goats were still producing plenty of milk. There was still food for the children. Once Brilliant Wisdom brought supplies, the only one lacking would be Laura, and God would take care of her as He always had.

But Brilliant Wisdom returned at the end of the day with food for her as well as supplies for him and State Ambition—a sack each of flour, rice, and cornmeal, some vegetables and a good supply of noodles. "My people asked me how it was with you, and I couldn't lie to them, could I?" he asked Laura.

"But it would have been better," Laura said, "if you had used this as an opportunity to depend completely on our Heavenly Father. Your people have been very kind to send you to us and provide your salaries. We mustn't burden them now by asking alms."

Brilliant Wisdom listened respectfully, his face bland. *He is young,* Laura thought. *It's hard for him to listen to God when he hears his stomach growling.*

One week later a Chinese evangelist visited and left two dollars. Five days after that, three Chinese strangers called on the family and left a dollar for the children. The family eked out their supplies, and Laura prayed day and night that her work would be acceptable to the Lord, and that any sin within the family circle would be dealt with and forgiven. Some days she fasted, too.

On the first of December the family used the last of their coal. So Laura moved their living quarters from the cold, dark kitchen into the sunniest room they could find in the mission and began burning sticks and stubble in an old kerosene can to cook meals and keep warm. Because she had promised not to cut down any of the trees on the grounds, their natural fuel supply was limited. It could last only if they did not burn fuel for more than two or three hours a day. Normally that would have been insufficient to keep them from freezing. Fortunately, however, the winter of 1932 was an unusually mild one, and they were well supplied with warm clothes.

On the evening of December 3, Laura and her two helpers again came to the end of their store of food. The next morning a Christian neighbor showed up before breakfast with a two-day supply of sweet potatoes. "Happy Plum Flower Richards," he said, "my friend and I were very uneasy about you all day yesterday."

Once again Brilliant Wisdom asked permission to visit his people in Peking. Once more Laura gave reluctant permission, and once more

Brilliant Wisdom returned with supplies for her as well as for himself and State Ambition. This time he brought ten pounds each of flour, cornmeal, millet, and rice.

Again Laura protested. "We need to trust in our Heavenly Father, not ourselves or other people."

His silent resistance met her words like a wall. "Trusting God has a purifying effect. It is necessary for keeping our walk with God close," she tried to explain. But she was not particularly good at explanations, and Brilliant Wisdom was not particularly interested in hearing them.

Laura felt more alone than she had since Canaan Home first began. Nothing seemed to be going right. The family kept running out of food and fuel. She had no money for the first $100 rent payment. The nanny goats were going dry, and she was still grieving over Apple Blossom. On top of all that, her helpers were resisting the way God had shown her the orphanage must operate.

She prayed as she worked through the day, snatched a quiet moment when she could to read her Bible, and stayed up late at night to pray. She reviewed the scriptures, decisions, and events that had led to her present situation at the Russian Retreat Place. Clearly, she felt, God had given her the task of raising the children, and clearly He had called her to do this by faith.

Now winter disaster threatened the family. It looked as if they would soon have no food, no fuel—and no visitors to bring help or spread the word of their plight. Perhaps she would soon have no helpers either.

She needed the two young men. Cooking and cleaning for her six children seemed all she could physically manage. How could she haul water from the spring, too, and tend the goats besides? Old Billy had grown so strong she could no longer control him. She needed the men's help, but not if their actions undermined Canaan Home.

"Let them be willing to trust You for their daily needs, dear Lord," she prayed. "That has been the foundation of this work." What God birthed by faith, his followers must nurture by faith.

Canaan Home's supplies continued to dwindle, and Laura gathered the family for a special time of prayer. Privately she told Brilliant Wisdom and State Ambition that there would be no more trips to the city for supplies.

Two days later, on December 16, the family found themselves with just enough food for breakfast, but not a crumb left over. For the first time since Canaan Home had begun, even the babies' supplies were completely exhausted. The goats had gone dry, so there was not even milk.

It was a beautiful, sunny morning. The sky curved above them like a great, blue bowl, and the mountains to the west stood out sharply. A hardy flock of sparrows twittered in the branches of the ancient pine. Laura brought her Bible outside to the porch after chores were done to read and pray in the sunshine while the children played nearby. Their chatter receded from her consciousness, so she missed the sound of deeper voices in the courtyard. She was surprised to look up and find a group of visitors making friends with the children. They gave the family flour, bread, and sesame.

"May I speak to you privately?" one of the women asked Laura. The other visitors wandered off with the children to look around the mission grounds. "You need to give up the orphanage, Laura," her friend said gently. "We can find good Christian homes for the children. You can come back to the Presbyterian mission and go into some other field of work."

Laura hardly knew what to say. Her friend's suggestion could not have come at a more discouraging moment—except for one thing. This friend and her companions had just brought the family's missing lunch. And their missing supper, too. In fact, the group brought them enough food to last most of a week.

So Laura thanked God, and kept on for five more days. Then, on December 21, the food supply gave out completely once again. For the second time since the orphanage had begun, even the babies' supplies ran out. After breakfast was served, nothing remained.

Once more Laura prayed for food. "Father, You sent me to take care of these little ones. I know that You love us and that You are willing to demonstrate how You take care of Your children, just as You promised in Your Word. We need that demonstration now. I only ask that You keep me away from anything that would prevent Your power from working in this family. These children are Yours, and for a short time You have given them into my care. Help me to be Your faithful steward."

Nothing happened. Lunch time came and went. There was no food, no meal to be served.

The day was so raw and windy that the children had to play indoors. They played peacefully together through the lunch hour, napped at the usual time, and never fussed over the missed meal. Laura kept praying.

A phrase from the Psalms touched her mind. "*I will offer to You the sacrifice of thanksgiving....*" If ever thanksgiving could be called a sacrifice, it was today. What might she give God thanks for on this stormy winter day, with six lively, unfed children, in an unheated room of a ruined temple building, isolated from her friends and family?

Well, the children *were lively*. She thanked God for the family's good health. The children were at a susceptible age for illness, and she had been unable to heat their living quarters properly this winter. Yet for months not one had been seriously ill.

She started thinking about the many invalids she had nursed in the past, which made her think, in turn, about special diets she had prepared for them. Sometimes people had had to go on liquid diets as part of their treatment—or even go without eating at all for a time. Did God have a special purpose for this skipped meal?

"Dear Lord," she prayed, "we are in China now where it is the custom for most people to eat only two meals a day. Please give us these two meals today according to Chinese custom, and we will praise you for your lovingkindness. I believe that you will not fail these children, according to the promises of your Word."

The afternoon passed slowly, and the sun was just beginning to go down behind the hill, when Laura heard pounding on the gate. Despite the bad weather, a large group of Chinese and Western friends had journeyed out to see them from Peking.

They brought a feast. Flour, rice, millet, meat, apples, salt, Chinese cabbage, carrots...and other supplies, too: tallow candles, matches, kerosene. Never in their short lives had the children seen such plenty.

Joy lodged in Laura's throat. It choked her. She could not speak to tell her friends how much their visit meant to her that day, that time.

"That was God's fast for us," she wrote home later. Usually, she explained, when God's people fast, they fast voluntarily. "But this time was better than a voluntary fast. God sent us His own fast to bring about a closer walk with Him."

It was the only time the Canaan Home children ever missed a meal for lack of supplies.

Christmas came four days later. Laura had not taught her children to expect toys or treats for Christmas, so for them it was a quiet, ordinary day. After morning chores, Laura settled the children on the porch and told them the Christmas story. Then they played in the sunshine.

At about eleven o'clock that morning, several Chinese Christians arrived at the gate, loaded down with bundles of clothing for the family. "We are from the Presbyterian church in Tienstsin," they told Laura. "Our people sent us to deliver these gifts to you before noon on Christmas Day. They sent this money, too." And the man handed her $108.50.

The rent money. Finally Laura had the money she needed to make the $100 payment.

The Christians from Tienstsin were still saying good-bye when a group of friends from the Presbyterian mission showed up lugging an enormous basket of apples, pears, bananas, raisins, popcorn, cookies, and candy.

And so the crisis passed.

Brilliant Wisdom and State Ambition went home and were replaced by the man who had been so worried about the family in December that he had brought them the two-day supply of sweet potatoes. He stayed and helped Laura for over a year and was astonished when she told him she had had nothing to eat for breakfast the morning he had brought the sweet potatoes to them. Enough money came in not only for food, but for coal, which probably saved the lives of the first kids born to the goat herd.

Several weeks after Christmas, a racket from the goat shed awoke Laura at midnight. She dressed quickly and rushed out to the shed to find a newborn kid in a shivering heap on the frigid shed floor, with its mother still in labor. Laura helped the nanny deliver the twin, then carried the two baby goats in straw-lined boxes into the kitchen to keep them warm by the kitchen stove.

When they were settled comfortably, she hurried back to the shed to check on their mother and discovered a third kid trembling on the floor beside her. She was astonished, because triplets were rare. She carried him inside to keep warm with his siblings, and all three kids survived.

The goat herd thrived, and the orphanage never again ran out of milk for the children to drink. In fact, the Canaan Home nannies produced so much milk that Laura made butter, cheese, and cottage cheese and gave away milk to neighbors who wanted it. The herd provided the family with meat sometimes as well and greatly reduced Canaan Home's overall expenses.

Even though the rent at the Russian Retreat Place was double the rent at Chao Yang An, when Laura totaled up and compared costs at the end of the year she found that the family saved money by moving there. At Chao Yang An they had paid $150 a year for rent, plus $70 a year for water, and $400 for milk and ice to keep the milk fresh. At the Russian Retreat Place they paid $300 for rent, but nothing for water or milk. The spring supplied all their water year round, and the goats produced their milk, with meat besides. So their expenses actually dropped $320 a year.

The babies who had been carried to the old mission through the rain on the iron bed shed their infancy and graduated to childhood. By mail and through visits, Laura's friends brought her news of what was happening in China and the world: how Chiang Kai Shek was building new roads, railroads, and schools to modernize China; how the Great Depression was devastating the lives of people throughout the world; and how Japan had taken advantage of the Western nations' preoccupation with their own internal problems to begin taking over large areas of Chinese territory. When the Japanese took over the province of Manchuria in 1931, Chiang Kai Shek did not resist, expecting the League of Nations to deal with Japan for him. But the League only protested; they did not intervene. So Japan took over the province of Jehol, too.

Chiang Kai Shek had other worries as well. The Communists created 15 rural bases in central China and established a rival Chinese Soviet

Republic. Within the Soviet areas, they beat and killed landlords, redistributed the property of wealthy landowners to the peasants, burned temples and churches, and killed pastors, priests, and missionaries. Chiang Kai Shek began "Annihilation Campaigns" against Communist strongholds in Hunan and Kiangsi provinces, forcing Communist leaders to retreat to a sanctuary in Yenan in the northwest. During this Long March of 1934-1936, Mao Tse Tung gained control of Communist forces and emerged as Chiang Kai Shek's chief rival in the ongoing Chinese civil war.

Laura's visitors also brought her news of great revivals spreading throughout North China. Hundreds of people who had merely been converted to Christianity were now being converted to Christ, friends reported. Even pastors, teachers, and church workers were realizing they had never been born anew. Dying churches were springing to vigorous new life.

But of all the news arriving at the Russian Retreat Place, the news that Laura was most eager to hear was news of Apple Blossom. In this she was disappointed. She never learned where the child had gone or what had happened to her.

More Stories from the Russian Retreat Place

Laura's letter written from the Russian Retreat Place, January 18, 1934:

Last summer I hoped to have some tomatoes and some were planted in the patch below us. They did not thrive because they were not watered regularly, and I was quite disappointed when told that only three plants were left. I told the man who cares for the goats to bring them to me, and I would water and care for them. They were three spindling little things, about one inch high and looked ready to die. I watered and sheltered them from too much sun, but for days did not know whether or not they would live. When the man saw that I wanted tomatoes so much for the children, he found some more and after a while all were growing. The children had plenty of good ripe tomatoes all summer.

Several months ago a Buddhist came to our door for the purpose of giving three dollars for the little ones. He did not stay long but returned again after a few months. This time I invited him to come in, as before he came in the summer and I was busy with the children out of doors. He seemed to be hungering for a new life, for freedom from sin. As I talked to him he confessed much sin and I told him about the blood of Jesus being able to wash away all of our sins. I told him of my own dependence upon the Lord in prayer and as I knelt down, he knelt too, while a Chinese woman and I prayed. This time as he was about to leave, he left four dollars for the children. I did not use the first donation which he left as I had promised our Heavenly Father not to use any money coming from unbelievers. But this time he seemed so sincere that after prayer I used it for the children. After this he sent a large grain sack full of peanuts and the man who brought it witnessed to his having become a Christian. A few days ago he came again and since the above was written. This time he again expressed his desire to lead a victorious Christian life.

For weeks and months I have had a deeper and deeper sense of my own unworthiness and have cried daily to our Heavenly Father that as the precious blood of our Lord and Saviour Jesus Christ has cleansed me from sin that He may indeed keep me pure and undefiled before Him, "a vessel meet for the Master's use." I know that I would have no power at all were it not for His Precious Holy Spirit, His long-suffering love for me. He has made me ashamed and confounded by the manifold mercies which He has showered upon us throughout the year.

Pray especially for me that I may have great power in intercession for the souls that are so in need of a Saviour.

These little children are like sweet flowers. One is of the frailer type with a mind which seems, in so many, to be a peculiar part of that kind of body. She is so bright and intelligent for one so small (not yet four years old) yet so affectionate. When I am caring for them I am especially careful of this little flower, although I try not to have it appear so as it might spoil her and not be good for the other children. Her name is [Charity]. On the day before Christmas she asked me, "Mama, where did I come from?"

I said, "The Lord Jesus sent you to me, Darling, and you know that He loves us dearly. And He not only gave me you, but He gave me Himself and has given Himself as a ransom for many."

The next day she said, "And where were you when I came?"

"I was over at Chao Yang An when you came. And don't you remember how five little babies were put in a little iron bed and carried by four men from Chao Yang An to Chuang Hua Ssu?" I think she does not remember it now although she did for a while.

9.

The Crippled Beggar

The Russian Retreat Place, 1935

THE DAY Laura invited the sick beggar man to live in the compound was the same day her daughters found the great long worm.

It was a beautiful fall day, with a blue sky and no clouds. Laura was hanging laundry on the clothesline outdoors and watching her children play in the front courtyard, like they did every day after breakfast. Rachel and Rose Mary, the four-year-old twins, were taking turns pushing each other on the swing, and five-year-old Sarah was packing dirt into a wooden boat. The family's only boy Samuel, nearly two years old and only recently come to Canaan Home, was chasing a mama hen and her eight chicks. He couldn't go fast enough to catch them, but he kept them on the run. The mama hen was squawking and Samuel was squawking, too, trying to sound like a mad mama hen. Charity, age five, was wandering all around the yard, looking for something with Lydia, not quite four years old. Lydia's hair and eyes were brown instead of black like her siblings, so the workers and the other children all called her Foreign Doll.

After much searching, Charity and Lydia finally came over to the clothesline and Charity said, "We can't find any worms. Where are the worms, Mama?"

"They have probably gone back underground, Darling," Mama said.

"They come out when it rains. But it's September now, and the rainy season is over. Look for puddles in the yard, and you might find a worm there."

Charity hadn't thought of that, but Mama was right. A few weeks ago the front yard had been full of puddles, and they had found lots of worms then, wriggling on the ground near the little pools. Now, though, the front court was all dried up.

"There's a big puddle in the back court," Charity told Lydia. "Let's go look."

She took her sister's hand, and they set off for the old orchard in the back courtyard near Mama's tomato patch. Pretty soon they found the puddle, but it wasn't big anymore like Charity remembered it. The two girls squatted beside the drying circle of mud and Charity thought about worms, so brown and fat and squirmy. If you touched one gently with your finger tip, it curled into a tight little ball, just like that.

Her eyes traveled over the ground looking for puddles. It felt shady and cool here under the tree. Over on the wall, where the tree branches did not reach, the sunlight poured steadily down. Suddenly Charity's eye caught a slight movement and a glint of green on the stone ledge. She rose up on her tiptoes to see better and stopped still in astonishment.

"Look, Foreign Doll!" she breathed. "Look on the wall."

A giant creature just like their worms lay stretched out longer than the stove poker. It was green as new grass and as thick around as a baby goat's hind leg. Charity and Foreign Doll held hands and stepped nearer to stare. The creature stared back. Its black eyes were flecked with yellow, and after a time it blinked slowly. Foreign Doll thrust a thumb into her mouth.

"You touch it and make it curl," Charity said.

They stepped closer, and the creature flicked out its tongue, fine and long as a blade of wheat. They had never seen any of their worms do that. Flick, flick. In and out, in and out flicked the funny black tongue.

Foreign Doll turned and fled, crying, "Mama! Mama! A great worm! A great long worm! Come see!"

Charity backed away from the worm and watched it until Mama arrived with Foreign Doll.

"That's not a worm, Darling," Mama said. "That's a snake. Charity, run to the kitchen and bring me the stove poker. Lydia, you go back to the yard and play by Sarah."

Foreign Doll darted away, but Charity hesitated. Now Mama was laughing. "Great long worm!" she said. She laughed and laughed.

"The goat man says snakes are poisonous, Mama," Charity said.

"Not all snakes, Sweetheart," Mama said. "This one is probably not poisonous, but I can't take chances with my precious children. I will have to kill it. Now run and fetch me the stove poker and don't worry. The snake won't hurt me."

Charity ran off. When she reached the front court, the gatekeeper was there looking for Mama. "She has to kill a snake in the back court," Charity said. "I have to bring the poker."

"Tell your mama that there is a visitor at the gate," the gatekeeper said.

So she told Mama when she fetched the poker.

Laura killed the snake and hurried to the gatehouse. Her caller turned out to be a crippled beggar who had had to crawl to get up the 75 steps to the mission gate. He was weak and shaky, and the back of his gown was slimy with the ooze from his running sores. "Will you take me in?" he asked. His voice was so low, Laura could barely catch the words.

"But this is an orphanage," she said. "I only take in little children."

"My family has turned their face away from me," he said. "I have no place else to go." He paused a long time. "I am too ill to beg…." his words trailed off, and he looked at her hopelessly.

"All right," Laura said finally. "Come with me." She led him to a small hut on the other side of the compound, away from the children, and found extra bedding and a bed. She had no extra clothes for him, but the weather was still warm enough for him to be comfortable in his summer gown.

Briefly the man explained his situation. When he was four years old, he had jumped from the family bed and dislocated his hip. His family was too poor to pay for medical treatment, so he grew up lame. He was now in his early 40s, and the hip had become tubercular, with seven large, draining ulcers.

Every day Laura bathed the sores on his hip and washed out his underwear, which became soiled quickly from the discharge of the ulcers. The family shared their food with him—millet porridge, cooked Chinese cabbage, tomatoes from the family garden, and steamed bread made from cornmeal and millet flour. Laura prayed daily that he might somehow come to understand the gospel and receive new life in Jesus.

At first the man gained strength. After a couple weeks he was able to limp down the hill with a cane to the spring to sit outdoors in the warm fall sunshine. Still, he never smiled and rarely spoke. Once, though, when Laura was washing his soiled underwear, he asked, "Why are you doing this for me?"

"I do it because of the Lord Jesus," Laura said, "and I hope that you will never forget the name of Jesus. This name opens the door of Heaven for all of us who believe in Him."

The man said nothing, and his face gave no indication that he had heard or understood one word she said.

That fall, Laura wrote to several places in Peking asking if they could take in the sick beggar, but no one had a place for him. So every day she told him about Jesus as she brought his meal tray, washed his clothes, and cleaned his oozing sores.

The days grew crisp and the nights became frosty. The sick man began to weaken in the chill. The disease seemed to have entered his spine, and the discharge from his ulcers became profuse. The cold bothered him, and he asked Laura for a coal stove to warm his little hut. Laura found one for him, but explained that the family had no coal and no money to buy any. "We must ask Jesus to send us coal," she told him. And not long after that, someone donated a large supply of coal to Canaan Home, enough for the whole family and the sick man, too.

But still the man was cold, so he asked Laura for winter clothing. "The only extra clothes I have are for little children," Laura said. "I have no adult clothing, and no money to buy any. But I have been telling you every day about Jesus and how he loves you. We must pray to him and ask for warm clothes."

Two days later, Samuel suddenly announced, "Vroom! Vroom!"

The family rarely saw or heard motor vehicles. The nearest road was two miles away, and motor vehicles seldom used it. Sure enough, though, the family now could hear the drone of a car growing louder and louder. All the children dashed to the gatehouse to look between the cracks in the gate.

A long limousine rumbled and bumped its way slowly along the trail leading from the village. It stopped at the spring below them. A lady stepped out and began pulling a large bundle out of the back seat. "These are all adult-size padded winter garments," she told Laura apologetically. "Nothing here will fit the children, but I thought you could take these clothes apart and make them over into winter quilts."

Thankfully, Laura laid aside the two best padded gowns for the sick man. She sent the others, a few at a time, to Mrs. Kao in Chao Yang An, to be torn apart and sewn into warm bed covers.

A couple days later, a large package arrived from Laura's high school friend Lois Lenski. The children crowded around the kitchen table curiously as Laura opened the package and drew out baby clothes, diapers, baby bottles, nipples, and a bottle basket. Lois Lenski's son Stephen had outgrown his baby things, so she had packed everything up and sent it to Laura.

Oh my, Laura thought as she drew out the tiny layettes, *the Lord must be planning to send a baby soon!*

Sure enough, three days later, five-day-old Grace arrived, carried in her father's arms up the steps to the mission gate. A few days later, the father returned, bringing Grace's twin sister, Gloria. Other gifts of baby supplies began to show up after that, and in the weeks that followed two-month-old Leah, 24-day-old Priscilla, and a brother and sister ages six and nine joined Canaan Home. All the newcomers were undernourished, needing special diets and specialized nursing care. The four babies needed to be fed around the clock.

Laura had been able to hire a local man to tend the goats, and the gate man's daughter still came from time to time. Now her workload had exploded, so she began crying out to God to send her help. "Lord," she prayed, "keep us from any situation which might not bring glory to Yourself."

A man named Forever Upward came in answer to her prayer. He took over the cooking and helped carry water.

The sick man seemed oblivious to all the new arrivals. His appetite failed, and he began to yearn for special kinds of food as sick people sometimes do. "Can you get me some peanuts?" he asked Laura one day.

"I'm so sorry," she said. "I have no peanuts and not a penny to buy them. But all our good things come from Jesus. I will pray to Jesus for peanuts. You do remember the name 'Jesus' don't you, and how this Name is the door, the entrance to Heaven?"

Laura prayed for peanuts, and several days later, someone brought a large flour sack full of peanuts "for the children."

"Will you share your peanuts with the sick man in the hut?" Laura asked the children. They agreed, so she brought the man his peanuts.

Next he asked for rice, which was considered a delicacy in North China, where millet and corn were the staples of the local diet. Again Laura had to tell the man that she did not have what he wanted. "But we can call upon Jesus, and He always gives what is best for us," she said.

A couple days later, a Chinese friend gave Laura several packages of food. One item in the package was a small paper sack, just large enough to hold about two cups. Laura thought it was salt, but when she opened it, she found it full of rice, just enough for the sick man.

By now it was December, and the sick man had become too weak to get out of bed. One more thing he requested. Could Laura bring him Chinese cakes? Once more she told him she would pray to Jesus and suggested he pray, too. And once again, the cakes came within a few days time, the gift of another kind visitor.

"Do you remember the name I told you?" Laura asked him one day after she had brought him the peanuts, rice, and Chinese cakes. "Do you remember who it is that forgives your sins?"

"Jesus," the man replied without expression. And then, briefly, "I believe."

Christmas neared, and the sick man became so weak that Laura had to feed him herself, by hand. One evening as she was about to spoon feed him his supper, he looked over to the other side of his bed and made a motion as though he were offering to share his food with someone there. Then he turned to Laura and courteously motioned to her to share his food as well. Politely she declined, and then began spooning supper into his mouth.

She wondered how the gateman's daughter was managing with the children in the other part of the compound. It was getting late—time to put the children to bed. And this meal was taking so long....

When she finished feeding the sick man, he said, "There is a bright light in this room. Where is it coming from?"

Laura saw no bright light. She had no idea what to answer. Then suddenly she thought of the person whom the man had seemed to see on the other side of his bed, the one with whom he had first offered to share his supper. "I believe it is the Lord Jesus coming to receive you," she said.

His face lit up with delight. In all his time at the orphanage he had never smiled before, nor had the stolid expression of his features ever changed. Laura had never seen such a dramatic change in anyone's face.

She covered him well with quilts, wished him good night, and hurried back to her little ones. Then she put them to bed, said her prayers, and immediately fell asleep. Early in the morning she checked on her patient. He was unconscious, and by noon he had passed away. So Forever Upward prepared the beggar's body for burial, and then searched out the man's relatives. They came and buried him near a little clump of trees not far from the lane leading from the Retreat Place to the main road.

Laura hardly had time to notice the beggar man's passing, for children came now in a steady stream. By New Year's Eve of 1937—scarcely a year and a half after the beggar man first arrived—the orphanage had nearly quadrupled in size to 26 children.

A father climbed the hill to the gate one day early in 1936 to give her his four-year-old daughter, and the evangelist, Glorious Aim, brought her two sisters, ages two and six. "Their parents came to my house last night with their five children, begging for food and shelter," he explained to Laura. "I took them all in, and the mother died during the night. So I have brought you the two little girls."

Esther was 11 months old when her neighbors brought her to Laura after her mother threw her out the door of her hut one day in a rage. The baby was nearly starved, and her back was injured so badly that Laura thought she would probably be a hunchback. Still, with the Lord, there was always hope for healing. On the advice of Dr. Harold Henke on the Presbyterian medical staff, she kept Esther tied to a simple slant board, with her feet higher than her head.

Every few weeks another baby or two arrived—unwanted, starving, abandoned, homeless....Some were too far gone to survive. A nearly starved baby with a cleft palate died a couple days after entering the mission, and a premature infant weighing under two pounds died also. His two-pound twin Nehemiah survived, however. Besides the older children who came, Laura took in 17 babies during a period of about 15 months, and 13 babies lived.

Somehow the supply of food and other provisions kept up with the increasing needs of the family. Laura was too busy to write to her supporters about the recent population explosion. Still, people mailed needed supplies and funds from overseas, and Christians in China, both Western and Chinese, sent provisions or journeyed to her remote mission to offer moral support and bring supplies in person. Laura continued to pray for all the family's needs, then lived within the limits of the provision that came. She was on the go every minute, it seemed, praying as she worked.

What a story! Florence Logan thought to herself every time she heard the latest orphanage news from friends who had been to Canaan Home. *And to think I tried to discourage her from starting all this!*

Florence's initial misgivings about Laura's plan to begin Canaan Home on faith had disappeared early in the adventure. *God hasn't called me to this kind of work or given me this kind of faith,* she had concluded after her first visit to Chao Yang An. *It isn't God's kind of project for me, but it is His for Laura.*

She tried to visit Laura whenever she could, but it was hard. Paotingfu was 100 miles away. Florence was in the Peking area infrequently. Even when she was there, it was difficult to make the trip to Laura's remote home at the Retreat Place. During her visits, she peppered her friend with questions and then passed on what she had learned to the Chinese Christians and Western missionaries in North China. A work of faith like Canaan Home, she believed, depends on the prayers and support of God's people. So she tried to inform God's people about the work. Florence wished, though, that there was a way she could be of more help to her friend.

Orpha Gould lived closer by, and she helped a lot. Douw Hospital in Peking, where Orpha worked, gave free medical care to any of Laura's children who needed it. Whenever Orpha could take time off, she stayed a few days at Canaan Home to help. The children pronounced her last name the way it sounded to them. They called her Nurse Gu.

After the children were tucked in bed and the interruption level declined, Laura and Orpha liked to reminisce. "Who would have ever thought when you and I first met each other in 1917," Orpha said one night, "that we would be mixing baby formula together almost 20 years later in the kitchen of a ruined Russian Orthodox mission, halfway around the world in China?"

"No one but the Lord," Laura said.

That set them laughing about their first reunion after the war. For a year and a half after their Red Cross unit disbanded in 1919, they had lost track of each other. Then came the day they both set sail for China as newly appointed Presbyterian missionaries. Laura had boarded her ship in the San Francisco harbor and found Orpha, standing at the rail.

"You should have seen your face, Miss Laura Richards!" Orpha giggled.

"And you should have seen your own, Miss Gould!" Laura laughed.

Each, unknown to the other, had signed up with the same mission board, which had then assigned them each to the same language school in Peking. They traded memories of that first year they had spent together in China, attending language classes and sharing a house with Florence Logan and a couple of other missionaries. They marveled at how fast the years had flown and how faithful God had been through all their adventures.

Laura was especially glad that Orpha was close enough to come and help when a new disaster fell in early January 1937. The trouble started unremarkably in December when a newly arrived infant was sent to Douw

Hospital in Peking for a few days to bring her severe diarrhea under control. The day after she returned, her nose began to run, her cheeks grew bright with fever, and a blotchy red rash spread over her whole body. "Oh no! Measles!" Laura said. "She must have picked it up at the hospital."

Ten days later, 17 children came down with measles in one day, and soon all but three of 26 children had broken out with rashes and fevers. Then most of the measles patients came down with infectious pneumonia. No serum for pneumonia was available so far from the medical centers of the western world.

The sounds of coughing and choking filled Laura's ears as she labored on day and night, making her rounds. She kissed burning cheeks, cuddled limp bodies, rubbed heaving chests, wiped streaming eyes. Anxiously she listened to baby Nehemiah's labored breathing and baby Johanna's soft, weakening cries. Coughing, barking, choking on mucus, vomiting phlegm…day and night she heard the noise of her children's lungs struggling to clear. Her heart twisted at the sound of it.

The babies worried her. She could see their strength failing. "Father, Your will be done," she prayed.

She had lots of company during the day, but little help. The owner of the Russian Retreat Place had decided to rebuild the structure that burned down, so the caretaker and local workmen were in and about the place daily. But they were not there to help her. She had to deal with the epidemic almost alone. Just before the crisis, Forever Upward had had to leave on a trip that he expected would take him several weeks. The goat man was around, but he was busy with the family's two dozen goats. Only the gatekeeper's daughter was available to lend a hand.

Every day she worked from dawn until midnight then rose at 3 a.m. to give the tiny babies their early morning feeding. Every other night she went without sleep to squeeze in a full nighttime shift, pushing on through the dark morning hours—sterilizing bottles, preparing formula, setting bread for steaming, boiling diapers, hanging endless washings on the clothesline.

On one of those sleepless nights, after she had given the tiny babies their 3 a.m. feeding, she decided to take advantage of her nighttime privacy and get a bath. She was completely alone with the children. Every other temple in North China kept a watchman stationed at the front gate day and night. But none of the local people were willing to stay on these crumbling temple grounds past nightfall on account of the ghost of the old Russian priest.

It was dead winter and bitterly cold. The kitchen's only source of heat came from the stove, an open Chinese burner. She warmed the water in the metal bathtub with the contents of a kettle steaming on the stove. Then she refilled the kettle and set it back to boil. She stripped off her padded gown and sank into the warm water.

The room was quiet. Only the muffled gurgles of Laura's bath water and the faint chorus of coughing from the bedrooms disturbed the stillness of the night. The warm water soothed her aching legs and tired back, and she bathed slowly, luxuriating in her few moments of solitude. She felt sleepy and her head ached, but she took no notice. Anyone would feel sleepy, on her schedule. She was too tired to stop and think that her drowsiness and her headache might be symptoms of coal gas poisoning rather than fatigue.

Laura finished her bath, wiped her body dry, and began to pull on her clothes. She was still in her underwear when she picked up the kettle of boiling water to add hot water to the tub. She could use this bath water for another load of laundry. No point wasting water that had to be carried 75 steps up from the spring.

She fainted sideways into the tub with the kettle still in her hand, pouring a stream of boiling water over her hip as she collapsed. The kerosene lamp fell to the floor but amazingly it did not break and start a fire. Laura herself heard no sound and felt no pain. She lay quiet, with her body slumped in the tub, breathing the deadly coal gas fumes leaking from the stove.

Laura Richards (standing) with her friend Orpha Gould (seated, on right). This photograph was probably taken around 1921 when the two women were in language school together in Peking their first year in China. Laura first met Orpha when both served the army as Red Cross nurses during World War I. Orpha became a Christian through Laura's influence. The two friends lost track of each other when their unit disbanded in 1919, but after each of them applied as nurses to the Presbyterian Board of Missions, they experienced a surprise reunion in 1921 on the ship taking them to China.

Family Report from the Russian Retreat Place

Laura's letter written from the Russian Retreat Place, December 17, 1936:

How grateful and how full of praise I am to our merciful Heavenly Father for His loving watch-care over us throughout the whole year.

Early last fall until almost Christmas I had a patient with a tubercular spine. During the time that he was here, four tiny babies arrived and for a while I had the work practically alone. The thing that impressed me so during these weeks and months was that I seemed to be having a warfare with the Prince of this world, but I thank God that His beloved Son has overcome the world and that we can always be victorious, as He is the great Leader.

During the past few months I can see a very marked development in the little ones who came when only a few days old, five and six years ago. They ask questions continually, love books and pictures, flowers, birds, and worms. Sometimes the very small ones run from the goats and the dog, but they usually aren't afraid of anything. I try to teach them to keep away from scorpions.

It is a joy to me to see the children happy and growing, and I believe that with the physical growth there is a desire for an increasing knowledge of our Saviour. Mischievous as many of them are, they love to talk about Him. It is my great desire that they shall every one know Him, and if He still tarries, that they may grow in Christian character and be of good service in the Kingdom of our Lord.

While most of them are more or less mischievous, still they all seem to be responsive to loving teaching. One of them often asks me whether I've had my breakfast or dinner. Some of the tiny ones come to the door and say, "Mother, I love you, and I love the Lord Jesus too." At Christmas time and other times, too, friends bring them cookies and candy. I do not give them much at a time so I usually have some in supply. Some of the four-year olds come to remind me, "Isn't it time for cakes and candy now? We've been good, and we will be good." And a five-year-old will say, "I'm most fond of that rice gruel that you're making for the babies, and my stomach doesn't ache either."

10.

Recovery

The Russian Retreat Place, 1937

Instead of drowning her, the bath water saved her life. First it cooled, then it turned cold, and finally it revived her.

Drenched and shivering, she heaved her body weakly from the tub and peeled off her soaked underwear. Her arms and legs felt numb. She found her winter gown and pulled it on, but she could not will her deadened fingers to fasten it. It flapped open, exposing her neck and chest. Groggily, she tried to hold it closed with her chin as she scraped her knees painfully forward along the brick floor, crawling beyond the circle of warmth that radiated from the kitchen stove. The pain of her burns and the shock of the cold kept her going.

She rested for a couple hours in the sitting room until dawn broke, and then staggered to the children's bedroom where six little girls slept soundly together in a big square bed, cuddled warmly together in small connected humps under the quilts. She could see them dimly in the early dawn.

She poked feebly at the nearest hump, and somehow managed to waken five-year-old Lydia. "Mama is hurt, Darling," she said. She wanted to make her voice sound calm and strong, but all she could manage was a faint whisper. "Run to the gatehouse and tell the goat man your mama was in an accident and got burned. Tell him to hurry and get help from Douw Hospital."

Foreign Doll shoved back the quilts and slipped from her warm bed onto the freezing floor of the bedroom. She raced outside to the gatehouse in her stocking feet. It was quite a distance from her bedroom. Laura slumped to the floor and closed her eyes.

After a while she became conscious that she was surrounded by crying children. Their forms blurred, and their wailing ebbed and increased, faded, and then rose again. She needed to get up, but she could not move.

Then somehow, her friend Pervading Peace, an elder in the Presbyterian church in Peking, walked into the room and asked, "What is the matter?"

But that couldn't be real. It had to be a dream because how could Pervading Peace possibly have walked a dozen miles through the hills from her home in Peking to this remote spot to arrive so early in the morning?

Her pain felt real, though, when Pervading Peace half-carried her to her bed.

Her friend shooed the children out of her room, examined her burns and disappeared. After a while she returned with badger fat and bandages, which she said the neighbors had given her. The neighbors said they were glad to help Happy Plum Flower, because Laura had often given them helpful medical advice and nursing assistance.

Then Pervading Peace explained why she had come. She said she had waked in the night, so troubled in spirit that she had tumbled out of bed in a kneeling position and started praying. As sleep left her, she became convinced that Laura was in serious trouble and she must go to her immediately. So she had started hiking west in the darkness of night to reach the Russian Retreat Place.

The neighbors' folk remedy greatly eased Laura's pain, and Pervading Peace left to cook the children's breakfast. Laura dozed off.

The next thing she remembered clearly was the welcome sound of two familiar voices. Lydia's errand had been successful. Somehow the little girl had conveyed the urgency of Laura's situation to the goat man, and he had managed to get a message to the people at Douw Hospital. Orpha Gould and a Presbyterian doctor had immediately driven out in the hospital car.

The doctor dressed her blistered hip, Orpha took charge of the orphanage, and news of the accident spread quickly through the Presbyterian community. Dr. Mackey traveled all the way from Paotingfu to help.

Dr. Mackey was in the bedroom with Laura when Orpha brought news that Johanna and Nehemiah had died of pneumonia. "Nehemiah only weighed two pounds when he came," Laura told them sadly. "He was doing so well for a premature baby. He had such fat, rosy cheeks...."

She was silent for a few moments. Finally she said, "My father...," but her voice trailed off and tears trickled from her eyes. She wiped them with her handkerchief and blew her nose. Then she said with an effort, "My father died, too."

"Oh Laura, no!" Dr. Mackey exclaimed. "When?"

"Months ago...but I just found out," Laura said. "The letter came on Christmas Day. It took a long time to reach me." First her father, now her babies.

A couple days later Dr. Mackey had to tell her that two more babies had succumbed to pneumonia. Laura could not stop crying.

Dr. Mackey tried to console her. "God knew what lay ahead of them if they had lived," she said. "Since He took them to Himself early, they will escape the trials and heartaches of the world."

Her brain registered the words. Probably those words made sense. If only she could take them in, if only her world were not so dark and frightening, if only her loss were not so heavy, pressing her down.

She could hardly move her body, but her heart raced with fear. She could not wrench her mind away from the edge of death—her death. What if she had died? What would her babies have done? Coal gas poisoning was fatal. What if she had not fallen into the tub? She could have lain unconscious in the poisoned air until she died. Or what if the water had drowned her instead of reviving her? What would have become of her children?

Grief and fear bore down like a huge boulder rolling over her body, mashing her into the bed. Her eyes kept leaking tears. Her arms and legs were heavy weights. In vain, she willed her unresponsive fingers and toes to bend. Was it her grief, or was it the coal gas poisoning?

Dead arms. Dead legs. Dead father. Dead babies.

Gradually, then in a rush, memories of her father filled her mind—warm memories, jumbled in space and time. Curling up on a scratchy mound of hay in the pungent barn and watching Father while he fed the horses and sheep and milked the cows. Snuggling cozily up against him in the sleigh with Harold and Mother at Christmas time as they squeaked over the snow to Grandmother and Grandfather Russell's. Trotting behind him through the earthy smelling fields as he plowed, and watching the little quails scurry from their nests.

Once, a mother quail fleeing from the plow had left behind a nest full of tiny eggs. Laura had gathered them up and placed them under a setting hen in the barn. Later she discovered a mound of delicate, empty half-shells in the hen's nest. The little quails had run off as soon as they hatched.

How old had she been when that happened? It must have been before she turned nine years old—before Mother died. After Mother passed away, Father took a civil service examination to become a rural mail carrier. Sometimes during school vacations, he took her along with him on his mail route. Those were companionable times—driving the team together along the hard dirt roads, poking newspapers and letters into people's mailboxes, chatting with neighbors on his route.

Once Father took her and Harold to the circus. Now, whenever she smelled popcorn, she remembered the heady mix of popcorn, cotton candy, lumbering elephants, and ladies soaring high overhead on the trapeze.

Father bought bicycles for her and Harold, too, when she was ten, so they could pedal the five miles from their farm in Swanders to Grandmother and Grandfather Russell's house in Sidney. He let them stay at their grandparents' for a few days every so often to visit with their mother's family and see their little brother Edwin, who lived with their grandparents and Aunt Jenny.

When she was 14, he moved the family closer to Grandmother and

Grandfather's and built a modern house in Sidney with a hot-air furnace, piped-in water, and acetylene lighting. The house was beautiful. It smelled so clean and new that first day they moved in, so fragrant with the odors of fresh paint and sawdust and newly laid linoleum.

Her father's life had been a hard one, looking at it now with the eyes of an adult. First, baby Paul had died. Then three years later, Mother had died, too, leaving him alone with three young children to care for.

Mother. Kind, firm Mother. After all these years, Laura missed her mother still.

How dreadfully quiet the afternoon seemed that day her mother died. Mother had been very ill with tuberculosis for a long time. She would have died earlier, someone told her later, except that the doctor had brought a great oxygen tank out from the city and revived her. But she had protested. "Why did you bring me back?" she had asked. "There were angels there, ready to take me Home."

Which of the aunts told Laura about that? She could not recall.

What she did remember—vividly—what she would always remember until she died herself one day, was the enormous stillness of Mother's final day and the dawning awareness of death on her little-girl mind.

That, and the voices.

They came from the room next to where her mother lay, and they said, "Laura shall have her gold watch and her rings."

She fled to the woodshed then and crumpled in a heap on the hard dirt floor, sobbing bitterly. "Oh God," she cried out, "if You will only let my mother live, I don't want her watch and rings!"

But Mother died anyway, leaving behind her daughter's bitter inheritance.

More than one inheritance, actually. Along with the unwanted watch and rings had come the unwanted—precious—gift of an aching heart. For she had learned compassion, had she not? If her mother had not died when she was young, would she have begun Canaan Home when she was grown? She knew just what a motherless child needed. Her mother's early death had shaped her life, had brought her here to Canaan Home.

What a long strange road she had traveled since then, to become mother to these children.

A funeral followed that terrible day of silence, and then Aunt Jenny took her baby brother away. Father began delivering mail, and he had hired a genteel-looking old lady with white hair to keep house for him and Laura and Harold. The housekeeper was quite elderly and liked to visit her relatives.

Laura and Harold attended country school over the hill. Every day when school let out they would climb the hill, and Laura would look down to their house to see if there was smoke coming from the chimney. If there was smoke, all was well—it meant that the hired lady was cooking supper. But if there was no smoke, it meant that the old lady had gone visiting again, and the children would have to find their own supper. Sometimes the cupboards were quite bare.

After two years of that, Father remarried.

Frances Shearer Richards was the new stepmother. She was a well-educated young woman, but undemonstrative and unused to children. She had no idea how to replace the mother her stepchildren longed for. What Frances Richards did know was how she wanted the farm to be run.

There were no more empty cupboards once Frances took charge of the Richards household, and there was no nonsense either. She was a strict disciplinarian and a thorough teacher. If the children's work displeased her, she made them do it over and over until they did the job right. Her standards were high. She expected Laura and Harold to handle adult-size workloads from the time they were 12. She assigned Harold all the work of a hired man outdoors. She taught Laura to do everything inside a farmhouse that a woman in the early 1900s would have to know if she were left to do all of it by herself.

Then, two or three years after the marriage, Frances developed the liver trouble that eventually caused her to die just after the Great War. After that Laura had to cook and clean for four people before she could begin her homework. At night she stayed up late studying and writing out her lessons. On washdays she woke up at 4 a.m. to do the family laundry as well as her regular morning chores before leaving for school. The schoolhouse was a mile and a half away. She and Harold usually had to run part of the way to get there on time.

It had been a lonely life. Every day she ached for her mother. Frances allowed no opportunities for her to ease her loss through friendships with other girls. Laura and Harold were not permitted to play games at the farm or invite other children home. Their only chances to relax and have a bit of fun were recess times at school or visits with their mother's family, the Russells.

Grandmother and Grandfather Russell were kindly people who thought that children should have time to be children—to run free and make friends. They disapproved of the way Frances was raising their grandchildren. "It's just not right," Laura had overheard them say. "How can the children keep up with their schoolwork with all that work she gives them? She'll break their health."

Yet God had redeemed those lonely years, Laura thought now. He had gathered up her bleak adolescence and turned it to good. Frances had taught her a hundred useful skills in the house and garden, and she had taught her good work methods, too: how to organize a mountain of chores, how to do them properly and efficiently, how to use up everything and not waste anything, how to plug away at a big job and keep going until it was finished.

Yes, Laura thought with gratitude, *my stepmother gave me sound training for one day running a household of two dozen children out in the Chinese hinterlands with no modern conveniences.* Even though Frances had not known how to mother a lonely child, she had had a strong sense of duty toward her stepchildren. Despite her poor health, she had gone to much trouble to raise them properly, according to the way she saw things.

And whenever the farm became unbearable, the Russell clan had offered a safe retreat. In the homes of her grandparents and her many aunts and uncles, Laura was always welcomed, always hugged, always loved.

She had always been able to go to Jesus, too. Her mother had taught her to pray when she was small, and her family attended church routinely. Somehow she had simply grown up believing. Jesus had been part of her life, every day. He was there, like Grandmother Russell or Harold. She could not remember a time when she had not known about Jesus and trusted Him, or when she had not talked to Him. As a teenager she started reading her Bible daily, and gradually she learned to recognize the soft tug of the Holy Spirit in her thoughts.

One Sunday when she was 17, a missionary came to speak in the little Presbyterian church her family attended. As Laura listened, a persistent summons pressed into her mind—a summons not from the speaker, but from somewhere inside her bones. Silently she agreed to that call. *This is what I shall do one day,* she thought.

It had been another ten years before she actually applied to a mission board to go overseas. But like the consciousness of her mother's absence, the consciousness of her promise to God stayed deeply with her. The one was pain, the other anticipation.

Laura remembered how she had graduated from high school and traveled to Minneapolis General Hospital in Minnesota to train as a nurse. One of her first duties there had been to help fumigate the diphtheria wards. She promptly came down with diphtheria and nearly died. The disease partially paralyzed her, and she had to learn to walk all over again. For a long time her eyes hurt in sunlight, too, so she had to spend the first three months of her recovery in a darkened room.

It had been a curious way to begin nurses' training—six months in the contagious building, beating a slow retreat from the brink of death. When she finally began ward duties again though, she understood what it felt like to be a hospital patient. The experience helped to make her a better nurse.

After graduation, she joined the Red Cross, met Orpha, and learned nursing in a war zone. At the time she had no idea that those nine months in France were a mere first introduction to wartime nursing. She knew little about the political upheaval in North China when she sailed for Peking. As it turned out though, all the nursing courses she taught in China had been conducted in a war zone.

Laura opened her eyes. She thrust her hand from under the warm quilts into the frigid bedroom air and tried to pick her Bible up from the chair pulled next to her bed. Her deadened nerves refused to cooperate, and the book dropped three times from her clumsy fingers back to the chair. She gave up the effort and tried to recall the exact words of a Bible verse passing through her mind:

"And we know that all things work together for good to those who love God, to those who are the called according to His purpose," the Apostle Paul had written.

Yes, for her it had been so. God had turned her bad times to His good purposes. He had taken each hard experience and used it to prepare her for what lay ahead.

Nor should she forget the parade of people He had sent her and all the different ways He had cared for her and the children since the first day she left Peking for Chao Yang An: those faithful Dutch working girls with their busy knitting needles.the Chinese cook from the tubercular hospital with his humble gifts of pennies and cabbages…the toothpaste tube with hand cream in it…her graduate nurses, sneaking money into the children's cribs and cabinets…obnoxious, prolific Old Billy…Dr. Henke, straightening out Esther's poor back on that simple board…Mrs. Kao, deftly transforming used clothing into warm blankets…the beggar man's coal and peanuts, warm clothes, rice, and Chinese cakes…

The beggar man. Something about the beggar man teased at her memory, and then she was reliving the scene when she had spoonfed the sick man his final meal. "*There is a bright light in this room,*" he had said. "*From where is it coming?*" Then his own face had flared bright as a lamp when she had said it was Jesus.

She had been so preoccupied with taking care of all the new children at the time that she had scarcely noticed the beggar man's question and her reply. It had seemed an everyday occurrence then. Now it comforted her. God must have answered her prayer and saved that poor man's soul. It must have been Jesus standing by his bedside when he saw that light. How loving and kind the Lord had been to give that wretched man the things he needed and even the delicacies he longed for before he died.

God had been loving and kind to her, too. Think of the good health she had enjoyed up 'till now. What a blessing to think that this was the first time she had been really ill since the first year of Canaan Home.

That was remarkable, come to think of it, for a woman who had taken up mothering in poor health at the age of 36.

Besides all that, He had sent Orpha. Dear, reliable Orpha whom she'd introduced to Jesus during the Great War. They had first met nearly 20 years ago in Fort Roots, Arkansas, and now here was Orpha once again, half a world away in China, cheerfully and amazingly available when Laura needed her so badly.

Laura's reminiscing turned to praise. And somehow, as she praised God, the fear that paralyzed her spirit ebbed away. Peace replaced it.

"Father, You know and You do what is best, and You have lovingly watched over us for all these years," she prayed. "So I am willing now for You to take every one of these little ones to Yourself, for they are all Your dear ones anyway. And Your promises are sure. We will meet again in Heaven one day."

Laura's burns healed in several weeks, but the coal gas poisoning left her weak and clumsy. It was months before she regained full use of her arms and legs. She was fully in charge of Canaan Home again, however, and had even taken in two more babies by July 23, 1937, when the U.S. Embassy sent her two messages. The first informed her that Japanese and Chinese troops were at war near her in the Western Hills and asked her to move the children into the city for safety. The second message arrived later in the day saying that the fighting had stopped.

The second message brought her a sense of relief. Unfortunately, it also brought her wrong information.

Laura's Childhood

Laura Richards (third from the right in the back row). These are the children who attended Laura's one-room school near Sidney, Ohio in the early 1900s. Her brother Harold wrote that he and Laura had to walk, "over one mile to High and grade schools in Sidney. After our daily chores we really had to hot foot it to (get to) school."

Laura with her brother Harold, probably taken around 1910 when Laura was 17 and Harold was 15. Laura's mother Cora Delle Russell Richards died when Laura was nine years old. Harold was seven years old and their baby brother Edwin was five months old. The Russell grandparents took Edwin home and raised him.

Letter from Laura Jane Eberhardt Cerling, to Jean Cerling Allen, August 4, 1976:

Cousin Laura's father remarried and my childhood impression from Mother's stories were that Laura had the traditional wicked stepmother. I'm not sure now how "wicked" she was—possibly she was just an ordinary woman trying to cope with raising two motherless children on a farm in the early 1900s. Both Cousin Harold and Cousin Laura had to work very hard. Mother said Laura had to do the family washing before going to school and both left home so they could finish their high school in town. My mother's brother, their Uncle Ed Russell, gave them help and a home so they could get their education.

Letter from Harold R. Richards to Becky Powers, July 13, 1984:

I will try to verify and explain about Stepmother and Laura. I know she did have a feeling of responsibility for us children, but as you say there must have been some deeper feeling for us. Otherwise she would not of cared so much about giving us so much strict attention and enforcing it. She just didn't express it.

At the time, certain disciplinary restrictions look out of place. However, both Laura and I have believed in later years that the hard going was good for us in the long run. Laura and I both have had a fantastic bringing up. You might say from the time we were old enough—ten to 12 years—we both carried responsibilities that grownups usually had….

Excerpt from Laura's testimony, written in 1957:

My mother taught me to pray at a very early age, and I have believed in the Lord since my earliest recollection. I do not remember when I received the Lord Jesus Christ into my heart as a little child, but I believe that I was very young. I have sometimes deviated from His pathway, but I have never doubted Him or His Word. There is great thanksgiving in my heart today for all the ways that my Savior has led me.

As I think of that little nine-year-old girl left without the love of a mother, I can see His guiding Hand, His disciplinary Hand, and the Hand that helped her to grow up with more compassion in her heart for little boys and girls who have had like experiences, than she would have had, had that mother lived.

Laura's letter from the Russian Retreat Place, August 20, 1937:

The little ones that our Heavenly Father called to Himself were some who had come to us when only a few days old and when taken were almost a year old. It was the second time since the beginning that my Heavenly Father had permitted me to see such sorrow of heart. Since then I have thanked Him often for that experience, for much came out of it to strengthen and help us.

11.

War in the Western Hills

The Russian Retreat Place, 1937

LAURA WAS TOO BUSY WITH THE CHILDREN and too isolated from the city to stay well informed about the world's political situation. She was only dimly aware of the war brewing in Western Europe, where Germany's Adolf Hitler had murdered his political enemies and then turned his country from a republic into a totalitarian state. Hitler was openly building up the German armed forces, operating munitions plants at full tilt, and eyeing his neighbors' borders. Italy had just helped herself to Ethiopia, and an ugly civil war raged in Spain. Germany, Italy, and the Soviet Union were all intervening, using the Spanish conflict to test their tanks and war planes in real battles.

Laura knew little about China's situation either. She was aware that Chiang Kai Shek had been kidnapped the winter before by one of his own generals. She was unaware though, that he had ransomed himself by agreeing to ally with the Communists in a common fight against the Japanese, who were exerting steady military pressure on China's northern provinces. After several months of negotiations, the two sides signed a working agreement on July 5. Two days later, on the night of July 7, 1937, a disagreement arose between Japanese and Chinese troops at the Marco

Polo Bridge. Chinese soldiers began firing, and Japanese troops returned fire. Both the Japanese and Chinese commanders-in-chief tried to settle the affair locally, but numerous repeated, inexplicable acts of violence over the next few weeks finally escalated the conflict into a full-scale war.

After that, the political situation began to affect Canaan Home directly. For Peking, with its famous temples and palaces, was a jewel that both sides wished to preserve. The fighting moved into the Western Hills.

On July 28, five days after the Embassy's messages arrived, Laura heard gunfire muttering in the distance. Since it was the rainy season, she thought at first she was hearing thunder. But the sound was too constant. As the day passed, the rumble grew to a roar.

That afternoon the gate keeper and the goat man lost their fear of the murdered Russian's ghost. They fetched their families and stayed overnight in an empty building on the orphanage compound, listening apprehensively to the thunder of army vehicles racing past on the main road two miles away.

The noise disturbed the children's sleep. Laura slept fitfully, too, between night feedings, wondering what the day would bring. What if the soldiers started fighting on the main road? What if they moved into the villages below? And what if they came up the hill and into her courtyard?

On the other hand, what if she should be so foolish as to forget the lesson God had taught her after the coal gas accident, the last time her mind became overwhelmed with "what if?" questions. She must use her head to fortify her faith. She drifted in and out of sleep, pondering the scriptures her mind dredged up, recalling the ways that God had shown her His power and love, dozing off, then waking again to praise her God.

In the morning machine guns began roaring again, very close now. A stream of terrified refugees boiled up the muddy steps to the old Russian temple and flowed through the gate. The Japanese army had caught up to the fleeing Chinese army on the main road, they said, and the Chinese soldiers were badly outnumbered. Hundreds of people of all ages, from newborn infants to tottering grandparents, crammed inside the compound walls. Some Laura recognized, like her nearest neighbors and several workmen who had rebuilt the burned-down structure on the property.

Exploding mortar rocked the hills. Airplanes screeched across the skies and dropped bombs at targets several miles away. The clamor of guns continued all day long. The courtyard grew smoky from the burning of the refugees' cooking fires. Laura tried to provide fuel, water buckets, medical advice, and calm direction, while tending her own 24 children in the crisis.

When darkness fell, as many of the refugees as possible moved into the mission's buildings to sleep. There was not space for everyone though, so scores had to camp outdoors. It was the rainy season, and during the night it poured. The people sleeping outside dashed to the nearest building to get out of the storm. Soon there was standing room only within doors. Nobody slept much.

Laura dragged herself out of bed the next morning to the sound of gunfire out by the main road. *This is a good opportunity to tell all these people about Jesus*, she reminded herself. But she felt sluggish and stupid from lack of sleep. She felt strangely oppressed, too, as if her every step and gesture was being opposed by an unseen force. She seemed unable to fight off her lethargy.

Heavenly Father, she willed her mind to pray, *bless me, strengthen me by the power of your Holy Spirit.*

"Do you have an American flag?" several voices chorused as soon as she stepped into the courtyard.

"Yes, I do," Laura said, "but it is packed away."

"Hang it on the front gate," the refugees begged. "Put it where the soldiers will see it. The Japanese will respect an American flag."

"But there is a cross at the top of the gate already," Laura objected, "and another cross on the hill back of us. If we must depend for safety on some outward sign, I believe the cross will be more effective than the flag."

"How can the cross help us?" an anxious young father asked, grasping a bare-bottomed toddler firmly against his shoulder.

"The United States is a mighty nation," Laura explained, "but the cross of Jesus Christ is more powerful than any government or any human authority. The cross of Jesus can save you not only in this life but in the life to come."

Another crowd of panicked villagers clambered up the muddy steps to the Retreat Place gatehouse, wailing and shivering. They said that Japanese soldiers had camped along the main road and moved into villagers' homes, raping women and looting shops and houses. Fear thickened the air of the courtyard, more stifling than the dense humidity.

"Do you have an American flag?" the refugees kept asking Laura. "You can put the flag by the cross."

Finally Laura set aside her work and located her flag. While she was searching through packages to find it, she discovered a bundle of gospel tracts. She passed out the tracts, and people seized them with eager fingers. They listened respectfully when she told them about the great opportunity they now had to trust in God—"the true God who is able to protect both soul and body from the enemy."

Fighting continued throughout the day. Chinese soldiers hid in the hills, and some of them pounded up the slope and banged on the orphanage gates. People watching nervously from the mission walls saw Japanese patrols scouting the area, searching for the escaping Chinese. Japanese soldiers killed three local herdsmen on the mission hillside.

After evening prayers with the children, Laura dropped into bed, exhausted. The noise of artillery fire punctuated her dreams, and she slept poorly.

During the babies' 3 a.m. feeding on July 31, Laura heard the heaviest artillery fire yet about one mile away. The noise dwindled then, and the battle ended later that morning with the Japanese as victors. For ten days more the mission remained crowded with refugees while Japanese troops stayed in the area. Villagers came and went for supplies and information, returning to the mission in terror and reporting stories of atrocities.

In one village where a number of Japanese officers had camped, the conquerors treated people responsibly and thanked villagers for feeding and housing their soldiers. In other villages, though, Japanese soldiers plundered houses and stores, shot and stabbed ordinary citizens on a whim, and raped, beat, and sometimes mutilated women and girls as young as ten or 12. With guns, clubs, bayonets, and knives, they attacked unarmed men who tried to protect the women.

While searching for escaped Chinese soldiers, Japanese troops shot without question any Chinese man wearing any article of clothing that resembled part of a Chinese uniform. They moved into private homes, seizing valuables and stripping the buildings of anything wooden—doors, rafters, window frames, furniture, farm tools. In some homes they left nothing but brick walls and dirt floors. They burned the wood to cook meals and keep warm. Apparently they did not know how to burn charcoal because even if supplies of it were available, the soldiers burned doors, plows, or craftsmen's tools instead. They burned a woman's weaving loom even though it was the only source of income she had.

They never came to the Russian Retreat Place though. One of the neighbors reported that when several Japanese soldiers asked villagers for directions to the mission, the villagers told them that an American woman was living there taking care of a number of little children. So the soldiers turned back. At the time, the mission was crammed to the gates with refugees.

It was a relief when all the villagers finally left. The children did best on a simple, orderly routine of regular mealtimes, playtimes, naps, choretimes, and bedtimes. Laura was glad to be able to get them back on schedule.

She was now caring for 24 children under age 11, a dozen of them less than two years old and still in diapers. The children's day began with a breakfast of cornmeal mush and vegetables at a table set up in the hallway near her bedroom. After breakfast, when the weather was fine, they took toys outdoors and played in the front courtyard. The oldest children took turns working alongside her at simple tasks.

Although it was the Chinese custom for children to eat as much as they could hold twice a day, Laura found that her children stayed healthier when she served them smaller portions of food, three times a day. So after playtime in the morning, the children came inside for a noon meal and then a nap. A snack and Bible stories followed. Then the children played in the front courtyard until suppertime. They played a little longer after supper, then put away their toys for the night. Each of the older children was assigned to help a specific toddler. At the end of the day, these children made sure their toddlers came inside for the night and started getting ready for bed. An evening blessing ended their day.

The family enjoyed a full week of this normal calm routine. Then the men in black appeared.

It was about ten o'clock the morning of August 18. Laura was in the courtyard with the children when she noticed a number of men sitting in scattered groups on the hillside opposite the mission. They all wore black, and they appeared to be resting alongside a trail that led to a stone quarry further up the hill. Two large white sacks lay amongst them on the ground.

"Who are those men in black?" she asked the goat man.

"I am wondering that myself," he said.

"Please go and ask them who they are," Laura said, "and what their business is among us."

The goat man trotted obediently off, and Laura watched him conversing with the strangers and making motions with his hands in the direction of the main road. Then he turned and started back to the mission. Laura noticed two of the strangers in black trailing him at a distance.

"They said they are soldiers escaped from the army," the goat man announced when he returned. "They wanted to know how to get to the main road."

Looking over his shoulder, Laura saw that the two men who had followed him were starting to come up the steps to the gate. *Something is wrong,* Laura thought.

But they were impeccably polite. "Have you eaten?" the men asked Laura, bowing courteously. They were curious to know, they said, what she was doing in such an isolated part of the country, and they wondered if she would be so gracious as to lend them her cooking pots and allow them to come inside to cook their food.

Laura smiled and paused before replying. Sometimes her problems with the Chinese language were convenient. People excused her long pauses as vocabulary lapses, when she was actually buying time to figure out how to handle difficult situations.

"I am taking care of 24 little children here," she said. "We have barely enough cooking pots to cook their meals. If I give them to you, I will be unable to feed the children. I deeply regret that I cannot lend them to you."

She ignored the request to come inside.

The two men received her refusal without apparent offense and returned to the group of men resting on the hillside. Laura went back inside the compound, but within a few minutes the gatekeeper called her back to the gatehouse. Three more men dressed in black stood waiting. They wanted to borrow the family's water pails.

"Yes, you may borrow the pails," Laura said, "but please return them as soon as possible. The family uses them almost constantly." She was reluctant to lend the pails but felt it was probably unwise to keep refusing the men's every request. This appeal, at least, did not include a demand to come inside the compound.

She watched the men fill the pails with water at the spring and begin toiling up the trail to the quarry with the full pails. She returned to her work. Within two hours the men returned the pails. They bowed deeply and thanked her courteously.

By this time the large group of men was no longer in sight on the hillside. They had apparently taken their two big white sacks and moved up the trail to the stone quarry, ignoring the goat man's directions to the main road. Laura wondered what it meant.

While she wondered, the peasants in one of the villages below the mission were hearing bad news. A distraught Chinese landlord appeared, asking if anyone had seen some bandits who had stolen two sacks of flour and $40 from him. The bandits had kidnapped two of the wealthy man's relatives and were holding them for ransom. The bandits had also kidnapped four other people from two homes near him, he said, including a mother and her four-year-old son. The villagers would recognize these bandits when they saw them, because they were all dressed in black.

By nightfall, everyone except Laura had heard about it.

Early the next morning when she came out to the gate house, she noticed a group of men in black standing by the steps to the spring. The man nearest her was sitting on the stone railing at the head of the steps and eating a large *lao-ping*—a kind of pancake the villagers usually ate for their morning meal.

"Have you eaten?" Laura asked in greeting.

The man scowled.

"We have some fine peaches, if you would care for any," she said. A neighbor had given the family the fruit. Peaches were considered a rare treat in the hill country.

The man refused with another scowl.

Laura turned to the other men, greeted them courteously, and began admiring their new clothing and the fine handmade shoes they wore. "Where did you get such nice new clothes and such fine shoes?" she asked.

"The people gave them to us," they replied.

"But they are so uniform and so new," she continued curiously. "They look as if they have been made to order."

The men gave no further explanation. Instead they began asking Laura questions about the children. "Where are they?" the men wanted to know. "May we see them?"

It seemed a harmless request.

Laura Richards (on the left) standing with Dr. Maud A. Mackey in front of the house Dr. Mackey shared with Florence Logan in Paotingfu. This picture was probably taken in 1940 when Laura visited the mission station en route to helping a Chinese woman start a new orphanage south of Paotingfu. Dr. Mackey was in charge of the Presbyterian Mission's Hodge Memorial Hospital for Women in Paotingfu. She and Laura remained lifelong friends after Laura resigned as superintendent of nurses at the hospital in 1928. In 1937, Dr. Mackey made an emergency trip to care for Laura when she suffered a near-fatal accident with coal gas poisoning, and Laura gave her old friend full-time nursing care from 1953 to 1957 during Dr. Mackey's final illness.

Orphan Memories from the Russian Retreat Place

Rachel's 1989 memoir, translated from Chinese:

I remember that place clearly [the Russian Retreat Place]. I couldn't forget it. When we woke up after our nap, Mama let those of us who could walk go to the back courtyard. The back courtyard was very big, with a lot of very tall fruit trees and a big stone table and stone bench. We sat down, and Mama gave us peanuts. We were too young to shell the peanuts, so Mama taught us how to use our two little hands to crush them on top of the stone table. When the peanut broke, we took the kernels out and ate them. After we finished eating, we sat there and Mama taught us to sing songs about Jesus. One of them was about "Jesus loves all the children of the world." Another one was "Jesus Loves Me." I knew those two songs were Mama's most favorite songs.

Mama cooked every meal for us and dished out each person's portion. We had cornbread and corn mush and vegetables. Before we ate, we had to wash our hands and sit in front of the table. Then Mama prayed for us. She taught us these good habits. Our kitchen table was in the hallway to Mama's bedroom. At noon she gave us cornbread and spread it with honey. When we were eating, Mama was working in the house while watching us eat.

Mama was dependent on her love for and her faith in God. Along with taking care of us, she was aware of the neighbors' needs, noticing if they had a disease or ailment. Some of the children who used to live nearby us have grown up. They say that the old people living there always talked about what happened at the orphanage.

12.

The Men in Black

The Russian Retreat Place, 1937

"THE SMALLEST ONES are still babies in cribs," Laura said, "but I will bring out the ones who are old enough to walk."

She rounded up the children playing in the front courtyard and led them out to the men in a cheerful, loosely knit parade. In all, there were a half-dozen toddlers and a dozen older children. Laura directed the older children to sit on the steps with the babies in their laps.

The man finishing his *lao-ping* continued to scowl. The other men's faces remained placid and unreadable.

"Why are the children here with you?" they asked.

"They are very poor," Laura said, "so I am taking care of them. When a poor child's mother dies or becomes very ill, the neighbors or relatives bring the child to me."

They seemed intrigued. Laura answered their questions, then she herded the children back into the compound and returned to her work.

Half an hour later the goat man and the gatekeeper arrived, bringing with them a carpenter from the village. Laura and the carpenter had become good friends during the winter and spring when he had helped rebuild the structure that had burned down on the old mission. The three men told Laura everything they had learned about the men in black.

The scowling man who had refused Laura's peaches had stolen the *lao-ping* he was eating that morning from a woman who had been carrying it to her husband working in the fields. The two white sacks she had seen with the men resting on the hillside yesterday must have been the sacks of flour they had stolen from the landlord whose relatives they kidnapped. The bandits had demanded $4 million in local currency for that man's relatives plus the four other captives, but today they had reduced the ransom amount to $1,000.

Laura shook her head in disbelief and dismay. "They asked to see all the children," she said faintly. "What have I done?"

She had dangled her lambs before wolves.

"They only kidnap rich men's children," the carpenter reassured her.

Laura said nothing. She knew she was poor. The villagers knew she was poor. But why should the bandits believe she was poor? To a Chinese bandit, all Americans were rich—and one who wasn't had friends who were. The bandits had already kidnapped a mother with a boy the same age as her bright-eyed Samuel. Why should they spare Laura and her children?

Each day after that brought more bad news. The men in black's main business appeared to be kidnapping. Every night they took more captives. In the darkness after the children were settled in bed, Laura could hear the sound of their victims crying out as the bandits forced them up the hill to the stone quarry. Sometimes after the cries, she heard shots. Then silence.

Someone from the neighborhood visited her almost daily, jittery with fear. When a kidnap victim's relatives failed to pay the ransom at the set time, the villagers told her, the men in black took the unlucky captives to the mountain across from the orphanage and shot them, or buried them alive. Daily, the neighbors reported to her the number and names of people taken in the night. Some were people she knew.

Each night after the children's bedtime prayer, Laura made a compact bundle of her large-print Chinese Bible and a few necessities. She placed the bundle on a chair beside her bed in case she was kidnapped during the night. "If they take me, Lord," she prayed, "please help me to give them your gospel of salvation."

More bandits continued moving into the area daily, and part of the gang moved to a temple farther back into the mountains to accommodate their swelling numbers. All the local stores closed, and the family's store of millet and flour dwindled. The U.S. Embassy sent Laura a letter stating that the Embassy had learned that several hundred bandits were taking over her neighborhood in the Western Hills. They urged her to move into Peking as soon as possible. Laura read the letter several times.

"*. . . move the children into the city as soon as possible.*" How was she supposed to do that? It had been hard enough moving three miles from Chao Yang An to the Russian Retreat Place when she had had only five babies and two young girls who were old enough to manage the hike. Now she had twelve babies plus twelve older children, hardly any of them old enough to manage even a three-mile hike, much less the ten-mile distance into Peking. It was true that the family would be somewhat safer living closer to the American Embassy, even though Peking was now occupied by Japanese troops. Also, it would be easier for volunteers to come and teach the children to read and write. She was becoming concerned, after all, about how to give the older children their academic education.

On the other hand, city life would be complicated. She would probably have to register the orphanage with city officials. It would be expensive, too. Rent would be higher, she would probably have to start buying water again from a carrier, and how would the family raise their goats and chickens? Without the supplements that their animals and garden supplied, the family's food costs would skyrocket.

In any case, there seemed no way to do it. The transportation problem was too great. So Laura decided to stay put and try to weather the crisis. Maybe something would happen to make the bandits go away.

But the men in black stayed and found another way to exploit the local people. Neighbors reported that the bandits were forcing the villagers to help them dynamite and plunder the Tomb of the Princess. Every day the people of one of the villages had to butcher a pig and carry it up the mountain to the men in black, along with two sacks of flour, vegetables, and other supplies. The bandits forced local carpenters, masons, and other skilled workmen to help excavate the tomb.

Opening the long passage to the door of the tomb took longer than the men in black expected, but after a number of days of hard work, they broke through and opened the door. Laura's carpenter friend told her that they found delicate leaves fashioned from silver and gold strewn over the remains of the princess's body. Precious pearls had been placed under her tongue, and a golden bowl rested at her feet. This bowl was so highly polished, the carpenter reported, that if a candle were placed inside it, it would reflect three candles.

All the time the excavation work was going on, the kidnapping continued. Nights were becoming noisy now with the barking of dogs and the echoing cries of terrified captives on the mountain trail opposite the mission. The children slept poorly through the commotion.

For several months Laura had been able to hire a village woman to help her do the laundry. The washerwoman now developed a nervous twitch in her left eye, and the gatekeeper's motions slowed almost to a halt, as if his limbs were becoming gradually paralyzed by fear. The children started to pick up the adults' uneasiness. One day when six-year-old Rachel was pumping the swing high above the courtyard wall, she suddenly screamed and tumbled out of the swing seat in a panic. She rushed over to Laura, sobbing. Laura put her arms around her, wondering what had happened.

"A bad man, Mama!" Rachel wailed. Her small frame shook, and Laura could feel her little heart thudding. "A bad man was looking at me!"

Laura looked over the wall. Rachel loved to swing. It was her favorite way to play. This morning she apparently swung so high she could see over the courtyard wall to the mountain facing the mission. One of the men in black was standing on the path, hands hidden in his black sleeves, staring in the direction of the mission. To Rachel it must have seemed that he was staring at her. The little girl didn't seem to know why he scared her. She said he was bad, that was all.

Laura kissed her daughter gently and told her that she and the other children were no longer allowed to play on the swings.

Soon after that incident, the Embassy sent a second urgent message, pressing Laura to take immediate action to move Canaan Home to Peking. War would erupt in her neighborhood soon, they warned. The Japanese were making plans to return and drive the bandits out of their stronghold. Laura carried the letter into her bedroom for a few quiet moments to think and pray.

It was now over three weeks since the men in black had first appeared. The family was nearly out of millet and flour, and there was no telling how long it would be before local stores opened again. Certainly they would stay closed until the Japanese moved in to fight the bandits, and the Russian Retreat Place was located too close to the bandits' stronghold to hope to escape the fighting. In fact, the Japanese would probably want to use the old Russian mission to house soldiers and store supplies. It looked like the time had come to find a new location for Canaan Home.

Laura sent a message to the laundry woman asking her to babysit the children for a day. She also sent a message to her friend the carpenter, asking him to accompany her into Peking in the morning.

A crashing thunderstorm drowned the cries of the bandits' captives that night, and it was still drizzling when Laura woke early. She checked the children. They were sleeping soundly. There seemed no point in waking them to say good-bye.

At the gatehouse, the laundress and the carpenter showed up promptly, glancing nervously over their shoulders at the trail to the bandits' hideout. Fortunately there was no sign of any of the men in black on the mountain. Laura hoped it would keep raining all day. Foul weather would make her journey less conspicuous. Perhaps she could go all the way into Peking and come home again without anyone noticing her absence.

The air was thick with the combined fragrances of damp fields, open toilets, and human offal spread out for fertilizer. Laura and her companion slipped and slid upon the wet grass along the narrow path through the villages to the main road. Laura's shoes soon became caked with mud. Her gown grew sodden and cold. At the main road, the pair hired rickshaws for the last eight miles into the city. The charcoal skies dripped on.

"I know a man who might be interested in renting a couple of courts to you," a Chinese evangelist told Laura at the Presbyterian Mission in Peking. "Most of his compound is vacant right now. There are Japanese garrisoned nearby, and he is afraid that they will take his place over to house more troops if they notice that his compound is nearly empty.

"I know about this situation," he added, "because the owner's brother-in-law, Nieh Shou Guang, lives in the back court. Mr. Nieh is a new convert who is helping us with refugee relief work at one of the chapels."

The landlord in question was a wealthy, high-ranking officer, and the evangelist's information was correct. The officer was willing to rent the two empty courts in his compound very cheaply in order to protect his property. His place was located near the Presbyterian Mission, and it was luxurious, with large buildings and modern plumbing in the kitchen and laundry room. Laura could hardly believe her good fortune. Imagine, hot and cold running water!

The new landlord nearly withdrew his offer, though, when Laura mentioned her goats. So she agreed to make arrangements with Chinese friends in town to take the family livestock.

After the negotiations, the evangelist found Nieh Shou Guang and introduced him to Laura. Mr. Nieh was a young man probably in his late 20s. He looked strikingly different from the men Laura was used to seeing in North China. His face was oval instead of round, without the angular cheekbones and pronounced, slanting eyes of the local people. He was taller than most of the Chinese men she had met. With his straight nose, large eyes, and high forehead, he looked more east Indian than Chinese. His mannerisms and courtesies, however, were pure upper-class Mandarin.

Mr. Nieh listened thoughtfully as the evangelist explained Laura's situation and described her work with the children of Canaan Home. "Clearly your greatest difficulty with this move is transportation," he said. "I will try to arrange for us to borrow vehicles from the police department—an ambulance to transport the children and trucks to load your furniture and livestock."

Mr. Nieh offered to arrange for truck drivers and said he would come along with the evangelist in the borrowed vehicles to direct the family's move into the city. Laura accepted his offer with gratitude.

Laura and the carpenter located the waiting rickshaw men and started home. The road was pitted with ruts and potholes, and the rickshaw's pace was a slow jolt. Laura closed her eyes and leaned back against the seat, recalling each of the children's faces and praying for them one by one. Tears trickled from her closed eyes and dripped down her neck into the collar of her gown. She cringed to think of her babies in the rough hands of the men in black. It was impossible not to worry.

At last the two rickshaws reached the place in the road where the path to the villages began. Laura paid the two drivers and trudged with the carpenter half a mile through the ripening cornfields to the first village. The day was still gray and overcast, but the rain had stopped.

In the village, the carpenter paused to talk with people he knew, and the conversation soon veered to the men in black. A few passersby joined in, and soon all were talking excitedly. Suddenly the carpenter looked up and drew in his breath with a hiss. One of the men in black was coming toward them. The group changed the subject abruptly.

"Let's wait until he passes," the carpenter said to Laura in a low tone.

The man in black passed the group without expression and without greeting. Laura and the carpenter watched him pad along the trail ahead quite some distance until he disappeared at a point where the path curved around a field of tall corn. Then the two companions said good-bye to their village friends and started for home, quickening their pace. Soon the sun would be setting behind the shadowed mountains, and they were anxious to reach home before dark.

They had walked only a short distance past the curve in the path when the carpenter glanced apprehensively back over his shoulder. There was the man in black behind them, following closely.

Rachel mailed this treasured keepsake from China, an undated photograph of the Canaan Home orphans probably taken at the Russian Retreat Place in 1936 or 1937. Outer circle, clockwise, Rachel in the center, then her twin Rose Mary, Sarah, two unidentified children, Dinah, Samuel, Patience (baby front center), Philip, Lydia (Foreign Doll), Charity, and Ruth. The babies within the circle are unidentified except for the twins, Grace and Gloria, inside the first wheeled vehicle on the left. Philip (squatting on the left) and Ruth (tallest, top row) were brother and sister.

Perceptions

1985 INTERVIEW WITH LAURA'S COUSIN,
LAURA JANE EBERHARDT CERLING,
WHO WAS 16 THE FALL OF 1937:

When I was 15, Mother started listening to WMBI [Christian radio station]. One night she said that she had decided to start going back to church, and she would go Sunday. My father and brother teased her about it, and I thought it wouldn't be nice if Mother had to go all by herself. So I went with her and I became involved with the young people's group. When I became a Christian at age 16, I was very drawn to Laura, but it was something I couldn't discuss [in the family] because there was the feeling that you shouldn't become very involved. Laura was strange. She wasn't accepted. The family didn't understand.

I don't know whether it was before or after I accepted Christ, but I always remember a conversation I overheard between my mother and father. I don't know if they were talking about me or just in general terms, but they said they didn't want anyone to become a religious fanatic like Laura. Now my father was a very kind man, and, as I look back on it, this was spoken out of the ignorance of his experience. To him, this is what it appeared to be.

LETTER TO BECKY POWERS FROM FLORENCE LOGAN,
WRITTEN JULY 26, 1986:

It seems to me that at least three remarkable characteristics stand out: First, the physical strength and fortitude to endure the hard work and endless hours. Second, her great skill and ability in caring for babies. How did she ever manage so many? Third, her quiet loving spirit at all times. There must have been dozens of times when most of us would have "blown our top," but I don't believe she ever raised her voice! Amazing! She was specially gifted for the special needs of her work.

13.

Mr. Nieh

The Russian Retreat Place and Peking, 1937

THE CARPENTER WHISPERED a warning. Laura dared not look around. Quietly but clearly she announced, "There is a stone in my shoe. Can you wait a moment while I remove it?"

She stooped in the path. The man in black passed them by without a word.

Slowly Laura took off her soggy cloth shoe, emptied it deliberately, and drew it back over her foot. The pulse in her throat galloped. Her legs felt shaky. She straightened, smoothed her gown, and started moving along the trail with the carpenter once again.

The man in black padded ahead of them at a relaxed pace, taking his time. The two companions slowed their gait to keep him in sight. Finally the man in black turned up the mountain trail toward the gang's hideout. With relief, Laura and her friend headed toward the spring.

Usually when Laura left the children with the laundry woman to buy supplies, the older orphans waited at the gatehouse to watch for her return. They liked to stand in a line at the gate, the woman had told Laura, where they rocked back and forth, chanting, "Mama, come back very soon! Mama, come back very soon!"

This evening they were massed at the gate in a terrified huddle, neither chanting nor making games. As soon as they saw her, they plunged headlong down the muddy steps. Charity tripped. Down, down the slippery stairs she tumbled, skidding and bumping and knocking her little head on the hard, wet stone.

Laura scrambled up to break her fall and lifted her gently. "Mama! Mama!" the child sobbed. "Where did you go, Mama? You weren't here! We couldn't find you!" A great red knot bumped out on the little girl's forehead. Laura couldn't keep back her tears.

"Mama! Where did you go?" the other children echoed, slipping and sliding down to the stair where Charity had fallen. They crowded around her, hugging and clinging and crying. Their voices were shrill with fear.

Laura set Charity gently upright and helped her up the stairs while all the other little hands clung to her. *I will never leave them again without telling them when and where I am going,* she promised herself.

She exchanged farewell bows with the carpenter and laundress, and she tucked the children into their beds with evening prayers. Then she dropped into bed like a stone.

Dogs barked. Captives cried. Gunshots echoed in the hills. Tragedy continued all around her in the darkness, and the children slept restlessly.

September 14 was moving day. Mr. Nieh met his friend the evangelist at the police station in Peking and arranged drivers for the borrowed police trucks and ambulance. He helped the men secure an American flag to each vehicle so that the bandits would not mistake them for Japanese soldiers and attack the caravan. The evangelist rode with Mr. Nieh in the ambulance leading the caravan so he could give the driver directions to the Russian Retreat Place. A bright blue sky arched overhead, and the sun's reflection on the city roofs shone like burnished gold as the caravan passed through the city's West Gate. It was going to be a hot day.

The evangelist entertained them with tales about Happy Plum Flower Richards. The stories intrigued Mr. Nieh. He hoped they would be able to rescue her orphanage without trouble from the bandits, although he was not looking forward to supervising a big moving job with children underfoot.

He reflected that before he had become a Christian, he would never have considered taking on a task like this. He had no use for children back then. Demanding nuisances he had thought them. But his attitude was starting to change. His new Christian friends had great respect for the potential of a child. They expressed compassion instead of contempt for children's weaknesses. They said Jesus taught that anyone who received a child in His name was receiving Jesus Himself, and that, unless a person became as humble as a little child, he could neither enter nor become great in the kingdom of Heaven.

The caravan sped along the main road until it reached the trail to the villages. Then it jolted slowly past villagers shucking corn in their fields. Mr. Nieh and the driver looked carefully every place they drove, but they did not see any of the men in black.

"I think that is their hideout," the evangelist said, jerking his chin toward the stone quarry in the side of the mountain across from the Russian Retreat Place.

The caravan halted at the spring below the mission. Mr. Nieh strode up the steps to the mission gate with the drivers following at his heels and glancing uneasily over their shoulders at the quarry. Happy Plum Flower Richards met them at the head of the stairway with a wide smile on her face and a baby clamped to one hip. She shook hands warmly with each of the men, making courteous inquiries about the trip from Peking. Then she led Mr. Nieh to the mission buildings and showed him what needed to be done.

Mr. Nieh directed the workers to load everything into the police trucks—cribs and beds, bottle racks and baby bottles, cooking pots and food supplies, bundles of clothes, piles of bedding, and stacks of diapers. Bleating goats and squawking chickens protested the adventure as the men herded and tugged, chased and carried them onto the waiting trucks.

Halfway through the move, two drivers dashed over to Mr. Nieh and announced that three men in black had come down the trail from the quarry. They were headed toward the mission. Mr. Nieh joined the gatekeeper at the gatehouse, watching the three men climb the steep stone stairway.

"We have a message from our chief for Happy Plum Flower Richards," one of the men told the gatekeeper.

Mr. Nieh waited in the gatehouse with the bandits while the gatekeeper fetched Happy Plum Flower. The three men in black ignored him. When the American woman appeared, one of the bandits said, "Our chief sent us to ask you not to go away. He said that if you and the children stay in this place, he will supply the orphanage with all the millet and flour you need, and his men will protect your children."

Happy Plum Flower looked surprised, then thoughtful. "Please wait here a moment," she said. "I have a gift for your chief."

Fifteen minutes later she returned with a Chinese Bible, bound in leather. "Please tell your chief that I thank him for his kind offer," she said, handing the book to one of the messengers, "and give him this book as a gift from me. This book will tell him how to receive eternal life."

The men accepted the book, bowed, and trotted down the steps.

"Mr. Nieh," Happy Plum Flower Richards asked, "do you think that was a genuine offer from the bandit chief?"

"Yes," Mr. Nieh said slowly, "I think it was genuine."

"What can it mean?" Happy Plum Flower asked. "Why would he make such an offer?"

"Only God knows the heart of the bandit chief," Mr. Nieh said. "These men have a reputation for being superstitious and unpredictable. It is reassuring. It appears that the men in black are not your enemies at least."

"Well, I do not intend to feed the children stolen millet," Happy Plum Flower said. "And even if we are safe from the bandits, the Japanese will probably want to move onto the mission grounds to fight them. We must finish loading the trucks."

It was dark when all the vehicles were finally loaded and ready to move. Mr. Nieh and the drivers helped Happy Plum Flower carry the babies down the steps. She settled the older children into the ambulance, handed each child a baby to hold, and then sat down herself with an infant in her lap. "Now don't let the babies cry," she told the older children.

The evangelist sat as passenger in the front seat of the ambulance again, and Mr. Nieh checked the flag on its hood to make sure it would not flap off. He could hear Happy Plum Flower singing with the children as they sat waiting for the ambulance to pull away from their home. He settled into the truck behind the ambulance, and the caravan set off, bumping loudly across the fields toward the main road.

"Look!" his truck driver suddenly whispered. The truck's headlights spotlighted the faces of men crouched beside the path alongside the main road.

The driver's face hardened into a grim mask. He turned the truck onto the road. Mr. Nieh could see that the ditches along both sides of it were filled with pale bandit faces, watching them. Mr. Nieh's body tensed.

The ambulance ahead of them picked up speed, and, to his relief, the bandits made no move to stop it. The trucks accelerated behind the ambulance. Soon they had passed the last ditch full of peering eyes. "They must have seen our lights and come to investigate," Mr. Nieh said.

"They were probably afraid we were Japanese soldiers coming to fight," the driver agreed. "When they saw the American flags, they knew it was Happy Plum Flower Richards moving into the city with the children."

Mr. Nieh allowed himself to relax completely for the first time since the trip home began. He wished he felt as serene as Happy Plum Flower had appeared all day. *How does she manage to stay so calm?* he wondered.

Something about this woman drew his attention like the melody of a nightingale piercing the chatter of magpies. How gentle she was with the children, and yet how firm. With only the gatekeeper's daughter and a local washerwoman to help, she had kept two dozen little ones occupied and under control all day so that they hardly interfered with the men's work. Yet there were so many of them! How did she do it? And then the way she had handled those bandit messengers…her words had been soft and gracious, yet she had clearly been in charge of the interview. A sparrow with the heart of an eagle she was, a mighty warrior disguised as a common peasant. Here was an adventurous spirit worth coming to know.

The children were worth a closer look, too. He never thought he would find children so appealing. Young Samuel had practiced imitating truck sounds all morning until, by naptime, he could mimic the noise of an entire moving caravan all by himself. And a vivid picture remained in Mr. Nieh's mind of the six-year-old twins, Rachel and Rose Mary, sitting solemnly in the ambulance, holding on their laps the other set of twins, the toddlers Grace and Gloria. It was odd how the one twin Rachel resembled Happy Plum Flower Richards. Rachel looked very like Rose Mary, her twin. Obviously they were sisters. Yet Rose Mary looked nothing like Happy Plum Flower, while Rachel resembled her somehow. Something subtle about her mouth and the shape of her face. Odd.

Perhaps now that this orphanage was moving into a section of his brother-in-law's compound, he could find ways to be useful to the Canaan Home family. Happy Plum Flower Richards probably had no idea how complicated the administration of the orphanage would become after she moved from the country into the city.

The caravan ran into trouble when they reached the West Gate of Peking at about 9 p.m. The city gates were closed for the night, and the Chinese soldiers at the entrance refused to open them. "Orders from the Japanese," they declared. Laura telephoned the U.S. Embassy. The Embassy then notified the Japanese authorities and they in turn ordered the Chinese soldiers at the gate to allow the orphanage into the city.

At midnight the family finally arrived at their new home. Helpers set up the children's beds while Laura prepared bottles for the babies. Then she settled down with her little ones for the night. It seemed odd, she thought, that midnight in a densely populated city like Peking should be so quiet compared to the midnights the family had been experiencing these last few weeks in the rural Western Hills.

Before the family was completely unpacked and settled in their new home, one of the little girls came down with typhoid fever, followed by whooping cough. Most of the rest of the orphanage followed suit. They were still whooping and hacking when they broke out with chicken pox. Several babies died in the double epidemic, but all the older children recovered.

Laura was still coping with fevers, coughs, and itchy spots, when a messenger from the bandits came to tell her that Japanese soldiers had attacked the men in black two weeks after the orphanage moved. The Japanese had killed several bandits in the battle and burned down a large part of the temple where many of the men in black had been staying.

The bandit chief sent Laura thanks for the Bible she had given him and explained that since he himself was illiterate, another man was reading the book to him. Laura was pleased to think that in this way two men were hearing the good news of Jesus. The messenger also told Laura that the men in black believed the Japanese would not have attacked them if only she and the children had remained in the area. Laura was astonished. Apparently the bandits regarded her as some kind of protective talisman.

I hope people are hearing about what God is doing at Canaan Home, Florence Logan thought when she visited the orphanage and heard Laura's tale of the men in black.

"Richie," she asked her friend, "are you finding time to write to your supporters to tell them what is happening here?"

"No," Laura admitted. "I'm so busy caring for the children that I haven't even had time to write letters to my own family."

"Well, I've often wished to find a way to do something useful for you," Florence said. "Now that you've moved into the city, it will be easier for me to visit and get information. Why don't you let me write your circular letters?"

Laura agreed, so Florence set to work writing down the tale of the men in black. She made no requests for donations in the letter because she understood her friend's requirements. Canaan Home was a faith ministry in the tradition of George Mueller's orphan houses in England and Hudson Taylor's pioneer mission to inland China. That meant Laura bent over backward not to manipulate people to give. She merely reported what God was doing. It was God's business to move people to give, not hers.

Still, Florence felt, God's work at Canaan Home needed a great deal more publicity than Laura was able to give it. While it was true that Mueller and Taylor had never asked for donations, their efforts had been publicized through pamphlets, news articles, and letters. Laura needed similar publicity, Florence thought, because Canaan Home's needs seemed more overwhelming than ever now.

The thousands of Japanese soldiers crowding into Peking took first pick of the city's provisions. Even for the rich, everything was in short supply—food, cloth, fuel, all the necessities of life. There was no scarcity, though, of widows, orphans, disease and hunger. Before the occupation, most of the children coming into the orphanage had been unwanted girls. Now desperate mothers brought their precious sons. "I would leave just this one with you," said one mother who came to Laura with two little boys, "but then his brother still would not have enough to eat at home." By Christmas, the number of children in Canaan Home had increased from 24 to 40—almost half of them boys.

After the New Year, someone brought Laura an eight-year-old girl with hydrocephalous. The child's body was the size of a three-year-old's, but her head was swollen larger than an adult's. Her legs dangled uselessly. Laura called her Tabitha, and for several weeks Orpha Gould worked with her daily, trying to teach her to walk. Tabitha never learned to do it, although she was bright and eager to please. She could speak plainly, and she learned the words to all the songs the children sang. Laura found a volunteer who moved into the orphanage to give Tabitha full-time care.

After that, people started bringing her children that the other two orphanages in Peking turned down for being too sick or too handicapped. Laura turned no child away. She took in children with severe malnutrition, beggars, the lame, deaf, blind, mentally retarded, even spina bifida cases.

Only once did Laura make a reluctant exception and refuse a child—two children actually. One January day in early 1938, a man and his wife shuffled up to Canaan Home and asked Laura to buy two babies they wanted to sell. The man was emaciated, with hollow cheeks and yellow dried-up skin. Laura thought he was probably an opium addict.

"We never buy little children," Laura explained, "but we try, with Jesus' help, to care for the very poorest."

She dared not offer even a copper penny for the babies. News of the sale would spread quickly and encourage the kidnapping trade.

"Some of my friends tell me I should stop taking in any more children," she told Florence that winter in Peking.

"And…?" Florence teased with a knowing smile.

Laura shrugged. "How can I refuse one of these little ones?" She pointed to Esther in the courtyard. "Look at the way the children gather around Esther," she said. "That little girl is so curious and full of fun. When she came to me, she was skin and bones. She was so malnourished, it took months to get her digestive system functioning properly. And her spine was so badly injured I thought she would be a little hunchback all her life. Now she is healed and whole, and this morning when I went out into the yard, I heard her arguing with the other children. She said, 'Did you say there is no way? Everything is possible with Jesus!'"

"'Out of the mouth of babes…'" Florence quoted. "She is living proof of her own words."

"As long as the Lord supplies," Laura said, "there will always be a way to find room for one more."

The landlord opened up some of the unused, extra rooms for them. Somehow the food supply stretched. The family was short on the warm winter over-garments that North Chinese wore outdoors over their padded winter clothing. Still, the high walls of the compound protected them from the winter wind, and they could stay inside if the temperature dropped too low.

As Mr. Nieh had predicted, Canaan Home's administrative and business affairs became more complicated after the orphanage moved into the city. Peking law required philanthropic institutions like the orphanage to be registered—a complex process that involved organizing a board of directors and arranging a series of long negotiations over several years with Chinese authorities.

Laura was poorly equipped to handle this. Her Chinese vocabulary was limited, she had trouble reading official Chinese documents, and she was unable to write Chinese characters well. She not only lacked the language skills necessary for managing the registration process, she lacked the social connections and cultural know-how she needed as well. Being female in a strongly patriarchal society was another handicap. Mr. Nieh possessed all these qualifications she lacked. He was a man, he had a fine high-school-level education from the Whampoa Military Academy, he was a Kuomintang Party member, and he was exceptionally well-connected. Many of his relatives and his former classmates held high government positions. He offered to oversee the registration process, and Laura accepted his offer with relief.

Along with the increase in children came—fortunately—an increase in donations. This, in turn, required more work keeping accounts and making receipts to donors. In addition, Laura now had to prepare regular financial reports for the board. Sometimes she was up until midnight with bookkeeping duties, and Mr. Nieh began staying up with her to help her with the Home's financial accounts and other business paperwork.

Mr. Nieh had been raised with servants and an upperclass disdain for physical labor, but nevertheless he also started helping Laura with some of the orphanage's heavy work. Whenever a new child came into the orphange, Laura took the child to the hospital for a complete check-up. Mr. Nieh helped by transporting the children on his bicycle, and he also took over Canaan Home's time-consuming shopping chores, buying food supplies and transporting the heavy loads back to the orphanage on his bicycle. Laura grew to rely on him more and more.

Mothering the Canaan Home children was becoming more perplexing, as the youngsters grew older and the family increased. How should she provide training for the older children so they could leave the orphanage and earn their own living as young adults? They all needed an academic education. How could she provide it? She needed extra wisdom, too, to deal with the rowdy, foul-mouthed street children joining Canaan Home. Abused, neglected, abandoned...these youngsters needed continual reassurance of love and acceptance. Yet they needed firm discipline, too, for their own good and for the protection of the other children. The boys in particular needed a strong, male hand.

Unfortunately, Florence's first attempts to inform American supporters about Canaan Home failed. The war with Japan disrupted the mail system, so Laura was unable to send Florence's letter about the bandits.

After Christmas, Florence composed a second letter for her, but that too proved impossible to mail. Laura set both letters aside.

Fortunately, though, Canaan Home's new location—about three miles outside the Forbidden City and a mile from the Presbyterian mission—enabled people to visit and bring donations more easily. Their visitors then spread news of the orphanage throughout the Christian community. The new location also made it easier for volunteers to offer assistance. Several adults moved onto the compound to help care for the children. A nearby Christian kindergarten opened its doors to the Canaan Home preschoolers. Two teachers taught the older children academic lessons at the Home. Another volunteer taught them songs and Bible verses every morning. One of the most interesting new sources of help turned out to be the next door neighbor's teenage daughter.

Mr. Nieh Shou Guang, standing beside Laura, became involved with Canaan Home when he helped Laura move the children into his sister's compound inside Beijing in 1937. He lived in the back courtyard of the compound and volunteered to handle general heavy lifting and business matters—buying supplies, accounting, and processing government red tape. As the orphanage burgeoned, his help seemed indispensable.

Reports from Peking

AN ENTRY FROM THE DIARY OF LORNA LOGAN,
WHO WAS VISITING HER SISTER, FLORENCE LOGAN,
IN PEKING, JUNE 8, 1938:

Miss Richard's orphanage is not far away, in a wealthy Chinese home, where they can stay for almost nothing because the owners want the protection of having foreigners on the property. She has more than 60 youngsters of all ages, all looking very nice and well-scrubbed. The property is a series of courtyards with rooms built all around them.

LETTER FROM FLORENCE LOGAN
TO BECKY POWERS, AUGUST 4, 1988:

Yes, Laura was not "out-going." She didn't try to draw people. Yet it is amazing the number of people that the Lord drew to her! I doubt if she ever gave a talk to interest people in the orphanage. Yet she had the courage to go to people when it was necessary.

LAURA'S LETTER WRITTEN IN PEKING,
JANUARY 24, 1938:

The increase in the number of poor children has been very marked within the last year. Many dear friends would advise us not to take in any more of these little ones because of the fear that we shall be unable to support them. But it seems that there is always a way to find room for one more, and a few weeks ago the landlord opened up the east rooms for us to use when every bit of available space had been used. So when our Heavenly Father provides the way in clothing and feeding those who come, shall I not then be willing to care for them?

He giveth more grace as our burdens grow greater,
He sendeth more strength as our labors increase;
To added afflictions He addeth His mercy,
To multiplied trials He multiplies peace.

When we have exhausted our store of endurance,
When our strength has failed ere the day is half done,
When we reach the end of our hoarded resources
Our Father's full giving is only begun.

His love has no limits, His grace has no measure,
His power no boundary known unto men;
For out of His infinite riches in Jesus
He giveth, and giveth, and giveth again.

Annie J. Flint

14.

Persistent Pearl

Peking, 1938

Seventeen-year-old Pearl hitched her silk gown above her pajama-clad knees and clambered up to her favorite place on the wall separating her family compound from the compound next door. There was always something interesting to see there after she came home from school.

Visitors trooped through the neighboring courtyard in sporadic parades —foreign missionaries with white faces and heavy accents, local Chinese pastors and their wives, students from Yenching University and the Women's Bible Institute, and members of various Chinese Protestant churches. Workmen scrambled in and out, repairing buildings and installing a modern toilet and additional plumbing in the bathroom. The landlord's brother-in-law, Nieh Shou Guang, wheeled his bicycle through the yard, coming and going on numberless errands.

But these adult activities held only peripheral interest for Pearl. What drew her to the wall were the children. After school, the yard was full of them—30 or more playing vigorously, and, on sunny days, an additional 15 or 20 babies in cribs. The oldest children were 12 or 13 years old.

When the weather was fine like today, a foreign lady and several Chinese helpers set up one or two dozen cribs in the yard so the babies could enjoy the fresh air. The foreign lady moved quietly and spoke softly to the children. Whenever she returned from a trip outside the compound walls, the children ran to her and she kissed every single one. They called her Mama, even though she was American and they were Chinese. At mealtimes, helpers collected the children into small groups, and then all the groups disappeared inside one of the buildings on the grounds.

Pearl had been watching the children play for several months, by this spring of 1938, and she was beginning to recognize some of them and figure out a few names. There was a strikingly beautiful girl about eight years old who was very responsible, like a little mother. If one of the toddlers fell or cried, she was usually the first to run over and help. Her name was Sarah. Then there was a fragile-looking girl about the same age named Charity, who preferred to play quietly, avoiding crowded areas of the courtyard. Charity was a dramatic contrast to the little chatterbox named Esther, who attracted crowds of children like a ripe persimmon tree drawing birds. Then there were two little girls about age six or seven who looked a lot alike. They seemed very loyal to each other and were probably sisters, or even twins. Some of the older children around age ten and up seemed rather rough. Pearl figured a few of them had probably been beggars once.

There were several handicapped children. There was a blind boy who liked to sit in the sunshine with his back against the courtyard wall. There were several crippled children, too, as well as a very strange-looking child with a toddler-sized body and a great big head, who sat propped in a crib in easy viewing distance from Pearl's perch.

One of the look-alike girls wandered over to the misshapen child in the crib. She peered at the disabled child through long bangs that half covered her eyes and asked, "Tabitha, what do you have inside your head?"

An enormous smile stretched slowly across Tabitha's big face. "Gold," she said. "There is a lot of gold in my head."

Pearl covered her mouth to stifle a giggle. The little girl wandered thoughtfully away, and Pearl sighed. *If only I could jump over this wall to be with these children,* she thought. *I would like to do something to help them.*

But what?

She could not offer to help cook their food. Pearl knew nothing about cooking. Her family's servants did all the cooking. She never even went into the kitchen. She couldn't offer to mend or make new clothes or help with the annual winter sewing. She knew nothing about sewing either. Pearl's family was giving her the finest upper-class education a wealthy Peking family could buy for a treasured daughter. Sewing was a skill taught to poor girls.

Pearl knew science and history and calligraphy. She could paint with watercolors and compose a poem or essay. She could speak English, and she played the baby grand piano skillfully. Her family was Christian, so she attended Bible classes, and her parents encouraged her to teach kindergarten Sunday School at the Presbyterian Church. She also directed the Sunday School music program. Pearl thought she could teach the orphan children songs and Bible stories, but the orphanage already had volunteers who did that.

A westering sun shone warmly down upon the stone wall where she sat, pouring golden light on the gilt tile roofs in the courtyard. Glints of turquoise and amethyst danced among the tiles. She ran her fingers through her short hair and took a deep whiff of the springtime scent of yellow briars, wood smoke, and supper cooking. It was time for her piano practice. She backed over the edge of the wall and dropped to the ground. Then she ran her fingers through her hair once more, this time thoughtfully.

Why, of course. That's what she could do.

She could help take care of the children's hair. That little girl who had been talking to bigheaded Tabitha needed her bangs cut. All the little girls needed their hair kept cropped short for easy care, and the boys needed their heads shaved regularly.

The next Saturday, Pearl showed up at the orphanage gate with a pair of scissors. The Chinese helper Pearl talked to seemed surprised by her offer to give the children haircuts. The helper hurried away to talk to the lady the children called Mama, who was on her way out the gate with a bundled up baby.

"Don't snub her," the American lady said. "Let her do whatever she wants to do to help."

So Pearl spent part of the day cutting hair and making friends with the children. After that, she came on Saturdays to cut hair.

One Saturday, a worker introduced her to the children's mama, Happy Plum Flower Richards. By then Pearl had thought of another way to help. "Honorable Lady Teacher Minister," Pearl said, "would you like me to take your children to Sunday School? I teach a kindergarten Sunday School class, and I can take the children to church and back."

Happy Plum Flower Richards looked delighted. "How thoughtful you are, Pearl!" she said. "And what a blessing you are offering me and the children!" She spoke with a thick American accent, and Pearl was glad that she had taken English lessons in school to help her decipher Happy Plum Flower's Americanized Mandarin. "I would be very, very pleased if you would bring the children to Sunday School. I can't take them myself because the babies need me. What time should we have them ready for you tomorrow?"

Pearl kept her face still and placid like a properly brought-up young Chinese woman. Inside, she glowed.

After that, Sunday School started for the Canaan Home children the moment Pearl entered the gate on Sunday mornings to take them to church. They sang hymns and gospel choruses all the way. "Jesus loves me..." they trebled. Pearl felt light with joy.

Through the sweltering days and thunderstorms of summer, Pearl continued giving the orphans haircuts on Saturdays and taking the children to church on Sundays. Then came the fall. The trees dropped their leaves, and the air smelled of roasting chestnuts. The nights grew cold, furring the roofs of the buildings with a morning blanket of frost. Pearl began donning her silk wadded gown and her winter shoes to ride her bicycle to school through the cold streets of Peking. Then one week, winter settled in for good, and she added a warm knitted cap, mittens, and her *ta ao,* a long, thickly quilted over-garment.

That Sunday she showed up at the orphanage gate to escort the Canaan Home children to Sunday School, looking forward to leading the weekly children's singing troop to church as usual. The children stood waiting in a row of wedge shapes, with their wadded cotton winter gowns hanging in a stiff slant from shoulder to ankle. They wore mittens, caps, and scarves, but not one of them wore a *ta ao.*

Pearl hardly noticed the lack until she and the children stepped outside the courtyard walls, and an arctic blast struck her face like a blow. One of the children gasped and started to cry. Then another started crying. A piercing wind pummeled the little group, and instead of singing all the way to church, the children cried. Once inside the church building, protected at last from the wind, they trembled and shook and whimpered until they warmed up. Then they were fine and enjoyed the Sunday School hour as usual. Once outside the church walls, though, they cried all the way home.

Pearl was beside herself. It was all she could do to keep from crying herself with them. Cloth was scarce and expensive in occupied Peking. The Christians at church had trouble clothing their own families. Buying material to make over-garments for all the older Canaan Home children would be an impossible extravagance.

"Mother, please let me take the train to Tientsin," she begged that night. "Let me go to see Grandmother and Grand Aunt and tell them about the children. Maybe they can give me the money to buy over-garments."

Her mother considered the request for what seemed to be a long time. "Yes, my heart," she said at last, "I think your grandmother will want to hear about the pain this problem gives you. You may take the train next Saturday to Tientsin."

Tientsin was 60 miles southeast of Peking, and the train trip took about two hours. Pearl knew that if she had asked permission to make the journey one year before, during the early months of the Japanese occupation, her mother would have flatly refused. The trip would have been too dangerous at that time for a teenage girl traveling alone. But the Japanese soldiers had calmed down by this winter of 1938, and Pearl had learned how to get by them without trouble. She just acted like an ordinary working girl going about her business and was exceptionally polite whenever she had to deal with any soldier.

Pearl's train chugged away from the Forbidden City along the Tartar wall through the towering South Gate. Looking out the train window, she could see blackened ruins of burned-down villages. The year before, Japanese soldiers had torched every village alongside the railroad for many *li*. Pearl glanced away from the scene and turned her thoughts to a happier subject. She could hardly wait to see Grandmother again—dear old Grandmother, with her watchful, kindly eyes and tiny bound feet wrapped in long yards of white bandage material.

Pearl entertained herself with memories of the days when she was small and had lived in an enormous clan compound in Tientsin with her parents, brothers, grandparents, aunts, uncles, and cousins. The clan was wealthy. Everyone had lived together until the family's import-export business expanded so much that some members of the clan had to move away. Pearl's uncle moved to New York City to manage the faraway office in America, and Pearl's father moved his wife and children to Peking.

Pearl missed living with Grandmother close by. She knew the old woman would want to hear all her news—all about the lessons she learned in school, the Sunday School class she taught, the music program she directed, and the orphans she wanted to help. Pearl knew that most rich Chinese women were indifferent to the poor, but Grandmother was a Jesus follower who took care of widows, orphans, and poor people. Grand Aunt was a Christian and would sympathize, too.

Grandmother had often told her the story of how she and Grand Aunt became Christians at the turn of the century through Pearl's grandfather. He had been a Chinese navy officer. When the Japanese destroyed the Chinese fleet in 1895, Grandfather's fortune had sunk with the Chinese armada. One day he was browsing through a local bookstore trying to find a good book to read, but all the books were too expensive. "Here is the cheapest book in my store," the bookseller finally said. "This book is called the Bible."

With his last cash, Grandfather bought the book. He read it from beginning to end and became a Christian. He influenced many people to become Christians—first his wife, brother, sister, and children, then later many of his neighbors and friends.

The family members were well known as Christian believers when the Boxer Rebellion erupted a few years after Grandfather's conversion.

Boxers searched the towns and villages to find and kill all Jesus worshippers. Many missionaries and Chinese Christians died, but fortunately all of Pearl's family escaped.

Grandmother said Pearl's father had been a baby at the time. Every night she crept into a neighbor's house to hide with her little son in her arms. Then one day Grand Aunt made a quick trip back to the house to get clothes. A Boxer caught her just outside. He held a knife to her throat, and demanded, "Are you a Christian?"

"Yes, I am," she said, and she knelt down to pray.

Just then another man came along. "Don't bother with her," he said impatiently. "She's just an unmarried female. The real Christian is in the house."

The men hurried inside the house to look for the "real" Christian, but fortunately, Grandfather was gone. So Grand Aunt escaped that day. Now she was very rich. God had blessed her in every way.

In Tientsin, Pearl described to her relatives everything that she knew about the orphanage history and what the American woman was doing for the children. "Happy Plum Flower Richards does everything by faith," she reported. "She never refuses any child who comes to her gate, and if she runs out of food, she prays. Then food or money comes. Although she has no money in the bank, nobody misses a meal.

"I have never seen anyone sacrifice herself so much," she said. "She does not live by an American standard. Instead she eats the food and wears the clothing of the poorest Chinese so she can take care of these children. Her clothes are getting ragged because any clothes people give her for herself, she makes into clothes and quilts for the children instead. You would admire her, Grandmother. Her voice is so soft and sweet, and she speaks so kindly. I have never seen her get angry, and I have never heard her criticize another person behind his back."

Finally, Pearl told her relatives how the children had stopped singing in the freezing cold on their way to Sunday School. "All the older children need a *ta ao*," she said.

Grandmother and Grand Aunt sent Pearl home happy, with enough money to buy a large quantity of warm material and batting. Canaan Home volunteers sewed the material into 35 red and black checked overgarments, each quilted with a half-inch layer of cotton batting. After that, there was no more crying on the winter trips to Sunday School. The youngsters sang again all the way to church and home. Pearl was content.

"I will miss the children and Happy Plum Flower Richards when I go away to college," Pearl told her mother as her high school graduation neared. "I won't be able to do anything to help them while I am gone. Do you think I could come back to teach school at the orphanage when I complete teacher's training?"

"Your future is in the hands of God," her mother told her. "You must obey Him step by step. He knows how much you love Happy Plum Flower Richards and the children. Right now you must pray for them and study hard. One day perhaps God will allow your paths to cross again and give you an opportunity to do more."

So Pearl left Peking and began teacher's college in another city. She came back to visit her family on school holidays and was always glad for news from the orphanage. And news there was. For one thing, Nieh Shou Guang proposed marriage to Happy Plum Flower Richards.

Orphan Memories

Rachel's 1989 memoirs, translated from Chinese:

[In this new place in Peking] Mama and the little children lived in the first court, and the older kids lived in the second court. Someone looked after us. The new home was in a very populous and active location, so we adopted a lot of children. Several people helped us take care of them. When new children came in, the first step was to give them a bath and change their clothes. Then Mama gave them a new name from the Bible. Because there were so many children there, we were separated into several classes, and each class had a person to take care of them.

All of us slept at the back courtyard at night. For sleeping we had to wear pajamas, and each of us slept in a small metal bed. If the weather was cold, we had cotton quilts. In the summer we had a blanket. At night, Mama often came to the back courtyard to check on us, seeing if all of us were going to sleep and if all of us were well-covered. If not, she would cover us up.

If any of the older children were sick, Mama would let them stay in the same room with the small children, because their room was just outside Mama's room. That way Mama could take care of them at night. Mama always slept like that. She worked in the daytime and took care of the smallest children and the patients at night. She couldn't get a very good night's sleep. One time my sister was sick with a high fever and convulsions. Mama let her stay in Mama's room so she could take care of her. I don't know what kind of illness she had. Today my sister has one remaining symptom. Her mouth is partially paralyzed. Mama gave all her love to all the children.

15.

The Marriage Proposal

Peking, 1939

REBECCA VOLKMAN TSAI GAZED CURIOUSLY at her fellow American, a petite woman sitting across from her in the elegant seat of honor in Mrs. Wu's sitting room. Rebecca had heard a great deal about this woman, Laura Richards, but she had never met her before.

With her brown hair pulled back in a bun and her common peasant's gown, Miss Richards looked out of place amid the Wu clan's classical paintings and ornate furniture. She appeared to be in her mid-40s, like Rebecca, with smiling brown eyes, a wide mouth, and rough-looking hands—which were to be expected if all the stories about the amount of work this woman accomplished were true.

She seems uncomfortable, Rebecca thought. *Perhaps she came to share a personal problem with Mrs. Wu and is disconcerted to find a stranger here.*

Mrs. Wu was a wealthy matriarch in the Presbyterian church who opened her home for Bible studies. Rebecca knew that she was a good friend of Miss Richards.

Mrs. Wu may have sensed Miss Richards' hesitations, too, for she embarked on a long, reassuring introduction of Rebecca Tsai. She described Rebecca as a staunch woman of prayer and a dear American friend who loved the Chinese people so much that she had become one of them by marrying a Chinese Christian translator. Then Mrs. Wu asked how Laura was coming along on solving her family's space problem.

"We have been searching the city for weeks for a suitable place to move the orphanage," Laura said. "Everyone has been asking around for us. No one has found anything we can afford."

So many children had joined Canaan Home by this spring of 1939, she explained to Rebecca, that the Canaan Home staff had crammed beds into every available room except the kitchen. Even the dining room had been turned into a dormitory. Since late winter the family had been eating all their meals outdoors in the courtyard.

"How will you manage when the rainy season comes?" Rebecca wondered aloud. "You need to find a bigger place right away."

Rebecca sympathized with Laura's housing problem. Other ministries also had trouble finding adequate space in the city now. Japanese soldiers had taken over nearly all the larger homes and buildings inside Peking that were either unoccupied or partially vacant, and it looked like the soldiers would be staying indefinitely.

Japanese forces now held all of China east of the line joining Peking to Canton via Hankow. This included the national capital and all the industrial and commercial centers. The Kuomintang government had lost its air force, arsenals, the best of its modern armies, its major tax resources, and all ports through which it was possible to import equipment and supplies.

In theory, the Japanese Imperial Army had taken over everything in China that counted. In reality, Japanese troops were swallowed up in the vastness of the Chinese interior, still unable to possess the land they had conquered. They held the cities, but they had trouble controlling the roads and railways that connected them. Behind the official front, a double war went on—a war between the Japanese and the Chinese, and a civil war between the Kuomintang and the Communists.

Officially, the two Chinese factions had laid aside their differences and united in a common struggle against Japan. In reality, neither Chiang Kai Shek nor Mao Tse Tung ceased their power struggle. While battling their common enemy, both men jockeyed for good positions from which to resume civil war against each other once the Western powers helped them force Japan out of China.

Everyone was affected daily by the strategies of the three rivals in this deadly double war.

To keep the country's resources out of Japanese hands, Chiang Kai Shek had decreed a "Scorched Earth" policy during the first battles against Japan. As his armies retreated, they destroyed railroads, bridges, highways, factories, palaces, and peasants' crops. Then Chiang Kai Shek and his government officials retired to Chungking, deep in the undeveloped, inaccessible interior of China, trying to preserve what was left of their strength. They left behind a leadership void that the Communists were quick to fill.

Mao Tse Tung saw the war with Japan as an opportunity for Communist expansion. His forces, officially known as the Eighth Route Army, infiltrated the villages of North China, concentrating their efforts especially near roads and railroads leading into Peking. In the villages, they set up an anti-Japanese government known as the Border Region Government. From the villages, they conducted constant, low-key guerrilla warfare. They harassed Japanese troops from the rear, ambushed supply convoys, conducted surprise raids on Japanese-held installations, assassinated Japanese officials and Chinese collaborators, and sabotaged railways, bridges, roads, and telegraph lines. They infiltrated the cities, too, to recruit followers and keep the Japanese army off balance through sabotage and surprise attacks.

The Japanese army responded with the "Three Alls" policy: Burn All, Kill All, Loot All. They doused civilians with kerosene and burned them to death publicly. They set homes on fire and shot the people trying to escape. They massacred, raped, and destroyed.

Villagers were trapped between daytime and nighttime masters. By day, Japanese soldiers ordered them to fill in the trenches that the Communists had ordered them to dig by night. By day, they paid taxes to the Japanese; by night, they paid another set of taxes to the Communists. They organized two sets of village leaders, one to deal with the Japanese, another to deal with the Communists. They suffered reprisals from both sets of masters for obeying the orders of the other. More and more, villagers who might normally have simply suffered and endured the Japanese presence now joined guerrilla detachments to survive. No matter what they did, they were in constant danger. As resistance fighters, they at least had a weapon.

Miss Richards' and Mrs. Wu's mutual friend, Miss Florence Logan, was still out in the Paotingfu countryside, training teams of young Chinese evangelists to preach in the villages amongst the terrorists and Japanese patrols. The Japanese tried to control the Chinese church, and Communist guerrilla fighters accused Christians of being unpatriotic. In their eyes, Christianity threatened the villagers' total commitment to the war of resistance against Japan.

Miss Richards said, that in her last letter, Miss Logan wrote that Japanese soldiers had fired five shots one night at a pair of young Chinese women evangelists she was training. They were on their way to a preaching service, and the patrol mistook them for resistance fighters. Fortunately the soldiers quit shooting as soon as the young women stopped and jumped off their bicycles. No one was hurt that time.

I wonder when Miss Richards is going to bring up the subject that really brought her here, Rebecca Tsai thought.

"My heart is at rest knowing you are no longer living in the Western Hills with the children," said Mrs. Wu. "The countryside has become so unsafe."

"The city is unsafe, too," Miss Richards said. "But the Lord is our Shepherd, and He spreads a table before us in the presence of our enemies."

She paused, and her mouth relaxed in a wide, brief smile. "Our housing need is causing us serious difficulty," she said, "but that is not the difficulty that is heaviest on my mind and heart today."

Ah, here it comes, thought Rebecca.

"As you know, Mrs. Wu," Miss Richards began, "Mr. Nieh has become quite involved in the daily affairs of the orphanage these past two years. His assistance has been so valuable, I don't know what I should have done without him. Now he has come to me saying he thinks I need a partner who is committed to this work for life. Also, he says the children need a father as well as a mother. So he has asked me to marry him."

Rebecca glanced at Mrs. Wu. The matriarch's face remained unperturbed, but her whole being bristled with interest. Miss Richards definitely had the elderly Chinese woman's complete attention.

"At first I was quite shocked by Mr. Nieh's proposal," Miss Richards said, "but I have been giving it much thought and prayer. I can see the advantages for the work, but I am very concerned for fear I might marry out of God's will."

Ten years ago, Rebecca thought, *my concern was the same—to be sure I was marrying in the will of God.*

She had caused a scandal, Rebecca had, with her marriage. Western society disapproved of racially mixed marriages, especially for white women. The U.S. Congress had even passed a law in 1924 causing any American who married a Chinese to lose his or her citizenship. Rebecca's friends had pressured her to change her mind about marrying a Chinese, and some of them even plotted to kidnap her to prevent the ceremony. Cooler heads pointed out that since she was an American, she had freedom of choice in the matter.

"Marrying outside of your race is a grave decision," Rebecca told Laura. "I am misunderstood. If you marry Mr. Nieh, you will also be misunderstood."

Rebecca told her something of her own experiences.

The marriage had isolated her in both cultures, Western and Chinese. The first Western pastor she and her fiancé asked to perform the ceremony refused to do it, and most of her Western friends and supporters rejected her. The mission society that sent her to China cut off all communication and support. Rebecca's father stopped writing to her, too, although her mother continued to write.

Then when she moved onto her husband's clan compound to serve her mother-in-law according to Chinese tradition, her in-laws persecuted her. They taunted her and called her "foreign devil." They invented ways to make her life miserable.

This was justified from the Tsai family's standpoint, because Rebecca's husband had betrayed his ancestors twice—first by becoming a Christian, and then by marrying a white Christian woman. This couple refused to kowtow in reverent homage at the ancestral altar. They paid no money to the local temple for ritual sacrifices that provided Mr. Tsai's late father with necessities in the World of Shadows. They would neglect his mother the same way when she died. Even worse, they trained their children not to worship their ancestors either, which could anger the gods and place the entire clan at risk. Clearly, the Tsai relatives felt, it was their obligation to punish this wayward couple until they returned to the path of honor and duty.

When Rebecca first married, she had thought she understood the difficulties ahead for her if she married a Chinese. She had thought she was willing to suffer for the love of her husband and for the love of Jesus Christ. She had been unprepared, though, for the kind of pain she was experiencing now, seeing her three children taunted and abused for being half American. Nine-year-old Becky Tsai was already saying she would never marry so that her own children would not suffer for their American blood the way she and Ruth and Daniel did.

How can I explain the difficulties of a marriage between two cultures to Laura? Rebecca wondered. *Marriage takes so much dedication. It's a hard adjustment for an independent-minded American woman who has lived single for twenty years or more, and marrying outside your culture makes the adjustment even harder. There is the language issue, too....I can't begin to explain to her how hard it can be for a man and woman to communicate, even when they both speak each other's languages, the way we do. But Nieh Shou Guang speaks no English, and Laura's Chinese is so inadequate! And then for her to begin a marriage while caring for so many children! How can it work?*

Aloud she said, "Any marriage is a serious decision. Since you have dedicated yourself to the Lord first and then to the children, you must be sure you hear the voice of the Lord before you take such a step."

She was discouraging me, Laura mused as she pedaled her bicycle home through the *hutongs*, the criss-crossing picturesque lanes that comprised most of the Peking street system. It was a windy spring day, and a gray haze of dust obscured the sun. Her eyes smarted, and her teeth felt gritty with fine Gobi sand. *Rebecca Tsai thinks Nieh Shou Guang will divert me from my calling. She thinks I should refuse him.*

The dust made her sneeze so hard that her bicycle started to tip. She dismounted and readjusted the rope tying a large sack of corn flour to her rear fender. Mrs. Wu had directed one of her kitchen servants to give Laura the flour to take home to the family.

Laura thought Mrs. Wu had seemed more matter-of-fact about Mr. Nieh's proposal than Rebecca Tsai—highly interested, but not surprised by the turn of events. "Where the mind and hands take hold, the heart will follow," she had said. "He is young and dedicated. He is helping you all day long every day. It is natural that this should happen."

Natural...but wise?

Natural...but within the will of God?

"You must be sure you hear the voice of the Lord before you take such a step," Rebecca Tsai had said. Rebecca Tsai was a deeply spiritual woman with an understanding of what it meant to hear God's voice. To her the phrase was more than a cliché. Nevertheless, she was using it to warn Laura that, in her opinion, marriage to Mr. Nieh would be unwise.

This is the most difficult decision I have faced yet, Laura thought.

The soft trotting of unshod hooves sounded just ahead and the hindquarters of a donkey emerged through the haze of dust several yards in front of her. She swerved her bicycle to go around him. An odor of donkey sweat and donkey dung followed her downwind.

For 16 years now Laura had lived in China. From the beginning of her work in Paotingfu, she had loved her Chinese students and staff. She had related to them directly, as human creatures, not as members of the Chinese race. Racial differences had begun to blur for her then and by now had lost meaning. Her question was not, "Should I marry a Chinese?" Her question was, "Should I marry this man? Is it within God's will for me to marry Mr. Nieh?"

She was now caring for over 60 children. Without her they would die. They needed food, shelter, education, and basic health care. They needed to be taught to work, to love God, and to care for each other. She had to stock supplies, keep financial accounts, train and administer a staff of helpers, negotiate agreements with city officials, and develop and maintain good relationships with donors. Was Mr. Nieh a provision from God to help her carry out this complicated work? In some ways he already seemed indispensable. If he hadn't taken over the financial accounts and municipal red tape, how could she have managed?

To the Japanese, the orphans were worthless; to Chinese officials, a nuisance. And the system was corrupt. If you didn't have money, you at least needed influence. But now the Japanese authorities had appointed Mr. Nieh's brother-in-law mayor of Peking, and the young man had many other relatives in high places, too. If he married her and became the official head of Canaan Home, he would use his family position and connections to keep the orphanage secure. Besides, in the Chinese culture, it was considered a disgrace not to have a father. By marrying him, she would remove a social stigma and meet the children's need for a father as well as a mother.

Nieh Shou Guang was nearly 20 years younger than she was. But surely age was no more a determining factor than race, if their marriage was within the will of God. And he was so enthusiastic, so zealous! It warmed her to the toes. She had begun to look forward to his company in the dark, lonely hours after the children went to bed and she had to stay up until midnight tending to the paperwork and financial accounts. She realized she liked having a little male attention, and...what a relief it was to think that perhaps she would no longer need to carry the burden of Canaan Home alone.

From the first, she had wanted Canaan Home to be a ministry that the Chinese people saw as their own. In many ways this had happened. Chinese Christians of many denominations throughout China supported Canaan Home with prayers, gifts, and service. Now Mr. Nieh said he believed he shared her calling—that taking care of the children could be his life's work just as it was her own. Was his proposal God's way of realizing her original goal more fully than she had ever imagined?

And Orpha approved. Orpha supported the idea of marrying Mr. Nieh. Orpha had been one of the few people who had supported her vision to start Canaan Home. People would oppose this marriage the same way they had opposed her decision to resign from the mission and start an orphanage. Might not Orpha be right once again, and the whole world wrong?

Another thought: there was the matter of fulfilling all the duties of a wife. What if she became pregnant? She was 46 years old, just a few years away from menopause. It could potentially be dangerous to become pregnant for the first time in her late 40s.

What should she do?

Laura braked to a stop in front of the orphanage, then wheeled her bicycle through the gate. All the children ran over for kisses and hugs. Mr. Nieh hurried out to unload the flour from her bicycle. His personality tingled with excitement. "Please join me inside so we may speak privately," he said. "I have important news."

So Laura kissed the children quickly and followed him into the kitchen.

"The tuberculosis sanitarium near the Summer Palace wants us to trade places with them," he said. "They will let us move onto the property they are renting at the old Lama temple, Kung Te Ssu, if we allow them to move their patients and medical staff here."

Shortly before the Japanese took over Peking, Mr. Nieh explained, Douw Hospital had opened a new tuberculosis sanitarium in the Western Hills region on the grounds of Kung Te Ssu, an old Lama temple which had not been used as a place of worship for many years. After spending quite a bit of money repairing the temple's living quarters, the sanitarium's medical staff moved their patients onto the compound, only to find themselves coping with a military invasion, followed by ongoing guerrilla war. It was impossible to provide the restful atmosphere their patients needed for recovery. It was difficult to give efficient medical care under wartime conditions as well. People going in and out of the city gate had to have passes and declare all the goods they carried on their persons. This made it hard to take patients back and forth into Peking for x-rays and laboratory work.

The sanitarium staff began looking for an alternate location inside Peking, but they experienced the same problems Laura faced. There was no unoccupied space to be had for reasonable rent payments. So, when they heard that Canaan Home was also looking for a new home, they wondered if Laura would be willing to make an exchange.

Kung Te Ssu had an orchard, a vineyard, plenty of play space, pasture for a few goats, and living quarters for about 100 people, children and staff together. She could have the property rent-free for three years if she agreed to the trade. Mr. Nieh had already discussed the proposal with his brother-in-law, Laura's landlord, and his brother-in-law was willing to negotiate with the sanitarium.

"Room for 100 people?" Laura asked in astonishment. "Rent free for three years? It sounds wonderful."

"The countryside is full of terrorists and Japanese patrols," Mr. Nieh reminded her.

"There are terrorists and Japanese soldiers inside Peking, too," Laura said. "We must pray about it."

Orphan Memories

Rachel's 1989 memoirs, translated from Chinese:

Some of the people who worked for us cooked for us and some took care of the children. Among them was an American. Her last name was Gu, so we called her Nurse Gu. She was taller than Mother. She loved children, too. Every day Nurse Gu took us to a big church, and there they taught us to sing, dance, paint, and play games. One time they gave us tea to drink. I had never drunk tea before, only plain water. I thought the tea tasted very bitter, so I poured it out, and then Nurse Gu punished me. I stood there and I cried. At last everyone went home. I didn't want to go. I was determined to cry forever. Finally Nurse Gu comforted me. At that time I had a very bad temper.

During this time, the orphanage adopted Tabitha, a paralyzed girl who had a very big head. She was eight years old, and she was very smart. Nurse Gu tried to teach her how to walk every day. Her head was twice as big as a normal person's head. Her legs were very thin, but Nurse Gu had the faith to teach her how to walk. After several days' practice, though, Nurse Gu realized that Tabitha's legs were too thin and her head was too big, and she had never walked before.

We often asked Tabitha, "What is inside your head?" and she answered, "There is a lot of gold in my head."

"Actually," Mama said, "there is a lot of water on her brain."

Tabitha learned how to sing a song real quickly, and one person was assigned to take care of her specially. During the daytime, her caretaker took her outside to get sunshine. She was the first paralyzed person to be adopted into this orphanage.

Mama knew another young Chinese man whose name was Mr. Nieh. He was tall. He acted as Mama's assistant, taking care of accounts and buying essentials. I remember he lived in the back courtyard.

When we first moved to this place, we ran out of food. Mama led all the older children in kneeling down and praying. The cook asked Mama, "What should I do without any food?"

Mama answered the cook, "We have faith even though we don't have food. So boil the water, and we will wait for food to come."

Soon after, someone sent us the food, along with money and apples. So we had no problems with that meal. I was too young then to remember this, so [Barnabus] told me about it.

Mama founded this orphanage to depend totally on God and have faith. Chinese and foreigners helped us with money and food. It seemed like we didn't live in this place very long because we had too many children. So we had to move again.

We moved to the suburbs near the Qing Long Bridge. At this time I was seven or eight years old. I did two things all day: eat and play.

One morning just after we woke up, Mama called all of the children to her room and told us, "From today on, all of us will call Mr. Nieh, 'Papa.'"

I already mentioned that Mr. Nieh was a tall man. He looked like a foreigner. He had a big nose and big eyes, and he spoke in a southern Chinese dialect.

(Continued on page 184)

OPPOSITE PAGE: ***Florence Logan thought this was Laura and Mr. Nieh's wedding picture, taken when the couple married June 2, 1939. Their interracial marriage scandalized Laura's family in the U.S. In the eyes of Chinese and Japanese authorities, however, their marriage transformed the orphanage from an American institution into a Chinese one. Dr. Chang Yu Ming and members of the Tsai family stated that Laura's marriage to Mr. Nieh was probably the reason why Japanese authorities eventually allowed Laura to return to Canaan Home after her Pearl Harbor arrest instead of keeping her imprisoned with the other Americans in Peking.***

He didn't take care of the girls. Because of us, Mama and Papa married, and they didn't have any children of their own. Mama went to the hospital to get an operation to prevent her from having children. Someone asked Mama, "Why don't you want children?"

Mama answered, "Because I've already got so many children."

Maybe at that time the operation was not very good, because after the operation, Mama was often in pain, sometimes acute pain. Sometimes she even fainted. I didn't understand what had happened because I was too young. I thought Mama was sick, but the older girls told me, "It's all right. She doesn't have a disease." [Sarah] explained it to me.

At that time, I was good at winning Mama's approval. After dinner I went to my room, changed into clean clothes, combed my hair, and then went to Mama's room. If Mama was not busy, I said, "Look! I'm clean!"

Then Mama would pat me on the head and say, "Oh, what very nice hair!"

I knew Mama liked clean children.

Mama was happy with me, and I was happy, too. Before long, all the rest of the children also came around to see Mama, and if she had time, she would play with us for a while. She hugged us and sang "Jesus Loves Me" with us. We sang the song in Chinese, and then Mama sang it in English. We very much liked to listen to her sing this song. It's strange that when we were growing up, Mama never spoke a single sentence of English to us, except "Good morning" and "Good night." Those are the only two phrases Mama taught us in English. After singing, we all felt happy and content. Then Mama took us around to look at the flowers. Mama especially liked flowers. If there were no flowers when we moved someplace, she would plant flowers.

16.

Living in the Old Temple Place

The Old Temple Place (Kung Te Ssu), 1940

CRACK! James Leynse whacked off the top of his soft boiled egg with an ornate silver knife, then picked up a matching silver spoon. He glanced across the table at his guest and grinned. "I hear, Laura," he said, "that you are still trying to rid Canaan Home of idols."

"That's right," Laura said cheerfully.

"You don't mean the boys are still sleeping with those great monsters in their dormitory!" Mieps Leynse protested.

"What's all this about?" 17-year-old Wally Leynse asked.

The Leynse family were sitting around their elegant dining room in Peking with Laura Nieh, sharing a simple breakfast of boiled eggs, muffins, porridge, and crisp, juicy pears.

"We use the Old Temple building at our new location as a boys' dormitory," Laura explained. "The boys sleep in the great hall, but the monks left behind rows of giant Buddhas. They are huge—towering, monstrous. The boys have to sleep with them."

"Ugh," Wally said. "I bet it gives them nightmares."

"The boys don't seem to be afraid of the idols," Laura said. "It's just that we could make better use of that space."

A couple weeks ago, she said, a Lama monk had come and asked to see the Old Temple. So she led him to the lofty, vaulted hall and opened the doors. There stood a towering Buddha—with a basket dangling on one arm!

"I apologized," Laura said. "I told him that one of the boys must have put it there when we weren't watching. And I said that some of the children are mischievous, but we think it is better for them to be mischievous than sitting around in corners. Then we would know they were sick."

"Why don't the monks move their idols to another temple?" Wally asked.

"We've tried to get them to do that," Laura said, "but the Lamas say there is no other temple large and high enough to hold them."

Wally excused himself to leave for school, and the Leynes began telling Laura the latest war news. There was plenty to talk about. Germany and Britain were raining bombs on each other's cities, and Germany had invaded most of northern Europe. Japan had just signed a military pact with Germany and Italy, which recognized Japan as the new leader in greater East Asia. The news closest to home was that the American Embassy had just advised American mission agencies to evacuate their people. A lot of wives and children were packing to go home.

"Three families sent us their used clothing to give to Canaan Home this week," Mieps told Laura. "I'm sure others will leave things behind for you, too. We will keep it all here, and you can take back what you can manage to tie onto the bike on each trip home."

"Thank you," Laura said. "Our population is pushing toward the 100 mark now. More clothing will be a great help."

"But the evacuation represents a great loss, as well," Mieps said. "You will lose many, many faithful supporters."

"Speaking of faithful supporters," Laura said, "what about you? Are you planning to evacuate, too?"

"We haven't decided what to do yet," Mieps said.

"We are still Dutch citizens," James explained. "The director has asked us to stay on in Peking to protect the mission's property and oversee its work in case war breaks out between America and Japan."

Laura asked Mieps then for her latest news from the industrial center for women, and James watched, studying the two women—his elegantly dressed Mieps, pouring out her heart to this drab woman in a shabby peasant's gown. Laura was no longer pretty and she was too poor to dress well. Yet there was a quiet radiance about her personality that transformed her whole being when she smiled. James could understand why Nieh Shou Guang had been attracted to her, despite their age difference.

James wondered about their marriage sometimes. It had startled everybody in the Christian community. Many had opposed the idea, including Mr. Nieh's pastor Wang Ming Dao. The pastor was concerned about the marriage because of the couple's age difference, their different backgrounds, and their different levels of faith. How could a woman nearing menopause satisfy the driving need of a young man's sexual appetite? Neither the Western nor the Chinese Christian community knew how to discuss this issue with a single woman contemplating marriage. And then the couple's backgrounds were wild opposites. She was an Ohio farm girl, accustomed to hard labor and making do in tough times. He was raised in oriental luxury where only servants did physical labor, and his primary duty was supposed to be preserving the power, prestige, and riches of his clan. It was hard to imagine anyone from his background persevering for long in the poor conditions at the orphanage—working hard and eating coarse peasants' food.

Spiritually Laura had the advantage of being raised in the church with Christian role models. She had an extraordinary gift of faith to go with her extraordinary calling. Even so, she had not begun the orphanage until after her walk with God had been tested through years of challenging responsibilities. Mr. Nieh had been raised outside of the church, and he was just a baby believer. Running an orphanage in wartime with nearly 100 mouths to feed required a mature, deeply rooted trust in God. Mr. Nieh seemed passionately dedicated to Laura and the orphans, but it could be easy to mistake human desires and human attraction for the call of God. Human passion would be insufficient for the trials ahead if, like seed sown on a pathway, Mr. Nieh's faith had shallow roots. For a while he might be carried along by the strength of Laura's unswerving trust, but how would he manage if he ever had to carry the full load of the orphanage alone?

It was more than a year now since Laura had married Nieh Shou Guang. Laura had always given the Canaan Home children an American name as well as a Chinese name. When she married, she had given her new husband an American name, as well: Samuel Kenneth Nieh. Privately and with Western friends, she called him Kenneth. With the children, she called him Papa.

To Chinese and Japanese officials, though, he remained Nieh Shou Guang. They considered him to be the new, fully Chinese director of Canaan Home. In the complex politics of occupied China, Mr. Nieh's Chinese citizenship and political connections immediately cut through a mountain of paperwork and simplified a host of official relationships affecting the orphanage.

Kenneth Nieh had dined with the Leynses a number of times now since the wedding. He seemed to be a quiet man and rather serious—cordial, well-mannered, thoroughly Chinese. Laura appeared to be happy with him.

They did not seem like newlyweds though. A man had to wonder. Maybe the Niehs' marriage was only a formality. After all, it was clear that the couple had not changed their sleeping arrangements after the wedding. Kenneth continued to stay in the boys' dormitory at the Old Temple, and Laura still stayed with the infants and the girls. Perhaps their marriage was primarily a legal step to safeguard Canaan Home from hostile government officials and allow the Niehs to live together as closely working partners without distressing the church.

People were starting to think of the Niehs' marriage as a kind of business arrangement. To James, though, it didn't seem like Laura to approach marriage that way. Was something amiss?

Well, it was none of his business. It appeared the Niehs' marriage must not be a union born of a romance, but of a rescue operation. Laura and Kenneth had taken their vows in order to save the lives of destitute children in a war zone. People should only admire them for that.

Meantime, it was good to have Laura visiting their home more often these days. Now that Canaan Home had moved outside the city wall to the Old Temple Place, the Niehs had to make frequent trips into Peking to buy food, pick up supplies, and run business errands. Sometimes they came together, but more often Mr. Nieh stayed at the orphanage, while Laura bicycled into town. The round trip was over 15 miles, making it impossible to ride into the city and complete much business before the West Gate closed at curfew. So the Presbyterians had given the Niehs a small bedroom to use whenever they needed to spend the night in the city.

James' concentration returned to Laura and his wife. He noticed that Mieps was telling Laura their family news now—how much they were all missing their eldest son Humphrey, who had left for Pomona College in California a few weeks ago.

Well, breakfast was long over. It was time to go. They all had more than a full day's work ahead, as usual.

Laura tied her collection of orphanage supplies securely to her bicycle and pedaled from the Leynse home to Douw Memorial Hospital for chats with a couple of doctors about the progress of the sick children she was caring for at home. They gave her medical supplies for her patients, and she added them to the burden on her bike. Then she bicycled out the mission gate into the crowded *hutongs*. Along her way, heaps of crockery, clothing, brass-ware, and pewter lay piled outside shop doors to entice potential buyers. Vendors shouted their wares, beggars sang songs and whined, and itinerant barbers plied their trade, snip-snipping on street corners. Rickshaw drivers trotted all around her, hauling almond-eyed matrons and old gentlemen with wispy goatees. When she reached the West Gate, she showed her pass to the soldier there and headed for home. She hoped she would get home before the noon meal.

A couple of fat little clouds floated in a sapphire sky, and the sun shone warmly on her back. The soft outlines of the Western Hills spread out before her, their bare slopes dotted with tile-roofed temples and pagodas. Beyond the shrines that littered the sides of the road, blue-clad peasants worked their fields and gathered ripe pears and apples from trees. The familiar whiff of open toilets wafted in a light breeze as she maneuvered her way carefully around creaky wooden carts, slow-running rickshaws, and heavily burdened pedestrians. From time to time, trucks full of Japanese soldiers hurtled past, honking. When she heard them coming, she slid off her bike and teetered on the edge of the road with the rest of the slow movers, trying not to fall into the ditch.

She passed several turn-off places where paths led to villages along the way. The crowd thinned, and the creaking of carts died away.

BOOM! BOOM! BOOM! Sudden thunder exploded.

Startled, Laura looked up at the sky. It was blue as a dayflower. No thunder ever pealed from a sky that clear.

The thunder boomed again.

She stopped her bike and turned around. The crashing sound seemed to be coming from the direction of a small sloping hill about a half-mile behind her. Were bombs exploding? Were soldiers shooting? What was going on?

Abruptly, a Japanese tank blasted over the top of the little hill and started roaring toward her down the slope.

Her heart stopped.

What should she do?

She looked around quickly and noticed a place just ahead where she could ease her bicycle into the ditch. She stumbled to the spot and wrestled the two-wheeler with its clumsy burden into the trench.

The tank must have seen her. Would it follow her into the ditch?

Panting, she laid her bike down and crouched beside it. The monster lumbered toward her, flattening a broad path through the fields of ripened corn and millet.

Finally it reached the road and crunched past, spitting pebbles.

Laura stood up and watched the big tank go up the hilly way, then turn off on a side path. It was moving away from her home, going in the opposite direction from the Old Temple Place.

She realized she had been holding her breath.

For a few minutes she sat down in the ditch, resting, and gradually peace descended on her spirit. The land was utterly still.

When she finally stood and looked all around, there was not a single vehicle, not a soul in sight anywhere. She hoisted her bicycle back onto the road and looked again.

Still no one. Nothing moved.

She started for home then, pushing up the rolling hills, coasting on the down sides, eager for a glimpse of the Old Temple's picturesque, towering roof. The grand old roof looked impressive, but when winter came, the great hall was impossible to heat. The boys had to undress for bed in a small, heated dressing room, then make a dash across the frigid floor for their covers.

The family's new home was beautiful, with two big courtyards. A flower garden flourished in the front courtyard along with shady, prickly ash trees and an orchard with peach, pear, and cherry trees. In the back courtyard there was a vineyard.

When the family first came, she heard about an elderly man who had been the former temple gardener and needed a home. She invited him to move in with the family. He tended the flowers in the front courtyard and taught the boys to garden and landscape. They planted a big vegetable garden in the back courtyard using a generous supply of seeds that Laura's father in America had sent her before he died.

All summer the family ate homegrown beans, bok choy, tomatoes, and other vegetables from their back courtyard. She was so thankful for the garden. Along with fruit from the trees, it provided an essential part of the family's food supply.

They had to keep the children out of it, of course. None of the orphans were allowed to go into the back courtyard without an adult supervising them. Last July, some of the older children snuck in and ate all the ripe grapes, proving the reason for the rule.

For a treat, Laura let one or two of the children go into the garden and pick tomatoes with her in the evenings after supper. How the children loved those tomatoes! For a snack every day after naps, the cook gave them a bowl of sliced pink and red tomatoes sprinkled with sugar—just the way she had loved eating them as a child. Her mouth watered at the thought.

She looked up at the sky. The sun was high overhead. Maybe she was thinking about tomatoes because she was hungry.

At the Old Temple gate she hugged all the children who ran to greet her, and then started pushing her loaded bicycle to the kitchen. Rachel raced after her. "Mama! Just because I didn't sweep the room, Miss Tung hit me!"

Rachel was almost nine years old now. Her dark eyes flashed with indignation.

"Are you hurt?" Laura asked with concern.

"No! But she hit me!"

"Did Miss Tung tell you to sweep the room for morning chores?"

"Yeeees," Rachel admitted. "but I didn't want to."

"So what did you do after she told you to sweep?"

"I just played."

"Rachel, next time you must obey Miss Tung," Laura said gently. "You are old enough to sweep now. God wants you to be a helpful child and do your share of the work."

"Yes, Mama," Rachel said, looking deflated.

Laura unloaded her supplies in the kitchen. "Has Papa eaten yet?" she asked the boys who were helping the cook.

They said he had not, so she told one of them to send Papa word that she would be waiting for him in the girls' dormitory. The cook spooned a double portion of vegetables into a container, added a couple thick slices of cornbread, and gave her two sets of chopsticks and two bowls. Laura and Kenneth always tried to eat meals together in relative peace and quiet by themselves, usually in Laura's bedroom.

In the dormitory, volunteer helpers were putting the children down for naps. She checked on the babies and the sick children, and then asked Miss Tung to come see her after she and Mr. Nieh had finished their noon meal.

It looked like things had run smoothly this time while she was gone. She believed in the power of a healthy routine for keeping order and getting a lot of work accomplished.

Whether she and Kenneth were home or away, volunteer helpers slept with the children and woke them at 5:30 a.m. Everyone had an hour to dress and clean their rooms. Then the whole family met for morning worship, followed by breakfast. After that the little ones had classes, lunch, naps, and play time. The older children split the day between school lessons and work assignments. The big boys gardened, cleaned buildings, helped cook and clean up after meals, and took care of the grounds, the chickens, and the goats. The big girls did laundry, cleaning, cooking, sewing, and also took care of the babies and little children. After breakfast, half the older children worked and half attended school. After lunch, they changed shifts. Then came suppertime, playtime, and bedtime.

Older children were in charge of meals. Little ones were assigned to sit at a particular table with other children their age, and two older children oversaw each table. The older children were supposed to make sure each youngster in their group came to the meal on time. They also brought food from the kitchen, supervised table manners, and made sure each one received his or her portion of food.

On Sundays, Christians from Peking came to Canaan Home and taught the children Sunday School classes.

Laura thanked God every day for the volunteer staff who made it possible to take care of so many small children and to have classes for the older ones. Whether the Japanese occupation lingered or ended tomorrow, the children needed good work habits, an academic education, and useful skills so that they could support themselves when they grew up. How could she and Kenneth ever manage to raise all these children by themselves without the help of these Chinese Christian teachers and caregivers?

Of course, the staff needed training, some more than others. Miss Tung, for example...Miss Tung meant well, and she was dedicated to the children, but she antagonized them. Laura wondered how to get across the idea that, as her grandmother would have said, "You can catch more flies with honey than with vinegar."

Laura was still turning the matter over in her mind when Kenneth came. They relaxed together over lunch. Laura reported that the first evacuees were packing to leave Peking, and she said that his new tactics for dealing with city officials in his negotiations to buy the quadrangle adjoining the orphanage seemed to be breaking the stalemate. He would have to go into the city again, though, to sign more documents. Kenneth said this was good, because they needed those rooms on the property badly. He didn't see how they could fit another child in the girls' and babies' dormitory. And he said that the gardener told him the pear harvest this year was the best he'd ever seen.

The children were stirring from their naps when Kenneth left and Miss Tung entered Laura's room, leaving the door ajar. Laura listened to the helper's report of the children's various activities during her absence, and they discussed Rachel's disobedience that morning during chores.

"Next time, if Rachel won't cooperate for morning chores," Laura said, "tell her she can't eat her next meal. If she won't work, she can't eat. Don't lose your temper, though, and hit the children. You might hurt them."

Miss Tung acknowledged her words with a bow.

As Laura moved toward the bedroom door to see Miss Tung out, she heard a faint, furtive noise just outside. When she opened the door, she saw Rachel skipping away from her bedroom toward the front door of the dormitory.

The little girl turned and gave her a wide, innocent smile.

A little too innocent, Laura thought.

She bit her lip to stifle a laugh. *That rascal eavesdropper!*

Reports from the Old Temple

Excerpt from a letter from Florence Logan dated August 11, 1940:

Yesterday we went on the bus out to visit Miss Richards. The buses are so crowded that the trip is not an unalloyed joy. However we were glad to see her and the kiddies. Some of them are very dear. We happened to take out a bunch of candy for them and had the fun of seeing them each receive a piece after dinner. One little scrap assured me that he had a yellow piece. (No idea why he thought that special.) We enjoyed watching them get their dinner. It was very well managed, various boys being in charge of the serving at each table.

Their beds are really a marvel: such attractive bedding and all scrupulously clean. They were wearing odds and ends of clothing, but their bedding was all uniform. In most poor homes the bedding gets awfully grimy, so it must be quite a transformation for these kiddies to have everything so clean. To train them to keep things so clean is no small item.

I do hope they succeed in buying an adjoining place of 35 rooms which they need very much. Dear Richie has no place at all for herself—just a wee room piled up with things. The big temple in which most of the boys sleep is an icy barn in winter and leaks in summer! Last summer it was like a sieve.

Richie may go to Paotingfu with me Thursday. She hopes to stay over a day and then go on down to Shihchiachuang to help a young Chinese woman who is starting an orphanage there.

Re-reading that later on July 27, 1987, Florence Logan noted:

Actually, that item is rather significant—that she was inspiring Chinese to follow her example! I had forgotten that bit.

Canaan Home orphans, probably taken in 1939 or 1940 on the grounds of the Old Temple Building. In 2006 the orphans identified the crippled boy in the bed on the far right as either Titus or James. They also said that the two babies in cribs were later adopted by high Communist government officials and that the children wearing the white hats had a contagious skin disease.

From Rachel's 1989 memoirs, translated from Chinese:

One time Mama was away for three or four days. During this time all the older children sneaked into the back courtyard and ate all the grapes. Papa noticed and asked us, "Who stole the grapes?"

Nobody answered.

So then he said he wouldn't let us eat breakfast.

Actually, I didn't eat the grapes. I ate the grape leaves instead, because I thought the grapes were sour. I took several grape leaves, put them together, and ate them—better than grapes. Still, I dared not say that I hadn't stolen the grapes.

That was bad luck for me, because the punishment was having our hand slapped. I thought it was fun, though. I learned from the other children. They all put their palm up (to be slapped) or they made their hand cool down first by putting it on the ground. Then Papa struck our hands one by one. Each one got ten slaps, including me.

Papa taught the children directly. If it was a minor fault, the punishment was to go without dinner. If it was a serious fault, he slapped the person's hand. He never explained to the person at fault the way Mama did. He just punished us, and sometimes we disagreed with him, so we didn't like him. We seldom saw him smile.

Mama's way of correcting us was different. She always taught us to use words from the Bible. For example, if we lied or if we stole something, Mama said, "If you do this, God doesn't like it. You should be an honest child." If children fought with each other, Mama would say, "You need to love each other. Even if you came here first, and he came here later than you, you can't hit him. You need to be united. Whether you are older than him or younger, you need to be united." Mama always used the talking method to teach us. She seldom spanked us unless we had done something serious. Generally if we made mistakes, she punished us by not letting us eat dinner.

Because we ate whatever we found, we often got diarrhea. Once we did that when Mama was gone. When she came back, she noticed the children's poor appearance and asked the teacher if the children had been sick.

"No," the teacher said.

So she told the teacher she was going to examine all our bowel movements to see if we had diarrhea. I didn't want to admit that I had diarrhea because then I would have to eat the sick diet, which was diluted food. They didn't give you cornbread if you were sick.

Mama examined our bowel movements one by one, and she didn't feel dirty or degraded. When it was my turn, she said, "I knew you must have diarrhea," because she had seen how pale and thin and yellow my face was. I had to sit at the table for the sick children and eat the sick diet. Then Mama gave us medicine, and we soon recovered.

Mama cared for all of us. If she saw poor expressions on our faces, she looked for the reason. One time, she made all of us take de-worming medicine. There were more than 100 children. Mama examined each of them and gave them medicine. After we had taken it, she wouldn't let us eat dinner. We took it the first time at mealtime. The second time was when we got up the next morning, before breakfast. This medicine seemed very effective. One boy excreted more than 100 worms, but a few had no worms come out.

Mama didn't mind the smell when she examined our bowel movements one by one. Whose love can compare with Mama's love? Thanks be to God who gave us Mama's love.

One day when we got up early, Mama told me that her relative was going to come to the orphanage to visit her. I don't know when he came, but Mama told me later that he had said I looked like her. She had replied, "No, she looks like my younger brother." I was very happy. I didn't care who I looked like as long as I looked like my mama's family. I was about eight or nine years old at that time.

I knew when I was young that Mama loved me. It seemed like something special. I didn't have my own mother, but I was willing to be the daughter of Laura Richards.

17.

Pearl Harbor Day

Peking and Paotingfu, 1941

PEARL HARBOR DAY came to Americans in China on Monday, December 8, 1941 instead of December 7 because of the international dateline.

Laura happened to be in Peking that weekend, staying at the Presbyterian missionary compound. She woke to the sonorous boom of a gong from the nearby Lama temple that wakened the gods to the duties of the day. She felt refreshed by the luxury of two uninterrupted nights of sleep. Quickly she slipped from beneath her quilts and dressed warmly for a morning prayer time and breakfast.

Suddenly, at eight o'clock, large groups of Japanese soldiers began pushing their way inside the compound residences. "Two hours!" an officer bellowed at the missionaries in Chinese. "We will give you two hours! The war has started! We have bombed Pearl Harbor! Pack your clothes, mattresses, pots and pans—all you can carry. Within two hours we will take you to an internment camp."

They all hurried to obey orders. By 10 a.m. Laura and her friends stood in a dazed huddle in front of the Leynse house with their belongings piled beside them. Gloating soldiers guarded them closely, and an officer gave them a fierce lecture in Chinese on the foolishness of American military strategy. He described in great detail what the Japanese army was going to do when they reached Washington D.C.

Laura had little more than her Bible, borrowed bedding, the family's flour, and the clothes she wore. She was unprepared for spending the rest of the winter in below-zero temperatures in the unheated buildings of the internment camp. And what would Kenneth and the children do if she was sent to prison? There must be some way to escape the camp and get home to the family.

It was a bleak winter day with a faraway sun that sat like a giant hailstone in the sky. The icy coldness stiffened her joints. James Leynse was recovering from typhoid fever, and they were all worried about him having to stand outside in the freezing air. He shivered and trembled, leaning against his wife Mieps. Orpha Gould waited with them. Orpha and Laura had shared hard times before during the first world war. Now it appeared that a second world war was sweeping them up together again. The war between America and Japan and their allies had finally come.

Laura stood quietly in the cold, praying. After the group had waited four hours, another Japanese officer bustled up, looking important. "Go? No go!" he announced in broken English. "Tomorrow go? Perhaps!"

The missionaries returned to their residences and settled down under house arrest to await further events. "Tomorrow" came and went.

Outside the compound, the Japanese began closing and sealing all the churches that had been begun by British and American missionaries. For the first time since the Boxer Rebellion of 1900, all the large chapels throughout Peking stopped services. Only the indigenous churches like Wang Ming Dao's Peking Christian Tabernacle remained open.

The imprisoned missionaries grieved as the Japanese began systematically seizing all American and British charitable institutions. They knew how much love and sacrifice people had expended through the years to start and maintain these ministries for suffering people. The Japanese had different motives for running the institutions than the Christians who started them. Douw Memorial Hospital was one of the first to be taken over, and Canaan Home's source of free medical assistance died with the new administration. "No more charity cases," the Japanese announced.

Dr. Henke had sometimes thrown up his hands in despair over the condition of some of the diseased, malnourished waifs Laura accepted into the orphanage and brought to him for care. He had done his best to rescue them. The Douw Hospital staff had saved the lives of many Canaan Home children, besides fitting the lame with artificial limbs, giving all the children regular medical checkups, and providing the orphanage with free medicine. Losing Douw Hospital's free service was a serious blow. So was the news that the Japanese had cut off all contributions from outside the country to Canaan Home and the other "enemy connection" churches and institutions.

Laura saw the list of charitable organizations that were going to be taken over by the Japanese. Canaan Home's name was on the list with a date scheduled for the transfer of administrations.

Still she felt hopeful. Perhaps the Japanese takeover could be averted somehow. In the meantime, she applied for a pass to travel between the compound and Canaan Home. Perhaps she would see her family again.

At Canaan Home on December 8, Mr. Nieh's friends brought news of his wife's capture and in seconds all the older children knew: "Mama's been caught! The Japanese caught Mama!"

The friends warned Mr. Nieh that Japanese soldiers were arresting all foreigners. Even though he was Chinese, he looked foreign. If he ventured from the grounds of Kung Te Ssu to buy supplies or try to get news of Laura, they warned, he would be arrested and imprisoned. He was afraid and began wearing a big gauze mask whenever he had to walk around the grounds of the orphanage compound.

The youngsters struggled to carry on their duties as usual—milking the goats, caring for the little ones, washing the laundry and hanging it on clotheslines in the dry, bitter wind. Every day, several times a day, they squinted through the cracks in the front gate, hoping to see their mother peddling home on her bicycle.

"Mama, come back very soon! Mama, come back very soon!" The

rollicking old chant from Rachel's baby days echoed through her mind as the long days passed. At night she and the other girls pulled the blankets over their heads and cried.

Down the railway line south in Paotingfu, Japanese soldiers arrested Florence Logan along with four other American missionaries and placed them under house arrest. They were forbidden to leave the mission compound for any reason, even to buy food, and the Japanese cut off their U.S. salaries. So they hired a Chinese cook to buy their supplies, pooled their funds, and rationed themselves. They had no idea when or how they would ever be able to get more money. They spent a lot of time praying for each other and for their friends in other parts of China.

Florence paged through *Now It May Be Told*, a ten-page pamphlet about Canaan Home that she had written a few months before. She prayed as she reread the text, and she wondered, *What are the kiddies doing today? And where is Richie?*

During the previous summer of 1941, Florence Logan had read *The Life of Trust*, by George Mueller, the book that had given Laura inspiration and guidelines for starting Canaan Home. Every few pages she thought, *The story of Richie's orphanage ought to be written up.*

Reading Mueller's story had inspired Richie to greater faith—and look at all that God had done through her as a result! Surely, Richie's story would be just as effective in showing people how to live the life of trust—and not only people in the U.S. If Richie's story could be translated into Mandarin, it could inspire believers throughout China.

It bothered Florence to think about how long it had been since Laura's American supporters had heard from her. Would they keep praying? Laura's family and friends had heard nothing from her since the Japanese takeover. They were ignorant of the dangers that the Canaan Home family faced and unaware of the way the orphanage had ballooned. Twice after the Japanese takeover, Florence wrote letters for Laura to send home, but each time the mail was blocked and Laura's letter went unsent. Florence herself, though, managed to send home a few reports successfully. Maybe she and Laura should try one more time....

Unfolding political events underscored her growing sense of urgency to write a report and mail it home while it still might be possible that summer of 1941. In Europe, Italy occupied Albania and Greece. Russia occupied the Baltic States and half of Poland. Germany occupied most of northern Europe and invaded her ally Russia. Germany and Britain were still bombing each other. Back home, the U.S. had adopted the draft and begun building up her army, air force and a two-ocean navy. War threatened between the U.S. and Japan. It felt like only a matter of time before the deteriorating international situation came to a head, catching her and the Niehs up in political disaster.

In August 1941, Florence visited Peking and proposed writing the report. Laura and Kenneth were delighted. "We've been feeling an urgent need for a written account," Laura said, "but we've been too busy to manage it ourselves."

So Florence postponed her return to Paotingfu and spent a week visiting the orphanage and gathering material to write a pamphlet giving the history of Canaan Home. She had to omit a lot of background information in order to get the account past Japanese censors. She could not mention, for example, how the prices of food and basic necessities had soared, nor how the refugees and beggars were multiplying, filling the Christian porridge kitchens with limp, staring women and silent, fragile children. She must not describe how hundreds of thousands of Chinese had fled the fertile provinces of the north to settle in the mountainous provinces bordering Burma and Tibet. From Peking alone, the students and faculties from over a hundred high schools and colleges had loaded libraries, laboratories and equipment on donkeys and moved into the mountains. Nor could she mention Japanese interference with the activities of Chinese churches, or the bombings, the atrocities, the terrorist attacks—all the crushing circumstances of life in an occupied country that made the orphans' situation so impossible and God's provision so miraculous.

Yet even without mentioning these political details, the Canaan Home story was remarkable. At the June 1941 board meeting, Kenneth reported that the orphanage needed $1,500 a month in local currency exclusive of clothing to care for 115 children. Each month in 1941, the necessary amount had come in through donations of money and supplies from hundreds of sources in large and small amounts. It was impossible to list all the people who had helped Canaan Home in one way or another over the last 12 years. Last-minute provision was so common at Canaan Home that the family lost track of all the incidents when they ran out of supplies, prayed, and received what they needed just in time.

Announcing Laura and Kenneth's wedding was Florence's second major challenge. This pamphlet would bring Laura's friends and family the first news of her marriage in 1939 to a Chinese national. How could they be expected to understand and accept Laura's reasons for marrying outside her race? Even many Christians in North China who understood Laura's living conditions had been upset. To many people, an interracial marriage was unacceptable under any circumstances. Many Western missionaries had opposed the marriage, and some of the Chinese Christian leaders also protested it.

People in North China saw the matter differently now, two years later. Kenneth had proved himself over and over by the way he applied his business ability to administer orphanage affairs and by his willingness to give up a comfortable life to care for the poorest and the most helpless. "I disapproved of the Niehs' decision to marry," Florence heard a Chinese elder report in a meeting, "but now I see that the work of Canaan Home could not have been carried out otherwise."

Florence finished writing the Canaan Home story at the end of August. For the cover, she used a photograph Laura had taken of Grace and Gloria saying grace before a meal. The Niehs then sent the report to Truth Hall Press to be published and mailed to the U.S. In October an enthusiastic young Chinese nurse translated the pamphlet into Mandarin. By the first of December, the report had been distributed to both the Chinese and the U.S. church—just before Pearl Harbor Day shut down mail service to America and closed the doors of American denominational churches inside China.

What will happen to Canaan Home now? Florence wondered. *Well,* she consoled herself, *if Laura has been arrested, the children at least have Mr. Nieh taking care of them.*

Mr. Nieh himself felt like he was drowning. First his wife was captured, and next most of the Chinese helpers left, one by one. It was too dangerous for them and their families to be associated with Canaan Home now because his wife was an American, an enemy of Japan.

The children cooked millet and cornbread until the corn and millet flour ran out. Then the family began eating black beans and bean cake, but how soon before that would run out as well?

All the children missed their mother. They were all crying, crying, crying. The toddlers and the babies whimpered and wailed, and the older children were quick to tears as they cooked and cleaned and cared for the livestock and the little ones. At night they cried themselves to sleep.

Over a hundred children to feed. Over a hundred children crying for their mother. Mr. Nieh did not know how to order the family's daily schedule with all the workers leaving. Normally he just did the accounting and paperwork. He felt trapped.

Would the Japanese ever release his wife?

It seemed unlikely. Probably he would never see her again.

Every day seemed like a month.

He couldn't leave the compound because he might be mistaken for a foreigner and arrested. He longed to get outside, ride his bicycle, talk to his family and friends, and hear some news direct from people who were likely to know what was really happening. He wished he could find a way to relieve the feeling of doom that hovered over him by day and kept him awake and restless in the night.

When he found out that the Japanese had set a date to take over Canaan Home, he despaired. He began dreaming about where he might go and what he might do when the Japanese sent his wife to internment camp and took over Canaan Home. He daydreamed about going back to Anhui Province where he was born, where people knew he wasn't a foreigner and he wouldn't have to hide behind a gauze mask. He had a good education and business experience. With a little money to invest, he could start a business and begin life over in the village of his ancestors.

And then, incredibly, the money came. The Presbyterian Church sent it to Canaan Home in a package. In wonder, Mr. Nieh counted it out: 130,000 Chinese dollars.

It was the largest donation Canaan Home had ever received.

How ironic. It was the largest donation Canaan Home had ever received, and now the Japanese would get it! They were going to take over Canaan Home, and when they did, they would take all this money.

It was too much.

He took the money and sent it to his younger brother in Anhui to buy property so he could start a new business and a new life.

The days passed, and still Laura remained under arrest in Peking. The Presbyterian Church sent a letter asking why Canaan Home had neglected to send a receipt for the large donation they had recently sent.

Mr. Nieh destroyed the letter.

Viewpoints

Memoirs of Laura's cousin, Laura Jane Eberhardt Cerling, relating how the Canaan Home report reached her family in late 1941:

Mother had gotten the letter during the day. I found out about it when I got home from business school. The envelope was so battered and torn up, it's a wonder anything on the inside survived. My mother said, "Laura has gotten married to a Chinese, and I don't want to hear anything more about it." My mother had also gotten a letter from my Uncle Ed, who was angry about it. I heard about both letters at the same time.

By that time I was a Christian. I thought—but I did not say—"Well, she wasn't planning to come back to the United States. He's a Christian, and it will give her help and companionship." I knew that they considered anyone who would marry outside of their race as doing something very bad. I did not agree. I didn't understand why they felt so harshly about it, but I knew enough to keep my mouth shut.

I had no inkling of what Laura was facing in China. We knew little about China. In school we had no geography, just social studies, which was essentially a kind of history. Laura's situation was extremely remote. No one could understand why anyone would go off that way.

Grace and Gloria saying grace at mealtime with other orphans. Florence Logan used this photograph on the cover of Now It May Be Told, *a pamphlet she wrote the summer of 1941 to record the history of Canaan Home. The pamphlet was also translated into Chinese. At least two newsletters that Florence had previously written for Laura during the Japanese occupation between 1937 and 1941 could not be mailed because of wartime restrictions. The pamphlet, however, made it through to the United States, bringing Laura's family the news of her 1939 marriage to Mr. Nieh.*

Excerpt from letter to Becky Powers from missionary Annie Kartozian, written July 1, 1984:

I did not know Laura in China although I heard of her orphanage in Peking's Western Hills. In late 1941 (before Pearl Harbor), I sent to her a Chinese woman who was having a child by a Japanese man who took advantage of her—she wanted to commit suicide and her cousin brought her to me. After she found Jesus as Savior, we got in touch with Laura through Presbyterian friends. Laura agreed to take my friend until the baby was born. Then the baby was left there and my friend came back to her Peking family. By that time we were restricted and I did not see her.

Rachel's memoir, translated from Chinese:

At this time [late 1941], Mama bought another quadrangle on the right side of the Temple. All the girls and the small children moved to the right side with Mama. Papa and the boys continued to live in the Kung Fu Temple. The youngest children stayed just outside Mama's room. Mama always kept the youngest children in the room beside hers so she could take care of them better. When we moved here, I started to work because there were so many children. I was ten years old. The routine was that the older children took care of the younger children, and we exchanged work once a month. For example, some took care of the children during the day, some at night, some washed diapers, and some cooked food. The youngest children were seven to ten days old. Each of us would take care of three or four babies.

18.

Under Siege

The Old Temple Place, 1942-1943

ALTHOUGH TIME DRAGGED for the Canaan Home children watching for their mother's return, it was really only two weeks before Laura was able to obtain a pass and return to her family in the Western Hills outside the city gate. She was fortunate. All the other American and British missionaries in both Peking and Paotingfu remained under guard, unable to leave their compounds. Laura's pass allowed her to travel in and out of Peking for supplies, and the Japanese permitted her to stay overnight at the Leynses' home on these visits. Her friends thought she was probably given the pass because of her marriage to Nieh Shou Guang, a Chinese citizen from a powerful political clan.

She returned home with food supplies and made a personal visit to each child.

"The Japanese are going to take over Canaan Home," Kenneth told her. "They've taken over so many places—Douw Hospital, the school for the deaf, the school for the blind, most of the nursing homes...."

"I have a sense of peace about this," Laura said. "God delivered me from house arrest. Now we must pray with the staff that He will deliver us from the takeover."

So they prayed and steeled themselves for the coming of Japanese officials on the scheduled day. Nothing happened though. The family went about their business as usual, and no officials showed up at the Old Temple's front gate. After several days, the Niehs received word that the official in charge of taking over Canaan Home had been called back to Japan. Much later Laura learned that he died there of typhus. His office unraveled in confusion and apparently forgot about taking over Canaan Home.

In the meantime, the Presbyterian Church sent Canaan Home a second letter asking once again for a receipt for their donation. Mr. Nieh destroyed the second letter just as he had the first. When the Presbyterian Church received no reply to either letter, they sent a third letter, this time in English. Since Mr. Nieh could read no English, he laid it aside with other orphanage papers, and, before long, Laura found it.

"What happened to the money that the Presbyterian Church sent us while I was gone?" she asked her husband. "They say that they never received a receipt and when they wrote us asking for one, they received no reply."

His evasions were more troubling than the letter.

Laura kept asking for an answer, and Kenneth finally admitted he had sent the money to his family in Anhui. She was so angry she could hardly speak.

"Why? What were you thinking?"

"The Japanese were going to take over Canaan Home," he said. "They were going to take the money for themselves."

"So to prevent *them* from stealing it, you stole it yourself?" Laura demanded. "The Presbyterians sent the money to care for the children. The money belongs to Canaan Home. Go to Anhui and get it back!"

So he left.

It got worse.

Laura had trained the six oldest teenage girls to take care of the babies and the little children at night. A couple of them took turns rising in the darkness to give the babies their 3 a.m. feeding and the others took care of any little ones who woke and needed attention. After Kenneth left, a nurse on Laura's shrunken staff came to her and said that she had just found out from one of these teens that while Laura was under arrest, Kenneth had forced his attentions on two of the oldest girls.

It was a nightmare. Her husband had betrayed her—twice.

Rape was the worst kind of disgrace for a woman in China. A raped woman was considered unclean. If the violation became known, no one would marry her, and she was socially shunned. Chinese society never forgot, never forgave. Many of the Chinese women who had been violated by the Japanese committed suicide afterward rather than face life branded by the social stigma of rape.

She dared not risk the girls' future by reporting what had happened, even if she thought the authorities would help her—which she knew they would not. Japanese officials cared nothing for Chinese orphans. And Chinese officials were focused on keeping themselves and their families alive and their possessions safe. None of them would go to any trouble for a molested orphan girl, especially when her violator was the son of the former police chief and brother-in-law to the mayor.

She would have to tell the Presbyterian Church that her husband had embezzled their donation. She would have to take one of the older boys into her confidence to help her write the Chinese characters to explain. The Presbyterians had to know the truth, but they would be as powerless as she was to get the money back. They were an "enemy connection" church now. For them, there was no justice.

And what about her marriage? Divorce was out of the question for her in either Chinese society or the Christian community. Even if it *was* an option, which it was not, divorcing her Chinese husband would mean taking back the official director role of Canaan Home. That would guarantee a Japanese takeover. She would be imprisoned as an American, and she would lose all the children.

She had already done the only thing she could—separate from Kenneth by sending him away.

He was unlikely to return, she realized now. With the money he had taken, he could do what many wealthy men in China did—marry a second wife or take a concubine. With all that money, he could be a big man in Anhui.

But what would Canaan Home do without him? What if the Japanese found out that Nieh Shou Guang had left for good? That he was no longer the director of Canaan Home?

She had never been so vulnerable.

And so it was that the early months of 1942 began for Laura with her Western friends imprisoned, her Chinese friends endangered, her food supply low, her overseas donations cut off, her husband as good as gone, her volunteer staff reduced to a couple of courageous Chinese and no relief in sight. It was a great encouragement, therefore, when a valiant new Chinese volunteer showed up at her gate—Pearl of the 35 winter over-garments.

Pearl had just graduated from normal school. Ever since she started teachers' training, she had dreamed of teaching one day at Canaan Home. Now she was determined to fulfill her dream, war or no war.

She moved into the girls' section of Canaan Home and dove into her first full-time kindergarten teaching assignment with the wholehearted energy and idealism of the young. She was especially fond of Tabitha, who insisted on sitting propped in her crib outside Pearl's classroom so she could join the other children singing all the songs. It lifted Laura's spirits to watch Pearl working with the children. She did the work of two.

Pearl's enthusiasm ran headlong into one major obstacle, however. The wealthy young woman's stomach rebelled at Canaan Home's meager winter diet, which consisted of salty vegetables, steamed cornbread, cornmeal mush, and millet cooked without salt and eaten without sugar (salt and sugar were too expensive now). The cornbread especially bothered Pearl. She gagged and could not get it down.

When Pearl started losing weight, her mother grew concerned. One day Pearl's brother showed up for a visit carrying a large box. "Mother sent you some good food," he told his sister.

"No!" Pearl was plainly shocked. "I can't do that! The children don't get special food. How can I eat special food?"

"Mother says you are getting too thin," her brother argued.

Pearl was silent, torn between her sense of duty to her mother and her sense of duty to the children of Canaan Home. "Take the food home," she said at last, "and tell Mother to pray with me that I will be able to eat the cornbread."

Pearl's brother left with the box unopened, and after that Pearl started finishing her cornbread at meals.

Laura continued to ride her bicycle into Peking for supplies, bringing news and encouragement to the missionaries imprisoned on the mission compound. She kept her overnight visits brief. She wanted to avoid being inside the mission compound when the Japanese decided to transport the missionaries to internment camp. If she was not with the other Americans when the day of detainment arrived, maybe the Japanese would overlook her. Maybe they would forget to send her off with the others.

She gave the children no explanation where their papa had gone. He left, and they did not know why. They gave it little thought though. They were distracted by a new and unexpected kind of trouble: for some reason, their mama had become bad tempered.

Laura herself only noticed that she was tired. Her body lay in bed like a dead weight in the mornings, and she had to talk herself into getting up. She felt like she was pushing her body around all day by sheer strength of will.

She had no energy, but her nerves were strung tight. She could no longer bear the sound of the babies' crying. She had always trained the girls to give close attention to the babies, keeping them clean and dry and feeding them milk and water on schedule. Now she began exploding into the babies' room in a temper whenever she heard an infant squalling. If the baby kept crying for no apparent reason, she took out her frustration on the girls, scolding and spanking.

She had spanked the children before only for serious offenses. Now she began lashing out, hitting them with the paddle just because she felt irritated or angry. The children's tears no longer touched her.

One spring day she noticed that 12-year-old Sarah had neglected to cover the outhouse seat properly. Sarah was one of the girls Laura relied on the most. She was so responsible that Laura could trust her with important duties like keeping track of donated supplies. But today Sarah failed her. The outhouse seat was left open to the flies. All Laura needed now, on top of everything else, was an epidemic of diarrhea and vomiting in the family.

"How many times do I have to tell you to cover the outhouse seat properly?" Laura scolded. "Now get in there, Sarah, and cover that seat the way I taught you."

Sarah scuttled into the outhouse like a cockroach scurrying for cover. She readjusted the seat with a quick, futile gesture, leaving it as badly disarranged as before.

For some reason, the sight of the partly uncovered outhouse seat infuriated Laura. Where were the child's eyes? Couldn't she see? Laura escorted Sarah to the big girls' room, shaking with wrath, and snatched the paddle en route. Then she paddled the girl before the horrified eyes of her peeping sisters.

"Now then, young lady, back to the outhouse and do the job right this time," she demanded. Sarah stumbled back into the outhouse with her eyes splashing tears, and Laura demonstrated the proper way to cover the outhouse seat. "Now you do it, Sarah," she directed.

Sarah failed again, and a second paddling followed. Finally, on Sarah's third attempt, she did the job correctly. "That's more like it," Laura said.

Laura left her in the outhouse and strode into the babies' room where Rachel and Rose Mary were on duty. The girls seemed cowed and nervous, avoiding her eyes and paying strict attention to their work. As she checked the diaper supply and inspected the progress of the babies' formula preparation, the scene with Sarah in the outhouse replayed in her mind unbidden.

Why was she so angry with Sarah? Kenneth was actually the one who made her furious. But he was not here. Was she taking out her anger at Kenneth on the children? She felt ashamed and overwhelmed. Life was so intense. Nothing was funny any more. Her sense of humor had vanished. She hadn't even noticed it was gone.

The days grew warmer. Springtime touched the air with velvet. With the help of the old temple gardener, the boys planted the biggest garden they could manage. One of the missionaries under house arrest in Peking gave Canaan Home two cows. Between the goats and the cows, Laura had enough milk for the babies, with some to spare for making butter and cheese. Chinese Christians continued to send contributions as best they could, despite their own great need and the danger of being found in contact with Laura. Fortunately the family had no concerns about making rent payments. The year before, a donor had paid the rent for the remaining 16 years of the Old Temple lease.

The number of children in the orphanage grew to 175. Laura learned that the Japanese were looking for older teenage boys without families and forcing them to work as slave labor in Japan's wartime factories. She began hunting for jobs, apprenticeships, and Chinese Christian families to take in her oldest boys. Eventually she was able to find places for about 60 of them.

Meanwhile, in Paotingfu, the Japanese government offered repatriation to Florence and two of the other missionaries with her under house arrest. Since Florence was no longer allowed to do her work or meet with any of her Chinese colleagues, she decided she might as well take her furlough now and come back to Paotingfu when the war ended. So, in June 1942, Florence left China on the diplomatic exchange ship *Gripsholm*.

The Japanese made no offers of repatriation to the Westerners under house arrest in Peking. So Laura's missionary friends continued to wait and wonder as the tedious days of their house arrest passed by. Laura brought her friends enormous juicy tomatoes from the Canaan Home garden that summer and fiery chrysanthemums from the courtyard flower garden to cheer them in the fall.

One day, a Japanese army officer showed up suddenly at Canaan Home with seven soldiers. Laura hoped he had not found out somehow that Kenneth was no longer living with them. But he merely shook hands politely and then asked to see her room.

She led him through the babies' room into her own bedroom, a plain 8-by-10 foot cubicle sparsely furnished with a bed, a couple cabinets, and nothing more. A curtain divided the room to give her privacy when sick youngsters moved into her bedroom for nighttime nursing care. The officer looked around carefully and turned up his thumbs. Upturned thumbs meant "good." A little finger pointed down meant "bad."

While he and his men were inspecting the rest of the compound, his soldiers stole the ripe tomatoes from the family's garden. A lot of people, both Japanese and Chinese, rationalized that it was all right to steal now from "the enemies of Japan," but Laura thought the officer would not have allowed his soldiers to do it if he had known about it. He seemed to be one of the moderate Japanese officials.

The stolen tomatoes were a loss. The children were hungry. Every scrap of food was precious. Getting food had become the primary concern of life, not only for Canaan Home, but for everybody.

The plight of the Chinese people under Japanese rule was growing steadily worse. The Japanese army tried to feed their armies and pay for the costs of war by confiscating harvests and stripping the conquered country of wealth and resources. People lost all initiative to produce because the soldiers took everything. As fall gave way to winter, inflation continued to soar, the economy crumbled, and the Japanese rationed the civilian population's scarce food supply. The quality of these rations steadily deteriorated. The family had to eat livestock feed, grains that had been stored too long, flour that tasted like gasoline, and potatoes from northeast China that had frozen and turned black. The famine was growing so serious that at the end of 1942, Pearl's family sent her to Shanghai where their clan had a more secure food supply.

No other Chinese dared volunteer any more, so the Canaan Home school closed completely down. The children had to carry on almost all the work, including the care of severely handicapped orphans like Tabitha and the spina bifida children.

Laura had always doled out the children's food carefully to avoid waste. In the past, though, if a child was still hungry after eating his portion, he could ask for more. The meal servers had increased the children's portions as they grew bigger and needed more food. Now, with a rationed food supply, Laura had to cut down the amounts and say no to extra helpings. There was no longer enough food. She tried to eat as little as possible so the children would have more. At suppertime, she kept back part of her food so the oldest girls could eat it when they got up at 3 a.m. to feed the babies.

Whenever she prayed for food, Laura found herself blaming Kenneth. How could he take all that money? He knew the children were hungry. He was as bad as those Japanese soldiers, stealing food from helpless orphans. And his daughters! His innocent, capable daughters! She had rescued these girls from being kidnapped or outright sold into brothels. How could he do this thing? How dare he do it?

Yet he had given so much of himself to the children. He had been so zealous, so enthusiastic, taking on mountains of accounting details and bureaucratic red tape for Canaan Home, making it officially possible for them to exist. He had used his clan influence to help them over and over. The marriage had been his idea, not hers. What had happened to all his good intentions, all his zeal? How had she misjudged him?

She would start out praying for food and the next thing she knew, she was no longer directing her thoughts toward God, she was delivering lectures to Kenneth in her head. And when the children interrupted these mental scenarios, she was irritated! She should be thanking them for it! Was she losing her mind?

God loved her, loved the children. He had convinced her heart of that, and she had to remember it, thank Him for it…

But why had He allowed this to happen? And why hadn't He stopped her from marrying Kenneth?

She disciplined herself to stop the mental looping the moment she became aware of it. She must not give in to despair and disorientation. She could focus on Kenneth's betrayal, or she could focus on God's loving provision in the midst of betrayal. Once again, during this worst year of her life, at this most desperate level, she must learn to live in God's presence through a sacrifice of praise.

I don't know why my girls had to suffer what they did, O Lord, but You assure me that whatever is done to the least of these is done to You. This happened to YOU, and You are going through this terrible time with them and with each one of us. Thank You for choosing to suffer with us. Thank You that despite this famine we have not yet missed a single meal. Even though there is not enough to eat, there is always something. Thank You that the family has had no serious injuries or fatal illnesses. Thank You that the Japanese have not taken over Canaan Home. Thank You, O Lord, for reminding me once again that my hope comes from You alone. Maybe I was starting to look to Kenneth to save the children… I acknowledge once again, O Lord, that You alone can save us. I am depending on You only to keep us safe and fed. May Your Kingdom come and Your will be done in my heart and in this home as it is in Heaven. O Lord, help me to forgive.

When thanksgiving brought perspective, she realized how well, under the circumstances, the family was managing as the year 1943 began to unfold. With Pearl gone to Shanghai, only her brave friend Pervading Peace, the equally brave Mr. Ma, and the temple gardener remained to help her care for over 100 orphans and several disabled elderly men that she had not the heart to turn away. A number of the orphans, like Tabitha and the spina bifida patients, were severely disabled. Caring for them and for all the babies and toddlers was strenuous work. Out of necessity, she had developed a system of assigning all the family chores to teams of six, with three older children paired with three younger ones. She trained them to build fires, cook, clean, sew and mend clothes, do laundry, garden, tend the animals, and take care of those who were too young, too weak, or too disabled to care for themselves. Somehow the children were still gaining enough strength from the family's inadequate meals to handle the burden. Somehow they were managing the workload of adults without serious accidents. Of course there was no school for them any more. But the middle schools, high schools, and colleges of Peking had had to pack up and take students away from their families into the mountains. At least the Canaan Home family was staying together.

The winds of springtime filled the courtyards with choking clouds of yellow dust. Temperatures warmed. The peach, pear, and cherry trees bloomed white and pink and Laura stopped in the courtyard between errands, breathing in whiffs of perfume and listening to the murmur of honeybees swarming among the springtime blossoms. The buzzing soothed her. It was time for the boys to begin planting the garden again.

She bought a clutch of baby chicks for the boys to raise for eggs and meat that spring of 1943. One chilly day, a sudden storm came up, and Laura dashed outside to get the chicks out of the rain. Her gown was completely soaked by the time she collected them all and brought them into the shed where it was dry.

Shivering with cold, she hurried to her bedroom to change into a dry gown. While she was pulling it over her head, a burning sensation shot suddenly into her back and jerked her muscles so tight she could hardly breathe. It was all she could do to lower her arms and pull the gown down over her hips. She sat on the bed and called for Pervading Peace.

Her old friend could do nothing for her though. The muscles of her back had twisted into a spasm that no amount of massage could unloosen. The pain crippled her so that she had to hold onto Pervading Peace to pull herself into a standing position. She could barely walk. She gave Pervading Peace instructions for carrying on without her, stretched out on her side in the bed, closed her eyes and tried to think of something besides her pain.

A Presbyterian doctor sent her morphine, which helped her get some sleep at night. When it wore off, though, the molten fire returned. "I don't want to become addicted to morphine," Laura told Pervading Peace. "There must be a better solution. Perhaps the Lord will heal me."

But He did not. Laura was still sick in bed when the Japanese sent a message ordering her to come into Peking immediately to be interned in a concentration camp as a prisoner of war.

Laura's note on this photograph says: "[Grace] and [Gloria], the smallest twins, one on either side of the teacher. She is holding one of the small ones." The teacher here may be Pearl, the young woman who insisted on coming to teach the children kindergarten after Pearl Harbor. Pearl was also the girl who took a train to Tientsin when she was 17 to persuade her relatives to donate money to the orphanage for warm winter over-garments.

Orphan Memories

"THE MEMORY OF OUR DEAR MOTHER LAURA MAY RICHARDS," ZECHARIAH'S 1988 MEMOIR, TRANSLATED FROM CHINESE:

Laura May Richards was an American nurse who left her country and came to impoverished, chaotic China. She lived an unbelievably hard life. She loved her work. She didn't care that her life was hard, but she gave poor Chinese people a lot of love.

Canaan Home adopted more than 200 children and several disabled old men. She loved all these people, and she took care of all these people, but not herself. During the founding of the orphanage, she withstood the difficult times, especially in 1940-45 when war, starvation, and disease spread through China. These orphan children were the poorest and the saddest. But she had faith, and she led all those children through the difficult times. It was a great wonder.

Among all of those children Mama loved, there were two that she paid special attention to besides the smallest babies. One of them was [Jonathan]. He was blind. The other one, a girl, Tabitha, was paralyzed. She could not take care of herself. During the most difficult time (1940-45), she sent [Jonathan] to a school for the blind to study. She gave Tabitha lots of love and patience. Every day she helped her get up. She put her dress on, washed her face, and did all the nursing work. Tabitha's urine and excrement would get all over her. She took care of her like that for several years. She loved people without condition. Her deep love was a very good example for the rest of us who didn't suffer diseases or handicaps.

As a parent, Miss Richards gave us a very good example of how to deal with difficulty. Because she was an American, the Japanese government put her under surveillance and restricted her freedom. Under these conditions she still led all of us in prayer every morning, and on Sunday we had worship. All of us had faith to live in the world as she taught us. In the end, she led all of us children through these deep valleys without losing anyone.

Comment from Priscilla at the 2006 orphan reunion:

"Although we were hungry, our hearts were still sweet. We knew that Mama loved us."

19.

Escape from Prison Camp

The Old Temple Place and Peking 1943-1945

SHE WENT NOWHERE. She stayed in her bed at the Old Temple Place and tried to breathe carefully. Her head held two ideas only. All other thoughts were swallowed up by the fire in her back. First, she could not go to Peking. She could not even make it to the outhouse, much less the city. Second, she could not leave the children. God had plucked them from death and given them to her for care. She could not leave the children.

One afternoon she heard a commotion in the babies' room outside her bedroom door, and the next thing she knew, four Japanese officers were tramping into her room. Their stern faces seemed unreal and far away. One of them marched up to her bedside. "Happy Plum Flower," the officer demanded, "all British and American citizens have been ordered into the city. You are the only one missing. Why are you not in Peking with the other Americans?"

She slid her body to the edge of the bed and pulled herself carefully into a sitting position, wincing. "I cannot go to Peking," she said. Her voice sounded weak and whispery. "I have all these children to care for."

"Any *amah* [household servant] can take care of these children," the officer retorted.

Her mind went entirely blank for several seconds. Then she remembered. "But I am too sick to go anywhere," she explained reasonably. "I have a serious illness in my back. I cannot even walk from here to the front gate. I cannot go as far as Peking."

"You must go to the city," the officer repeated. "I will post a guard. As soon as you can walk, you must leave for Peking."

He stalked out, leaving two armed soldiers on duty at the door to her bedroom. There was nothing for Laura to do but lie quietly and pray.

Whenever the girls came in to empty her chamber pot or check on her, the soldiers pestered her to pack her belongings and start walking to the city. "The children are frightened," Pervading Peace told her when she brought her dinner. "They want to know why their mother is being guarded by soldiers with guns."

On Sunday, a group of Chinese policemen arrived to replace the Japanese guard. The head policeman, Officer Fu, came into Laura's bedroom and said in a kind tone, "Happy Plum Flower, I also am a Christian. I was very upset when I received this assignment because I wanted to be in church today. But now that I find myself in a Christian place after all, I am no longer disappointed. I am very happy to be here with your family."

Later Laura heard him talking to the children in the next room, encouraging them with passages from the Bible to trust the Lord and not be afraid. *What a surprise!* she thought. Surely God was working out His plan, some way, somehow.

Selma Nelson, a Scandinavian missionary with an official pass, came to the orphanage to help. After a few days, when Laura was well enough to walk carefully, Selma took over as acting director of Canaan Home. Officer Fu told Laura he would do whatever he could to help her wrangle permission to continue on at Canaan Home. He gave her several documents and told her to take them to the Japanese Embassy.

She was in too much pain to pedal her bicycle, so she pushed it seven miles to the West Gate. The Chinese policeman on duty actually turned white when she asked him to admit her to the city. "Why are you at liberty?" he asked. "All the Americans are supposed to be assembled for the trip to the North China Internment Center. You should be with them. I cannot give you permission to enter."

Laura felt sorry for him. If he did the wrong thing, he would be in trouble with the Japanese. He probably figured it was better to do nothing than do the wrong thing.

"Do you know Officer Fu?" she asked him.

"Yes," the policeman said.

"May I telephone him?" she asked.

The man reluctantly agreed. When she had tracked down Officer Fu by telephone, she handed the receiver to the worried policeman. Officer Fu assured him that it was proper to admit Laura into Peking with instructions to go directly to the Japanese Embassy. So he allowed Laura to limp through the gate pushing her bicycle. Each step sent a flash of fire from her back all the way to her toes.

The first official she went to see at the Japanese Embassy threw a temper tantrum. "You are late!" he shouted, pounding the desk with his fist. "Why haven't you obeyed orders? You should have come to Peking and had your papers in order a week ago!" He berated her soundly for several minutes, then ran down like an unwound clock. He seemed unsure what to do. Finally he told her to go see another official upstairs.

Climbing the stairs was agony. Laura found the best way to do it was to turn sideways facing the wall, grip the banister with both hands, and pull herself up one stair at a time. By the time she reached the door of the second official's office, she was shaking.

The second official was gracious. He asked her to be seated and questioned her kindly about her illness and her work with Canaan Home. Some of her strength returned as she rested in the chair. "I have no interest in politics," she told him. "Officer Fu will vouch for that. I am only interested in taking care of my children. May I have a pass to go in and out of the city so we can buy the family's rations?"

"If the Chinese authorities permit it, then I will get you a pass," he said.

Laura knew that the Chinese had no authority over such matters under Japanese rule. He must be trying to get rid of her without seeming to be rude to an elder.

"Aren't your people in charge?" she asked innocently. "Don't you have the last word in these things?"

What could he say—"No, we're not in charge?"

The officer regarded her thoughtfully. Finally he said, "If Officer Fu will vouch for you, you may apply for a pass. However, it will take 50 days to process the application, and you must remain within the city gates during that time."

One step at a time, she told herself after the interview as she stumbled along the street pushing her bicycle to the Presbyterian Mission compound. *One step at a time.*

Staying inside Peking for 50 days while the application was being processed seemed like an impossible condition to meet. Where would she stay? When the missionaries left for the concentration camp, which they were supposed to do any day now, the Japanese would take over all the compound residences. They would hardly allow an American enemy to continue staying there when so many Japanese civilians working in Peking factories needed housing. Asking her Chinese friends to allow her to stay with them was out of the question. To the trigger-happy Japanese soldiers, taking in an American meant taking in an enemy to their emperor. It could mean her friends' lives.

But, one step at a time. The first step was being allowed to apply for the pass, and the second step was being able to go to the Leynses' now—Day One of the 50-day process.

She spent the night with James and Mieps Leynse. Although James had recovered from typhoid fever, he remained in poor health. So the Japanese decided not to send him to the concentration camp in Weihsien, Shantung Province, with his sister and the other Presbyterian missionaries still in North China. Mieps was allowed to remain with James to take care of him, and the couple continued to stay in their residence on the compound, with Japanese soldiers on guard duty prowling through the rooms of their house day and night.

This made it possible for Laura to stay on at the Leynse residence after Orpha Gould and Laura's other friends departed for the concentration camp. Two of the missionaries each gave her a gift of $100 when they said good-bye. They told her she was to use the money for herself.

Their gift was enough to pay for an extended stay in a good hospital to find a better treatment than morphine injections for her back. Laura respected the medical staff at the German Hospital and thought they might be able to treat her. So she entered that hospital and spent the next three weeks receiving short-wave treatments and looking at pictures of Hitler posted all over the building.

And reflecting.

Step by step, God was providing a way for her to avoid the prison of internment camp. And step by step He would help her to avoid the prison of bitterness. Then she could forgive Kenneth not only with her will, but with all her heart.

The writer of Hebrews said that the way to avoid bitterness was to fix your eyes on Jesus. When she looked at Him, what did she see? Jesus, too, had been betrayed by someone close to Him. He, too, had been robbed. Laura's husband had violated two of her adopted daughters. God's own chosen people had tortured and killed God's only Son. "Father, forgive them, for they know not what they do," Jesus had prayed.

People had been cruel to Him, deliberately cruel. Yet, He seemed to be saying that even when people were being deliberately cruel, they didn't actually realize what they were doing. The spiritual realm, that great battleground of real good and real evil, was invisible to them. If they had really seen that cosmic reality, they would have been robbed of the ability to choose, too terrified to do anything, good or bad. It was the same with Kenneth: "Father, forgive him. He did not know what he was doing."

Through the lenses of her own pain, she was gaining a glimpse of the depth of suffering Jesus had endured. Whatever she suffered, He also had suffered. He understood, and He would help her through it.

When Laura left the hospital she felt weak and shaky, but her pain was gone.

Mieps and James Leynse welcomed her back. She rested in their home for a couple more weeks until they received a message early one morning saying that the Japanese were going to imprison them in the British

Embassy the next morning. They had 24 hours to prepare to leave.

Laura helped Mieps pack, praying silently. Only one week remained of the 50 days she must stay inside Peking while waiting for her pass to be approved. With the Leynse home closed to her now, she needed a place to stay during that time. She would also need a place to stay overnight for future trips into Peking for food rations and other supplies. Where could she go? What should she do? Through the night she prayed for a new refuge.

Pearl happened to be in Peking that night, too, home on a week-long holiday from her teaching job in Shanghai. She was unable to sleep. Finally, early in the morning, she slipped out of bed and crept out of the house. Her mother heard her and hobbled on bound feet into the courtyard, where Pearl was wheeling her bicycle out of the compound gate. "Pearl!" she exclaimed in astonishment. "Where are you going? It's six o'clock in the morning!"

"I couldn't sleep," Pearl said. "I have a feeling that Happy Plum Flower is in trouble. I'm going to the mission compound to see if she needs me."

"Then go!" her mother said. "Come tell me when you find out what is wrong."

At the Leynse residence, Laura explained the situation.

"You keep praying," Pearl told her. "I'll go talk to my mother."

The young woman hopped on her bike and pedaled away. In a few minutes she was back. "Mother said to tell you that you can stay in our single room," she announced.

"Oh, Pearl, I couldn't do that," Laura protested. "I would bring trouble to your family. You have Japanese living right next door to you! It's too dangerous."

"Honorable Lady Teacher Minister," Pearl said stoutly. "My mother said that you are God's servant. She said that if God protects you, He will protect us, too. If God wants you to stay in our house, no one can come near us."

Pearl saw tears rise suddenly in the American woman's eyes. "All right," she said. "I will come."

Laura gathered a few belongings and tied her family's flour sacks to her bicycle. As she and Pearl pedaled their way out of the compound, they saw two Japanese soldiers marching toward the Leynse home to demand the house key. Six Japanese families milled at the gate, waiting to move into the Leynse residence.

Pearl brought Laura into her home and introduced the frail-looking missionary to her mother. "Happy Plum Flower has been very ill," Pearl said. "I have never seen her skin so white or her cheeks so thin."

"Allow me to show you your room, Happy Plum Flower," Pearl's mother said. "You may rest there, and I will go to the kitchen to fix you a big, hot breakfast." Pearl's mother was a practical woman as well as a wealthy one.

"I will make sure Happy Plum Flower has a good, big meal here whenever she comes," she promised her daughter. "I know that whenever she takes food home, she doesn't eat it. She cuts it up in pieces for all the children. She needs good food to get well."

Laura was still weak when she returned to the Japanese Embassy a week later, finally reaching the end of her 50-day waiting period. The application process had been complicated, the red tape endless. If Officer Fu had not personally intervened, she would never have managed to get the pass approved.

And to think that she and Officer Fu had met only a few days before she started the application process. And that the only reason they met was because she had been so ill.

One step at a time.

At the embassy, the official who finalized approval of her pass told her that she would have to appear every 30 days before the head officer at the Japanese barracks halfway between Canaan Home and the city gate in order to have her pass renewed. Then, at last, he handed her the precious pass. Balancing the family's heavy sacks of flour on her rear fender, she made her way out of the city with the hard-won document in her hand. To her surprise, the Chinese guards at the city gate did not even glance at it.

• • •

It was a muggy day in late spring. The sun shone warmly through a dense thicket of fluffy clouds, shooting an occasional ray of pure light through the moving patches of blue in the sky above. Laura pedaled her bicycle slowly along the familiar road, stopping often to rest and to thank God for her freedom. The sun had dropped low in the west by the time she glimpsed the marble pagoda on Jade Fountain Hill. At sunset she reached the Old Temple Place.

There was a small hill in the front courtyard where the children liked to stand to see over the courtyard walls. Two boys were standing atop the hill and saw her first. "MAMA!" they screamed. "Mama came back!!"

Nine-year-old Samuel opened the gate and dashed to the back courtyard-yelling the news to the boys working in the garden. "Mama came back! Mama came back!" The older girls came pouring out of the girls' and babies' quarters. "Mama came back!" Little bodies collided into her, hugging and clinging. She tried to kiss each face, embrace each child. The kisses started tasting salty, and then she realized that she and the children were all crying. Her legs felt shaky.

She heard the voice of Pervading Peace say, "Your mama is very weak and tired. We must let her go to her room to rest."

Laura wobbled over to the girls' building, and a beaming Selma Nelson shook her hand warmly. But Laura could not bear to go for a rest until she had seen all her babies. She gazed at each one in his or her crib and then retired to her bedroom.

"Everybody is delighted that you are back," the old temple gardener told her the next day. "We knew the Japanese could never make you stay away. When the soldiers came, the neighbors all said, 'She wouldn't leave those children if an airplane came to get her!'"

Laura learned that Japanese people were especially fond of flowers. Flowers were rare in wartime Peking, but she had some in her garden. So 30 days later, she made a beautiful bouquet and presented it to the officer in charge of the Japanese barracks when she came for her pass renewal. He and his staff were delighted. So after that, as long as her flowers bloomed, she brought a bouquet each month along with her request for a pass renewal. The Japanese granted her requests routinely. Fortunately no one asked any questions about her husband, who was still, on paper, the official head of Canaan Home.

She struggled to manage the official paperwork with Silas, one of her boys, to help her fill out forms and write correspondence in Chinese characters. Always the threat hung over her head that the Japanese might discover that Kenneth was gone.

And always the struggle for food pressed in on the family. The boys labored in the garden, and while the family waited on the harvest (and later when they ran out of garden supplies and rations) they ate wild greens, wild vegetables, and tree leaves—anything edible they could find. After harvest the adults and older children ate the leaves and stems of sweet potatoes—food that was normally considered swine feed—saving the sweet potatoes themselves for the babies and the few disabled old men who lived with them.

In the midst of famine, Laura did not forget her imprisoned friends, the Leynses. As Dutch citizens, they were ineligible for Red Cross packages until late in the war. They had to hire a Chinese servant to sell their clothes and books and buy them food to eat, and James Leynse became weak with pernicious anemia. When Laura could, she brought ripe tomatoes into Peking and left them at the embassy gate for the Leynses and another prisoner, J. Leighton Stewart, president of Yenching University.

The wheat harvest of 1943 was a good one, but the Japanese confiscated it all. Wheat was not to be bought in Peking for any amount of silver. Instead of wheat, the military rationed deflated bean dregs for people to eat. Deflated bean dregs had formerly been used for fertilizer. All the millet flour and corn flour was adulterated with material like ground-up peanut shells. People tried to make their millet stretch by mixing it with sawdust before eating it. The most destitute peeled the bark off trees and ate it mixed with clay. By the end of that winter, the trees in and around Peking were stripped of bark. When Laura rode her bicycle into Peking to buy family rations, she saw dead bodies of people who had died of starvation.

Sometimes she found herself wondering how Kenneth was spending the money he had taken, and then anger would wash through her again like waves and she would find herself thinking things like Kenneth was the one who deserved to be lying there dead in that ditch....But no, she checked herself, she had told God she wanted to forgive, and she would forgive. *Forgive ME, Lord. I refuse to entertain these fantasies of revenge and I release these wrongs—all this suffering Kenneth has brought on us. I won't retaliate. I turn this over to You to right the wrong. And I pray mercy for Kenneth.*

It seemed impossible that the family could stay alive that winter. All of Canaan Home's contributions from outside China had been cut off for two years. Except for Miss Nelson, none of the Western missionaries inside China who had once helped the orphanage could help them any more. They were all imprisoned or no longer in the country. Local Chinese were at risk of losing their lives and endangering their families if they were caught helping an American. How could Laura possibly get the clothing, food, and fuel she needed to keep over 100 children alive?

Yet, somehow, she managed.

Some of the missionaries who were in the concentration camp had given their furniture and other valuables to Chinese Christians before they were imprisoned. They instructed the believers to sell these goods if Canaan Home needed money. The believers did so, risking their lives to help, and these funds helped the family survive the winter of 1943-1944.

Through the fall and winter, Laura continued to pray for the ability to let go of her grievances as she worked through her anger and pain. By spring a settled forgiveness had birthed in her heart, and with it, a deep concern for Kenneth's soul.

She was still surprised, though, when he came back. More than two years after she sent him away, Kenneth appeared one day at the gate, as broad-shouldered and handsome as ever, but looking a little anxious now, his dark eyes appealing. He brought with him a big package full of bamboo bowls as a gift for the children.

He was frank and earnest. It turned out that he had not been a big man in Anhui after all, even through he had returned to his poor home town as a major property owner. The people there said he had brought shame on them by marrying an American. They snubbed him. His conscience bothered him, too, fretting him through the day, invading his dreams at night. He was going to sell his house and fields, he told Laura. God had revealed to him that he should return to the family to ask for forgiveness and reconciliation.

Laura said she would send for a Chinese pastor to discuss it.

She had to admit she was glad to see him again. But reconciliation was easier said than done. Obviously, coming back this way was a hard thing for Kenneth to do. God must be convicting him of his sin against the family, and he appeared to be responding. She had a responsibility to encourage that process. Yet she could not allow him to move into the family and come back into contact with the girls as if nothing had happened.

Reconciliation required forgiveness first, and she *had* forgiven. She had faced up to the wrong and what it cost her, she had owned up to her anger and pain, she had mourned her losses and willed to forgive it all. She had repented of her own sin. She had opened her heart and received from God the ability to let go of her grievance and turn the matters of understanding and justice over to Him.

But reconciliation also required repentance on Kenneth's part, and real repentance was a lot like real forgiveness. It meant you faced and admitted the sin, not minimizing or excusing it, not denying it or pretending it hadn't happened, not glossing over it, but dealing with it directly and turning away from it decisively. Like real forgiveness, real repentance could take time.

For Kenneth to come back this way...he must still love God, he must still love her, he must still care for the children...but she had to think about what was right and best for the whole family. Maybe God was pushing Kenneth to return at this time because she could no longer hide his absence from the Japanese, because his physical presence was an absolute necessity. Always, it seemed, political questions ruled the family dilemmas.

The Chinese pastor came and talked with both of them. And in the end, Laura decided to take Kenneth back, but with safeguards in place. Sadly, she arranged for all six of the oldest girls to move to an orphanage in Tientsin. Then she used precious orphanage funds to hire a man to be doorkeeper for the east campus door, with one of the older boys helping him. Kenneth was no longer allowed to move freely from the boys' to the girls' side of the orphanage.

Telling the children exactly what Kenneth had done would create new and unnecessary hurt, she felt. Only her scribe Silas knew about the money—but not about his sisters—and he was a close-mouthed boy who confided in his journal instead of the other boys. Providing details would do more harm than good, and anyway, the children would be unable to understand those details within the big picture of wartime politics. Still, she could not let their father simply return home after an absence of more than two years with no explanation to the family.

She held a meeting with the Chinese pastor and the children. Simply she explained that Papa Nieh had done bad things, but now he was sorry and he wanted to come back to the family. Would they forgive him and let him return?

Of course they said yes.

Laura was still unsure that Kenneth had honestly faced the gravity of what he had done. She set out to explain, to teach him from the Bible. Every night he came to her room to pray and repent, then returned to the boys' dormitory. At that time she did not realize that a wife cannot be her own husband's marriage counselor.

The famine dragged on. There were even more dead bodies lying about now, and the family continued to have to stretch their rations with leaves and wild edibles. They used up the funds from the sale of the missionaries' furniture and other valuables.

When every source of supply seemed to have dried up, a businessman from Tientsin stopped by at the family's front gate, curious to know why there were so many children coming and going in the courtyard of the old Lama temple. The Niehs gave him a tour of the property, answered his questions, and told him the story of Canaan Home. Several days later the man returned with a couple other businessmen. After they had all toured the orphanage and asked a number of questions, the men conferred together and then promised the Niehs that they would begin sending coal, food, and other supplies regularly.

They kept their word, and, because of their help, Canaan Home survived the winter of 1944–1945. By that time, inflation had driven Adolf's wages up to $600 a month, compared to $20 a month in prewar prices. Inflation and scarcity combined had driven prices so high that an egg cost $5, a loaf of bread was $15, and a ton of coal cost $750 in Chinese currency.

By that time, too, Pearl's parents had joined their daughter in Shanghai where it was easier for them to obtain food. Pearl's grandfather arranged for Laura to stay with a relative so that Laura would continue to have a place to stay overnight when she went into Peking for the family's rations.

The piercing cold of winter gave way to the dust storms of spring. Specks of emerald appeared along the branches of the trees, and the boys set to work preparing soil and planting a new garden.

The Niehs had no radio, and the Japanese military strictly censored the news. So they were unaware when Allied forces entered Germany on two fronts that spring of 1945, or when Adolf Hitler committed suicide and Germany unconditionally surrendered.

In Europe, the Second World War came to an end, but at Canaan Home in occupied North China, life continued as usual. Every morning Laura gathered the family for morning prayer. Then the children worked. Laura and Kenneth continued to eat at least one meal a day together, and Laura still woke through the night to help take care of the babies, the sick, and the handicapped children. On Sundays the family still set aside all work except the most necessary tasks. They spent extra time in worship and Bible lessons. Every 30 days Laura gathered a bouquet of flowers from the garden to give to the Japanese officer who renewed her pass. Regularly she rode her bicycle into Peking for rations.

Then, one summer day, the faraway events of World War II finally broke in on the Canaan Home routine. It was a fine Sunday morning, August 19, 1945. The children were outside playing in the yard when they heard airplanes whining overhead, too high to be seen. One of Peking's two major airfields was located behind the orphanage grounds, so the children were used to hearing Japanese bombers. But these planes sounded different to them. The pitch was higher, more cheerful sounding.

The children stopped their play and listened intently. "Americans!" they shouted suddenly. "The Americans are coming! The Americans are coming!"

The planes flew lower, circling the airfield. Then specks of black began dropping from the planes. As the specks descended, they turned into seven floating blossoms of pink, blue, and white. Down, down they dropped through the sky, and tiny figures could be seen dangling and swaying from their billowing brightness. They drifted so close to the orphanage grounds that it almost seemed like they were putting on a show just for the benefit of the children. Finally they landed in the airfield.

A young Chinese man ran over to their front gate then and announced that the war was over. The Americans had wiped out two major Japanese cities two weeks before, he said, destroying each with a single, new kind of bomb. Japan was unable to retaliate or defend herself from such power. The Japanese emperor had surrendered.

So the United States had defeated Japan, and now American Marines were parachuting into Peking to free the Westerners being held prisoner at the British Embassy. The Leynses should soon be free. Canaan Home's isolation from the rest of the world was ended.

Wartime Reports

Laura's untitled memoirs describing her stay with the Leynses in 1943:

While it was indeed a very serious time for all of us, still there were times when we laughed heartily. One afternoon when I was about to enter the sitting room at the Presbyterian Mission, there I saw a Japanese soldier sitting before the fireplace, his shoes off and his stockings hanging up to dry.

Another time, when I was holding a skein of yarn to be made into a ball, a Japanese soldier walked in and took the yarn from my hands, placing it in the right position on his own hands. Then one evening, one of the soldiers came in, and taking a lady's hat off the rack, tried it on his head. He then turned his head this way and that to see how beautiful he looked. He may have been laughing at us since the Japanese ladies did not wear hats. He did so many funny things and would appear suddenly as from nowhere. We called him George the Spy.

This happened just before all of these mission friends went to internment camp.

Excerpts from Zechariah's 1989 and 2001 memoirs, translated from Chinese:

During World War II, people were dying. You could see dead bodies lying anywhere. With famine, pestilence, and the brutality of the Japanese, it seemed that death had opened its mouth to swallow all that it could find. Many times during these years, the home had no food for more than five days. We lived on wild herbs, tree leaves, and whatever we could get. Mama ate the same food with us. Before we ate, we always sang a hymn of thanksgiving and praise. "We thank our Heavenly Father for protecting us..." Then we would start eating. Many children swallowed half of their food before Mama started. She shared her food with them. We really didn't understand Mama's heart.

Our neighbors knew about the difficulties of the orphanage, but they couldn't help. Their own situation was no better. We heard them saying, "Those children and their American mother will starve to death in a day or two." Yet on the brink of death, it seemed as if the living water would flow out of the rock. Someone brought us cornmeal and potatoes. We survived. We experienced this kind of situation many times. Winter would be worse, with the famine and the cold. Some of the children cried, shivering with cold. It pierced Mama's heart. Then a miracle happened. Camels loaded with coal came to the home. We didn't know who sent them.

"We went through fire and water, but He brought us to a place of abundance." In 1945, the Japanese surrendered and that ended World War II. Great changes took place in Canaan Home. Wheat flour, milk powder, clothes, and canned food all came to the Home. Things we had never dreamed of, things we had never seen before and could not even name, all came to the Home. "The Lord's name is to be praised" was a truth deeply imprinted in my heart.

Miss Richards always paid a lot of attention to the children's moral education. She taught the children to believe from their heart, recognize Jesus, confess their sin, repent and be reborn, and believe Jesus. She used this as the moral standard for being a good person. In this area, there was a good result. The children really learned from her and believed Jesus. Usually she taught the children by combining words and personal example. She asked the children to love each other and to especially take care of those weaker.

Besides that, Miss Richards also paid particular attention to teaching children to love work while they were still young. She taught them to do whatever they could by themselves. So after she had founded the orphanage 20 years, the children who had grown up could do all the routine work by themselves. The older children took care of the younger, and the stronger took care of the weaker. They lived like a big family.

20.

The Marines

The Old Temple Place, 1945

A couple days later, two tall American Marines sauntered curiously up to the orphanage gate, apparently intrigued by all the children they saw in the yard. Laura came to the gatehouse to meet them, her long hair braided and wrapped about her head in a neat crown of mingled gray and brown. "Good morning," she greeted them pleasantly in her soft Midwestern twang. "How are you today?"

Both men's mouths dropped open at the same time, as if they had rehearsed it. "An American!" one of them exclaimed. "What are you doing here?"

"Taking care of my children," Laura said. "Come inside, and welcome to Canaan Home."

The three Americans had plenty to talk about. The Marines brought Laura up to date on the most important events of the wars in Europe and Asia. One of them also said he had met James and Mieps Leynse two days before at the British Embassy. He said James had insisted on visiting the Presbyterian Mission compound to ring the bells of the mission chapel. Her friend was weak and ill, but exuberant. News of his release had spread quickly, and crowds of Chinese had flocked to the compound to greet him and rejoice. Japanese civilians and military dependents were still living in the houses on the compound, so the Leynses and other Embassy prisoners were remaining at the British Embassy temporarily. The men told her that her friends at the concentration camp in Weihsien would have to remain there also until things settled down. The Japanese army had not yet been disarmed or formally surrendered the city.

The two men were incredulous when they learned that Laura had never set foot in an internment camp throughout the war. As far as she knew, she had been the only American officially at liberty in North China.

She walked the Marines to the front gate and watched them stride away. A pleasant mix of emotions flooded through her—joy, relief, hope.

The Marines' rescue and the good news they brought from the world beyond did not mean the famine had ended. Food was still scarce. Inflation still wiped out the value of the family's meager funds overnight. The Chinese church was still ravaged by starvation, disease, and political oppression. Contributions from overseas were still cut off. Their missionary friends were still in prison camp. The students who had volunteered their services to Canaan Home during their vacations were still far away in the mountains near Tibet. In short, both their support and their support systems were still under siege. But the coming of the Marines meant that the siege was lifting. The beginning of the end was here.

The family had much for which to be thankful. During these famine years, when thousands of people had died of starvation or rampant epidemics, and when wealthy families like Pearl's had moved away to get enough food, poverty-stricken Canaan Home had not lost one child to hunger or disease. None of the children had become seriously ill either. Douw Hospital's services under Japanese administration had been unnecessary.

Still, the children were badly undernourished. They needed a careful program of nutrition and plenty of good food to bring them back to full good health. The family had suffered a famine of mind and spirit as well. For two years there had been no school and no academic progress.

Spiritually they had missed the ministry of the church, too. Before Pearl Harbor, Christian volunteers had helped give daily Bible lessons, teach Sunday School, and plan special weeks of concentrated spiritual training and challenge. After Pearl Harbor, Laura had managed to prevent the children from being exposed to the false religious teachings of Shintoism. But she had been so absorbed in the tasks of day-to-day survival that she had been unable to give much energy to the children's spiritual training. The family needed a fresh touch from God.

Lord, You know the children need food—food for body, mind, and spirit, Laura prayed. *Send us what we need! Most of all, send us Your Holy Spirit to come and be our teacher.*

The world war in Europe and Asia may have ended, but the civil war in China merely moved on to another phase. As soon as the Americans defeated their common enemy Japan, the Kuomintang and the Communists dropped their wartime truce and began maneuvering openly for control of all China.

Most of Chiang Kai Shek's Kuomintang troops were in southern China when the Japanese surrendered, while most of Mao Tse Tung's Communist troops were in the north. The Communists had grown strong in numbers and expertise during their eight-year guerrilla war with Japan. Communist troops who had been camping in the Western Hills now moved their camp to Peking's West Gate and demanded that the Japanese army turn the city over to them.

The Japanese refused. Only the Kuomintang had the authority to disarm them, they insisted. The Kuomintang, however, were unable to transport troops into Peking to handle the takeover. The Communists controlled the northern railway lines and surrounded both Peking airfields. They refused to allow Kuomintang troops to land on the airfields or travel through North China by train.

So August passed and then September, with the situation in stalemate. Finally, on October 7, a contingent of American Marines in Jeeps thundered through the gates into Peking and disarmed the Japanese. Three days later, in a colorful ceremony held in the great courtyard of the Forbidden City, the United States formally released China from the Japanese invaders. Kuomintang troops moved into Peking, backed by U.S. Marines. The Communists dismantled their camp and moved back into the villages of the Western Hills.

When James and Mieps Leynse visited the Presbyterian Mission compound, they found their former home a filthy shambles. The house had been turned into a makeshift apartment for Japanese military dependents, with one family to a room. Each household had set up a chimney-less stove on the floor for cooking. They had stuck their stovepipes through windows and stored coal against the walls. They had also pulled the cupboards off the walls and broken them up for kindling, removed bathtubs, wrenched off water taps, flooded ceilings, and pulled down electrical wiring. A refuse heap four feet high lay at the back door of the Leynses' house. Almost every tree on the grounds had been chopped down and burned for fuel.

The mission's church buildings and schools were basically undamaged, but Douw Memorial Hospital had been plundered. No equipment or supplies remained in the dispensary, the operating room had been stripped, and scarcely a bed, bathtub, or wash basin remained in the building.

U.S. troops supervised the task of returning thousands of Japanese troops and civilians to Japan. Businessmen, missionaries, diplomats, and other Westerners returned from internment camp. Some, like Orpha Gould, stayed on in North China. Others, like the Leynses, returned home. Dr. Henke came back on the first Liberty ship allowed into North China. He moved into the Leynses' former residence with several Chinese co-workers and re-opened Douw Hospital.

Throughout China, inflation spiraled out of control. Peking regressed to a barter economy, and the Niehs wondered what to do. The family had nothing to trade on the market for food, and even the poor-quality food supplies they had were almost gone.

Then one day, late in the fall, Frederick Pyke, a Methodist missionary friend who had just returned from concentration camp, brought U.S. Navy chaplain Harold Flood to visit Canaan Home. The chaplain began trucking groups of Marines out to visit Canaan Home on Sunday afternoons to play with the children. Each time they came, the Marines brought big tins of candy and gifts of money—not worthless Chinese currency, but American dollars, as good as gold in the Peking marketplace.

In December, Chaplain Flood brought a group of men out to give Canaan Home a large offering that the Marines had collected especially for the children's Christmas celebration. "We'll leave the party details to you," Chaplain Flood told Laura, "but we want you to use all the money for a big banquet and Christmas presents for everybody."

Laura counted the money incredulously. "I can't spend all this money on food for just one day," she protested. "Even with gifts for every child, it's far more than enough. Couldn't I use some of it for millet and coal?"

"But we wanted it all to go for the party," the men said. "Buy lots of food. Make it special. Make it the best meal the kids have ever eaten."

"You'll kill them with kindness," Laura said. "Their stomachs are still recovering from the famine."

Finally the men agreed to let the family spend part of the money for a good supply of grain, coal, and other supplies.

On Christmas Day, two truckloads of Marines drove out to the orphanage, with Chaplain Flood leading the way in his Jeep. The children sang a grace before the meal, and then ate until their stomachs could hold no more. At the end of the feast, the staff stood on one side of the room laughing at the Marines, who circled the tables with big grins on their faces, patting the children's tightly rounded tummies. "Oboy," they said, as they rubbed each firm little belly. "Oboy! Oboy!"

Then the children opened their presents, and the men helped them try out all the new toys and games.

The evening ended with a carol sing. The Americans sang the old familiar songs in English, and the children responded to each carol by singing it in Chinese. Then a throng of 100 children followed the men out to the gate, waving good-bye and singing a song of thanks as their visitors drove away.

The Marines continued to come often throughout the winter and early spring of 1946, bringing tins of candy and toys along with gifts of money. The young men shed their military manners and dove back into childhood. It was hard to say who had more fun, the children or the Marines.

Laura thanked God fervently for the Marines' generosity, and the children's condition improved with better food. Still, Laura continued to long for spiritual breakthrough. *"Send Your Holy Spirit now to come and be our teacher,"* she often prayed. *"Let His cleansing power come and be in our midst."*

One morning, she settled a group of twelve boys aged seven through ten in a group to look at a series of prints illustrating Bible stories painted by the old Dutch masters, a gift to the children from James and Mieps Leynse. Winter was beginning to merge into spring, so the day was cold, but not bitter. The boys pressed together in a cozy huddle, thrusting their cold hands up the sleeves of their padded jackets for warmth.

After reviewing some of their favorite prints, Laura reminded the boys what she had been teaching them: that when our first parents sinned, their sin brought death, and human nature became twisted so that now we all sin. We take advantage of other people, we steal and we lie and we do other bad things. We insist on having our own way even if it hurts somebody else. God is holy, and we cannot live in His presence in this sin condition. Then Laura showed the boys Rembrandt's painting of Jesus hanging on a cross flanked by two thieves, with radiance streaming down from a cavernous sky like a spotlight. Jesus died on a cross and rose from the dead, she taught the boys, in order to overcome the power of sin and death and give them the gift of eternal life with God in Heaven forever.

"Our Heavenly Father longs to have you live with Him in the Heavenly Home," she told them, "but to receive this gift, you must believe from your heart, repent of your sins, and choose to accept this gift of His salvation."

Eight-year-old Solomon listened intently. "Is it really possible for boys like us to be saved?" he asked wistfully.

"Of course!" Laura said. "Of course it is possible for little boys just like you to be saved."

Solomon's face broke out in a smile of delight. "Ezra! Titus! Gate of Righteousness! All of us, come on!" he urged his brothers. "Let's be saved, just like Mama said."

"I can't, I can't!" Gate of Righteousness cried.

"Why can't you?" Solomon asked.

"I've been too bad," Gate of Righteousness said. "I've sinned too much."

Solomon and five of his brothers pressed up close to Laura and asked her to pray with them so they could give themselves to Jesus. But all the time Gate of Righteousness hung back, whispering, "I can't! I can't!"

The half-dozen boys who prayed with Laura changed after that. Laura noticed a distinct improvement in their attitudes and behavior. Apparently, their brothers noticed the difference, too.

One week later when Laura returned from a trip to Peking, nine-year-old Simon ran to her and announced, "All the boys want to be saved!"

Oh those mischievous boys! she thought. *What are they up to this time?*

Above: *Canaan Home orphans skipping rope at a 1945 Christmas celebration with some of the American Marines who liberated Peking. Under the direction of Chaplain Harold Flood, the Marines made many visits to the orphanage from the fall of 1945 through the spring of 1946. They loved to play with the children, and their generous donations made it possible for the Niehs to buy desperately needed food and supplies.*

Opposite page: *Chaplain Harold Flood's note on the back of this photograph reads: "Protestant orphanage—Children are standing at their tables eating their Christmas Dinner. Mrs. Nieh (who is in charge of the orphanage) is standing in front of me..." Chaplain Flood remained in contact with Laura for the rest of her life and supplied written memoirs for this book.*

Liberation Reports

Rachel's memoir, translated from Chinese:

One Christmas, a lot of American soldiers came. They gave us each a gift. They spent Christmas together with us and we sang songs and prayed, and we had a wonderful time. We saw that each of these American soldiers had a small Bible with them. I felt strange. I thought, They believe God. Why do they fight in a war? Because I thought that God didn't like fighting in wars and those who believe God shouldn't fight each other. They spent a half-day with us. Mama seemed very happy, and we were all very happy, too.

Letter from Florence Logan, Nov. 8, 1946, returning to Peking after the war:

Jessie Mae (Henke) and everybody had waited for dinner until we got there. Laura Richards was there too and it was grand to see her looking well. There seem to be a lot of very high-class people helping her now. Later saw Mr. Nieh. He is really a handsome man and seems to be as good as he is good-looking.

Letter from Laura to U.S. friends, January, 1947:

So you see the Canaan Children's Home has come through the war as a living testimony to God's faithfulness and miracle-working power. May these little lives thus marvelously preserved be very precious and useful in the Lord's sight in the days to come.

21.

The Teacher Comes

The Old Temple Place and the Dowager's Boathouse, 1946

"WHY DO YOU THINK all the boys want to be saved, Simon?" Laura asked. She was sure he was teasing her.

"Ezra has been crying like a fountain," Simon explained. "He cried so much he couldn't eat his dinner. He took back a washcloth he stole from the girls and asked them to forgive him. Now all the boys want to come to your room to talk to you."

Laura eyed the boy thoughtfully. "First I need to take these supplies to the kitchen," she said. "Then I will go to my room, and you may tell Ezra to meet me there."

She deposited the food supplies in the kitchen and then wheeled her bicycle across the lane to her room in the girls' section of the orphanage grounds. The drooping figure of a ten-year-old boy in padded pants and a jacket awaited her. "When may we come to your room, Mama?" Ezra asked, wiping red, swollen eyes. He licked a tear off his upper lip.

Before Laura had time to reply, a throng of little boys appeared from nowhere and crowded into the open door of her room. They threw themselves down on the floor and began sobbing out child confessions of their sins. *This is no prank,* Laura thought in astonishment. *I know they've never seen anything of this kind before. They can't be making a play of repentance.*

Laura stood dumbstruck in the middle of the room for several minutes, with the boys sobbing all about her. Finally she knelt by Zechariah, the boy nearest to her, and asked him gently, "Don't you think the Lord has heard you now? You have asked Him to forgive you. Don't you think He has forgiven?"

She knelt by each boy in turn. The room gradually grew quiet until all the boys had risen and were standing on their feet, drying their eyes on the backs of their sleeves and the fronts of their jackets.

"Why have you all suddenly become so concerned with your sins?" she asked.

"It was because of the boys who became Christians last week," they told her. "They changed so much we decided we wanted to become Christians, too."

A couple mornings later, Laura awakened to the sound of childish voices on the other side of the privacy curtain in her bedroom. She peeked around it. A half dozen five- and six-year-old girls in padded gowns knelt in a row on the hard concrete floor, trebling earnest prayers. Sarah was kneeling with them.

Sarah looked up. She was 16 now, a strikingly beautiful girl with an air of quiet competence. Her dark eyes gazed straight into Laura's puzzled amber ones, and she smiled. "They came to me last night, Mama," she explained, "and they asked me to wake them up in the morning to come pray. They want to be saved like the boys."

After that, the kindergarten girls showed up with Sarah for prayer every day. Sometimes they came quite early in the morning and woke Laura up to join them.

At dinnertime, Kenneth reported that he had discovered Noah in the gatehouse that morning, kneeling in prayer. The boy was reading his Bible faithfully, too, he said. Now Gate of Righteousness whistled and sang as he did his daily chores, and he began sharing with the family some praise songs he had composed. Gate of Righteousness had never made up music before.

Soon afterward during family prayer time, one of the oldest girls burst into tears. "Why darling, what is the matter?" Laura asked her. "Are you feeling ill?"

"No, Mama," she said through her tears. "Let me come up to your room to pray. I want to become a Christian now, too."

And so, as winter melted into spring and the spring dust storms gave way to the torrential rains of summer, the school-age children began turning their young lives over to the service of Jesus Christ. The Christians in Peking spread the news: "There is a revival among the children at Canaan Home!" they said.

Meantime, in the Western Hills and throughout the rural areas of North China, social war was breaking out. Sometimes it began with villagers who lynched hated informers, tax collectors, and village officials who had collaborated with the Japanese. Sometimes it started with large landowners who had run away to safer areas seven or eight years before, and who now returned and ordered their bodyguards to kill the peasants who had taken over their properties in their absence. At other times, when the Eighth Route Army left, war-weary peasants first welcomed the Kuomintang Army and then grew rebellious when the returning government overturned the Communists' tax, rent, and interest rate policies, badly needed social reforms that the poor had assumed were permanent.

While all this was going on, the family moved, in June 1946, from the Old Temple Building to another compound half a mile away at the Dowager's Boathouse. This new location with 200 buildings—more than large enough for Canaan Home—had originally been built by the Empress Dowager at the turn of the century when she restored the royal Summer Palace. The Dowager's Boathouse shared a wall with the Summer Palace. By using a ladder and peering through a broken-down part in this wall, the family could catch a glimpse of the Empress Dowager's fabled Marble Boat moored near the Bridge of Floating Hearts on the calm surface of Lake Kunming. Once a year, the older children enjoyed a field trip touring the arched bridges of the Summer Palace.

Originally the Empress built the Boathouse compound to house her military guard. During the Japanese occupation, it housed low-ranking Japanese officers and Chinese soldiers who collaborated with the Japanese. These soldiers vandalized the compound before abandoning it, hoping to make it unusable for Communist guerrillas. They stuffed the artesian well with peanut hulls, smashed windows, shattered all the chandeliers, and generally left the place a shambles, badly in need of extensive repair.

The Jade Fountain was also nearby. In the days before the 1911 Revolution, when China was still ruled by an emperor, the clear, sweet liquid from this pool produced the royal household's water supply. The emperor would drink no other water. His servants drove an oxcart 40 *li* (about 13 miles) from the Forbidden City to fetch it for him in great wooden containers. For the Niehs and their children, it was just across the yard. They could help themselves to a drink of the emperor's water any time.

A stream flowed from the Jade Fountain through the back courtyard of the Boathouse compound, providing the family with a clean, clear source of water for the boys to irrigate the vegetable garden and for 13-year-old Samuel to raise ducks for eggs and meat. The Qing Long Bridge spanned this stream at the back of the Summer Palace.

Several volunteer Christian workers moved into the new place with the family to help care for the children and re-open the school, and a woman evangelist began teaching the children daily Bible lessons.

The family's food supply continued to be a problem. Reverend Flood dropped off another generous offering from the Marines as a parting gift before he returned to the U.S. in the spring of 1946. But that money was used up by summer. Dr. Henke, now on an international relief committee, personally saw to it that the orphanage received supplies when any were available. Other friends helped, too. Unfortunately, though, the Kuomintang government was financing its military operations against the Communists with the printing press. This outpouring of newly printed currency was neither backed by tangible assets nor public confidence. So the rate of inflation soared, wiping out the value of whatever money the family received.

One day a large package of provisions from the Red Cross was delivered to the Boathouse. When the Niehs opened the package they found that, along with other supplies, it contained a big packet of cigarettes.

Cigarettes brought a high price on the Peking black market. If the family sold these cigarettes, they could make a lot of money to use to buy the food they needed. Laura and Kenneth decided that the cigarettes provided them with a good opportunity to teach the children that the ends do not justify the means for Christians and that believers must live out Christian principles under pressure. At their next family gathering, they showed the children the packet.

"Cigarettes contain a harmful drug that poisons a person's body," Kenneth told them. "People become addicted to this drug when they start smoking, and they will pay a lot of money on the black market for cigarettes. But God doesn't want us to hurt our bodies, so we are going to burn this packet rather than poison someone else with this drug."

Then he and the older boys burned the cigarettes at the back of the compound.

A few days later a check came in the mail for the exact amount of money the family would have received if they had sold the cigarettes on the black market. When their neighbors heard about the incident, word spread through the surrounding villages. The story of Canaan Home's cigarettes was even published in the daily news.

Too soon, though, the large sum the Niehs received after burning the cigarettes was swallowed up by stampeding inflation, combined with the sheer volume of food needed to fill the stomachs of 115 growing children.

Then one day in July, a man named Mr. Raetz showed up at the orphanage gate. "I am from the China Children's Fund," he told Laura, "and I wonder if you would tell me about the work you are doing here?" So Laura gave him a tour of Canaan Home, beginning with the dormitories and schoolrooms.

Like most Western visitors, Mr. Raetz seemed flabbergasted when he saw the stark, bare rooms of Canaan Home, the dearth of equipment, and the severity of some of the children's congenital deformities and handicaps. "How did you manage to keep children like these alive through the war?" he asked Laura. In his eyes she could also see the question he was too polite to ask. *And how can an American woman choose to live in such poverty?*

"I am rich," she said, smiling. "I am rich in children and rich in the goodness of the Lord."

The children's clothes might be patched and worn, but the children themselves appeared cheerful and neat. Even though the orphanage rooms seemed barren and poor, they were either very clean or in the process of being cleaned by youngsters wielding brooms and mops. Everywhere Laura took Mr. Raetz, children were studying, working, or tending to other children younger than themselves.

In the kitchen, Laura introduced Mr. Raetz to a group of boys steaming cornbread on a cumbersome brick stove. When Laura and her guest left the kitchen, a series of sharp reports sounded from the back of the compound. Mr. Raetz looked around uneasily. "Isn't that gunfire?" he asked.

"Yes," Laura said. "It sounds like a little skirmish at the airport behind us."

The U.S. had assigned General George C. Marshall to attempt to persuade the Kuomintang government and the Communists to work out a compromise agreement. But at the same time peace talks were in progress, the U.S. was continuing to provide extensive military and financial aid to the Kuomintang. This embittered the Communists and encouraged the Kuomintang to hope that they could get what they wanted if they just hung on long enough. Neither side trusted the other, but Chang Kai Shek and Mao Tse Tung both knew that the Chinese people were sick of war and wanted peace. They had to go through the motions of peace negotiations or the people would turn against them.

An uneasy truce now prevailed in the Peking area due to the presence of U.S. troops during the peace talks. As arbitration dragged on, though, sniping incidents and skirmishes increased in the countryside. Canaan Home existed in a civil war zone full of Kuomintang soldiers and tough, confident Communist guerillas.

Laura gave her guest a tour of the Boathouse grounds, beginning at the back courtyard where the boys had planted the family's vegetable garden near the stream flowing from the Jade Fountain. It was a sunny day, and a group of six girls were taking advantage of the good weather to wash the family laundry in the stream and lay the clothes out on the grass to dry. Esther, now a tall, straight-backed 12-year-old, was the center of her sisters' attention, as usual. Her broad face lit with glee. As they worked, the girls were giggling over some story Esther was telling them in lilting Mandarin. They sounded like a flock of birds twittering.

Laura introduced Mr. Raetz to the six girls. "This young lady must be your natural daughter," he said when Laura introduced Rachel. "She looks so much like you, Mrs. Nieh."

"That's what everyone says," Laura agreed with a broad smile. "But nevertheless, she is my adopted daughter, just like these other girls. She and her twin sister Rose Mary were among the very first children who came to Canaan Home."

Mr. Raetz strolled over to inspect the family's luxuriant tomato patch. "This is quite a place," he said. "You certainly have accomplished a great deal with very little, and I know you will manage funds well. The China Children's Fund will take responsibility for 100 of your orphans."

Laura was so shocked that she hardly maintained enough presence of mind to thank him and escort him to the gate. She rushed to find Kenneth. "It's as if he dropped from Heaven," she said.

With that burden rolled from Laura's shoulders, she could concentrate her full attention on overseeing her huge household and school and also on checking to see that the older children in apprenticeships were doing their duty and being treated fairly.

By the fall of 1946, 60 of the older children were either self-supporting or preparing to become so through apprenticeships or further studies. Two boys were truck drivers, several others worked in offices or factories, a number of the older girls were nurses, the deaf and blind children were enrolled in special schools for the handicapped, and one young man was an engineering student at Yenching University. The older children who earned money delighted to come home for visits laden with gifts and treats for their younger brothers and sisters.

Those living in the city reported that Peking was jammed with refugees fleeing from the fighting in the countryside. The Presbyterian mission had opened a soup kitchen and refuge for the homeless in a Confucian temple four blocks from the mission compound. It was completely packed. Each family spread a quilt on the floor, and that was all the space they had. Dr.

Henke's wife Jessie Mae, who returned to Peking with her children in September of 1946, told Laura that her family could no longer picnic in city parks. The parks were so crowded with hungry refugees that opening a food basket would cause a riot.

Conditions worsened as autumn gave way to winter. In January 1947, General Marshall left China, denouncing both sides in the negotiations. Civil war was inevitable, and by March all pretense of peace talks ended. U.S. troops remained in Peking, however, for several more months.

The Kuomintang captured several of the boys who were living on their own and forcibly conscripted them into the army. One young man managed to escape capture by clambering out a window and running off. Conscripts who ran away after capture were beaten when caught, and they could be shot as deserters. The Kuomintang army was so hungry for conscripts that they even came to Canaan Home to draft two young men, one crippled and the other with mental retardation. Laura had been unwilling to send these two older boys to live outside the orphanage because she was afraid people would take advantage of them. The army quickly released the crippled man because he was too disabled to fight. The family never heard from the other young man again.

In contrast to the Kuomintang's strong-armed recruiting tactics, the Red Army swelled with volunteers. The Communists turned the territories they acquired into "Liberated Areas" where they promised liberation from the woe and wickedness of the old social order. They made good on the promise by taking land from landlords and redistributing it to former tenants. In gratitude, many of the poor peasants who received plots of land donated a son to the People's Liberation Army. From June 1946 to June 1948, 1.6 million men joined the Red Army from Manchuria, where the Communists redistributed land earliest and most completely.

The People's Liberation Army brought actors, actresses, and teachers to the villages for political education and agronomists for agrarian reform. The Communists were good listeners when it came to local gossip. They were adept not only at gaining information about enemy movements but also about which villagers had been victimized, which families had been evicted by landlords, which women were mistreated by their mothers-in-law, which tenants owed the most taxes. They used this information to recruit soldiers, develop popular social and political policies, and establish groups such as a Women's Association or a Poor Peasants' Association.

For centuries the poor had suffered in silence. "A poor man has no right to speak," was an old saying from Shansi province. The People's Liberation Army untied the tongues of the poor, training them in rudimentary democratic gatherings of village assemblies and poor peasant associations. They aroused and solidified the villagers' class consciousness by setting up "Speak Bitterness" meetings, where one by one the villagers poured out bitter-water stories and related their woes to their social status as peasants. The rest of the village repeated the complaints in chorus, then plotted and carried out vengeance en masse. The stored-up hatred of years overflowed. Soldiers paraded guilty landlords from town to town, and villagers armed with pickaxes, pitchforks, and shears hacked them into little pieces along the way. Some terrified landowners reacted with counter-terrorism, murdering rebellious tenants. Sometimes they ordered their men to bury entire tenant families alive. This only hastened the day of their destruction.

While this avalanche was crashing down on the heads of landlords in the Liberated Areas, China's economic situation continued to careen out of control. The value of paper money people received as wages plummeted. People felt they were being robbed, but the Kuomintang government dealt with dissatisfaction by forbidding dissent. People who complained either disappeared or landed in jail, accused of being secret Communist agents.

Secret Communist workers did in fact infiltrate the city, mingling among ordinary people as rickshaw drivers, vendors, factory workers, and minor officials. They stirred up discontent while they waited for their soldier comrades to defeat the Kuomintang army in control of the city. It was Mao Tse Tung's plan to defeat Chiang Kai Shek and then place thousands of dedicated intellectuals in administrative positions in every Chinese city, town, and village to ensure complete Communist control throughout China. To prepare for this future takeover, trained Communist students organized cells in all the colleges and universities. There they battled pro-government students and encouraged dissatisfaction with school administrators and government officials. They led protests, organized strikes, and tried to penetrate every organization on campus, including Christian groups.

Micah, a Canaan Home orphan who was studying engineering at Yenching University, told the Niehs, "There is so much political pressure from Communist and pro-government students that it is almost impossible not to get involved in the political situation, one way or another."

Micah joined an enthusiastic new Christian organization on campus, the Peking Christian Student Fellowship, which was part of China Inter-Varsity Fellowship (CIVF). The group had been born the summer of 1945 during a revival among university students in the wartime capitol of Chunking. These were students who had fled to Szechwan province for safety during the occupation. When they returned to their home provinces, they spread the revival rapidly to universities and colleges throughout China.

The Niehs' good friend Wang Ming Dao spiritually nurtured the fledgling fellowship in Peking. When the group needed a place to hold a ten-day summer prayer conference, he asked the Niehs to let them use the orphanage complex at the Dowager's Boathouse. With 200 buildings on the property, there was plenty of extra space for all the students.

Wang Ming Dao was the pastor of the Peking Christian Tabernacle. He was a slightly built, scholarly looking man who was known throughout China partly for his prolific writings, but even more for his courage during the Japanese occupation. He had risked his life by refusing Japanese orders to print Japanese slogans in his quarterly publication, put up a picture of the Japanese emperor in his church, and join the Japanese-sponsored North China Church Union. He was in high demand as a speaker in church services and conferences all over China.

The students' summer prayer conference was a big event for the Canaan Home family, who sat on the grass every night with the students and listened to the preaching. The air was sweltering and heavy, and throngs of mosquitoes whined and swarmed above the crowd. Wang Ming Dao was one of the speakers.

"All readers of the Old Testament are familiar with the story of David and

Goliath," he began the first night, pushing his round-rimmed spectacles onto his nose. "Goliath was the champion of the Philistines, and he was feared by the whole army of Israel. Yet David killed Goliath, and so delivered the people of Israel from the Philistines."

The pastor brushed a stinging insect from his forehead with an air of preoccupation and looked straight into the eyes of the students seated on the grass before him. "He did it with one small stone," he said, slowly and emphatically.

"Strange! Truly strange! The potentiality of one small stone," he said, "was so vast that it could achieve deliverance for all the people of Israel."

Laura sat near the back of the crowd with big-headed Tabitha snuggled in her lap. Her good friend Wang Jing-wun, the pastor's wife, sat next to her, keeping her eyes fixed on her husband's slim, gowned form behind the podium.

"In effecting this deliverance, God needed only one small stone to kill the champion—the fierce champion from whom everybody fled in fear," Wang Ming Dao said. "Similarly, when God effects deliverance today, He can use even the weakest of believers to achieve that which, without Him, is impossible even for an army."

The older children from Canaan Home as well as most of the members of the pastor's congregation were seated in the audience. Laura's eyes traveled over the orderly rows of seated children, slapping at mosquitoes while keeping their attention fixed on the speaker.

"The people around David were under the impression that only the use of the sword and spear and javelin could defeat a powerful enemy," Wang Ming Dao said. "But God made use of what man overlooked—a stone."

He paused. The stream murmured. Mosquitoes whined. Otherwise, all was quiet. Laura could see her children posed still as a photograph, drinking in the pastor's words.

"Nowadays," he went on, "there is a common impression that it is only people with learning and ability and position and wealth who can achieve anything great. But God uses believers who are foolish and weak and poor and lowly to do wonderful things for Him."

Tabitha's eyes had gradually closed as the preaching went on. Her giant head pressed heavily against Laura's shoulder, and she began to snore softly. Laura absently kissed the smooth jet crown of her head.

"In I Corinthians 1:27-29 the Word of God says, 'But God has chosen the foolish things of the world to put to shame the wise,'" Wang Ming Dao read, "'and God has chosen the weak things of the world to put to shame the things which are mighty; and the base things of the world and the things which are despised God has chosen, and the things which are not, to bring to nothing the things that are, that no flesh should glory in His presence.'

"God could do wonderful things like this in days of old," the pastor ended, "and He can do wonderful things today. He alone is worthy to be praised."

The fluting sopranos of Canaan Home's youngest singers blended sweetly with the vigorous voices of the university students in a closing hymn of praise. Laura could not sing over the lump in her throat. So she hugged the misshapen child on her lap and looked around her, surveying her large family with affection.

Here they are—the despised, the poor, the lowly, the weak, she thought. *They are the things that are not—not powerful, not connected, not regarded, not wanted. They are nothing in this world. Yet they can be smooth stones in the hand of God....*

After ten days, the conference ended with a flood of warm farewells from the students and members of the Peking Christian Tabernacle.

Canaan Home had many close ties to Wang Ming Dao's church. Two of the church deacons were members of Canaan Home's board of trustees, and many of the orphanage's volunteers also came from the congregation. During the famine years after Pearl Harbor, some of these Christians had secretly sent supplies to the orphanage at great risk and sacrifice. Also, the older Canaan Home children who were working or studying in Peking attended the Peking Christian Tabernacle.

That fall of 1947, three more teenagers from Canaan Home joined Micah at Yenching University. The Peking Student Christian Fellowship followed up their summer prayer conference with a series of evangelistic meetings, during which many university students were converted. The Communist students gained converts also, however. Student demonstrations multiplied within the city and throughout the nation.

In the midst of this political and spiritual ferment, a new and troubling issue began to emerge for Gate of Righteousness and some of the other boys now living on their own. It seemed that some people in the community had a poor opinion of their father. They gossiped that he chased women and someone even intimated that he had embezzled orphanage funds and used the money to start a factory. He lived a double life, they said, deceiving their mother and the rest of the family.

Gate of Righteousness began to wonder. Why had Papa left Canaan Home during the Japanese occupation? The family had really needed him. He should have been there to protect them. Why had he left and where had he gone? And what had Mama meant when he returned and she asked if the children would forgive him because he had done bad things? What bad things? Had he been unfaithful to Mama? Had he funneled orphanage funds to his clan?

Gate of Righteousness began to look at his father with new eyes, and what he saw made him uneasy. Unlike Mama, who worked harder than a peasant for the family day and night, Papa seemed to avoid physical work. He did the bookkeeping and left it to the boys to cook, clean, tend the livestock, and work in the garden. Mama shared the children's lot in life completely. Whatever the children had to eat, she ate the same, and if someone gave her a treat, she cut it in small pieces and shared it. If she was running errands in the market for the family at mealtime, she bought something cheap to eat from a street vendor. Papa, on the other hand, kept special food aside for just himself, and when he went into the city, he ate in good restaurants.

Gate of Righeousness thought that Papa appeared to be less committed to the children than Mama. He decided he needed to know whether there was any truth to the gossip about his father.

Meanwhile the warm days and crisp nights of autumn gave way to the freezing cold of winter. By December 1947, Communist forces had gained considerable territory in Manchuria, the east, and in much of the countryside, Chiang Kai Shek's stronghold in the south. Inflation had spiraled until Kuomintang troops could no longer buy themselves enough food with the paper currency they received for wages. To eat, soldiers sold their personal weapons and other supplies. Their commanding officers did the same, taking advantage of their greater access to materiel. In this way the Communists acquired millions of American dollars worth of Pacific War surplus equipment and supplies which the U.S. had given Chiang Kai Shek. Kuomintang troops and officers sold it to their own enemies.

During the spring and summer of 1948, the Communist army established a firm grip on the rural areas surrounding Peking and tried persistently to choke off the Kuomintang army's vital supply lines by blocking roads and sabotaging railways. U.S. troops moved out of Peking early in the fall. Rumors began spreading that the Communist army had taken Paotingfu and was heading toward the city. The American Embassy advised all American women and children to leave the country. The sounds of explosions and gunfire became common in the Canaan Home neighborhood.

Then early one cold winter morning, the earth suddenly shuddered and the sky poured down an agony of sound. Laura jolted upright in bed and jammed her fingers in her ears. It did no good. The monstrous boom of exploding shells and mortar shook the floor and traveled to her eardrums through her bones.

It was December 13, 1948. The battle for Peking had begun, and Canaan Home Orphanage lay trapped in the center of the combat.

Revival Reports

Zechariah's memoirs, translated from Chinese:

Mama not only helped us through times of difficulties, she spread the seeds of the Gospel in our hearts. It was on a winter night. We were worried because we thought Jesus was coming, and we had to prepare to meet Him. Our hearts must be cleansed. Simon was the one who told us this. We didn't know what to do, so we all went to Mama, and she prayed for us. That was the first time that I realized that I am a sinner. All of us confessed our sins. Some said they stole food, and some said they fought with others, cursing people. We asked Jesus to cleanse us. While we were praying, many were in tears, some crying aloud. This lasted about two hours until peace came to our hearts. It was the first time that I had ever experienced this.

The next day the neighbors asked us, "Why did you cry last night? Did your American mother beat you?"

We answered, "No, we repented of our sins."

They didn't understand, but later they could see we were all changed. The neighbors were surprised that we became different kids. What a change there was! The spiritual change transformed everything. After that, even when things were difficult, we had peace in our hearts and we got through much easier.

Laura's note on the back of this photograph reads: "A group of children taken with a stranger." The children with the bald heads are the same children who were wearing white hats on page 196. The orphans said in 2006 that these children had a contagious skin disease on their heads. Laura sent them to the Peking Union Medical College hospital, where they were all cured, but came home bald. During their two-week hospital stay, Laura visited them every day, and people at the hospital asked them, "Why does this foreigner visit you?" They were surprised when the answer came, "She is my mama."

Memoir from Laura Richards Nieh, "Old Temple Building":

...As I let them (the boys) in, they almost fell to the floor, prostrating themselves around the room. They were crying and confessing their sins, and there were little puddles of tears on the cement floor in front of them. I was amazed.

Rachel's memoir, translated from Chinese:

Mama was very careful about the way we grew up. I remember one night when Mama was lying on her bed. She called four or five people to come to her room. I was among them. I sat near Mama, and Mama let us kneel beside her bed. She talked to us from God's Word. Mama told us to believe God, not to commit sins, and if you sin, confess it and repent. Then kneeling, we confessed. Mama also prayed for us, and we felt happy and relaxed. Mama was very happy. After that I remember that all the boys and girls in the orphanage were confessing their sins to Mama. Then all the people were united again and helping each other and not committing sins. We were very happy the whole day. It was not like before when we dared not see Mama and we lied to Mama. After that, if we knew something was a sin, we wouldn't do it.

One summer, many students came here for a summer camp. Sometimes Mama told us to sit beside them and listen. Although we were young at that time, Mama let us feel from our hearts that God loved us. They let the children take part in the conference along with the visiting students. Through this experience, we were able to know God more deeply. We listened to the singing and they gave testimonies of their experiences. At that time I determined to follow God, but soon afterwards my determination faded.

22.

In the Center of Combat

The Dowager's Boathouse, 1948

It was still dark outside. Laura lit a lamp and hurried to the babies' room. They were all howling. Their little faces were contorted with crying—mouths stretched wide, eyes screwed shut—although no one could hear them over the stunning din.

The younger twins, Grace and Gloria, now 12 years old, burst into the room on her heels. "Sarah sent us to tend the babies," Grace shouted in Laura's ear. "She wants to know what they should do with the little girls!"

"Bring them here!" Laura screamed back, plucking a frantic baby from one of the cribs. She kissed a great salt tear from the little one's cheek. The baby snuggled into Laura's shoulder, pressing her cold, wet face into Laura's neck.

The older girls and the women teachers herded the little girls into the babies' room. The family gathered for prayer, cradling the babies and huddling close to each other for comfort.

"O Lord, You are our refuge and our fortress, our God in whom we trust," Laura prayed, recalling the familiar words in Psalm 91. "Deliver us! Calm these little ones, we pray, and cover them with Your feathers. Give us refuge now under Your wings. We have no power against these bullets.

Shield us with Your great faithfulness and Your unfailing love. Give Your angels charge over us to keep us safe. We thank You for Your promises and we give You all the honor and praise for our deliverance."

When the children were calm, Laura retreated to her bedroom to continue praying. The older girls minded the younger children. They took turns standing at the window and watching artillery shells splash harmlessly into the stream.

For three hours the guns were unrelenting, and then, briefly, the grueling volume seemed to lessen. During the lull, the outside door slammed open, and Samuel bolted into the room, clutching a big can of water. An acrid odor like the smell of popping fireworks drifted into the room with him.

"Samuel!" Laura exclaimed. "How did you get here?"

Again the guns began to boom.

"By crawling!" Samuel shouted cheerfully. He looked like he had been rolling in a dust pile. Patches of ground-in dirt decorated the knees of his wadded winter pants, and his jacket was streaked with dust. His dark eyes shone with excitement. "Papa said when the mortar shells burst, they scatter straight out. So the closer you keep to the ground, the less you're likely to be hit by shrapnel."

He set the water can down by the door. "I brought you water. What shall I bring you from the kitchen?"

It was past the family's usual breakfast time. Normally the family breakfasted on hot millet mush boiled in four cauldrons on the big old Chinese stove. Today, cooking was out of the question. It was too dangerous to take the children through the yard into the kitchen to eat or to run back and forth fetching enough cooked food from the kitchen to feed over 60 children here in the babies' room. Laura sent up a prayer of gratitude for the large supply of easy-to-prepare powdered milk, beans, peas, and ice cream that Canaan Home had just purchased from a huge stockpile of food the U.S. Marines left behind.

"Bring a carton of bean powder," she yelled over the din, "and a carton of powdered milk for the babies."

Samuel dashed out the door and returned a few minutes later with a carton each of powdered milk and powdered beans, nestled into a big pan piled with bowls, spoons, and baby bottles. Fourteen-year-old Ezra tagged at his heels, toting another full water can. Laura prayed with them briefly, then sent them crouching back to Kenneth, pressed to the earth by the noise and flying shrapnel.

For two days artillery roared constantly over the orphanage grounds, and the airport at the rear of the compound caught fire. Kenneth and the older boys fought the fire away from the orphanage grounds. They ran absolutely necessary errands on their knees, crawling from place to place, dodging shrapnel. Bits of shell landed in the yard, exploding into flame and ashes, and a shell fragment ripped through a corner of one of the buildings.

The cruel noise hammered on. It bit into the brain and numbed the mind until Laura wondered if it had destroyed her sense of time. The fight seemed endless.

Finally the battlefield shifted east, closer to the city. With ears ringing, the Niehs emerged from the children's dormitories to assess, with awe, the lack of damage to the orphanage complex. The airport just behind them was a pile of smoldering ruins. Many soldiers and civilians had died or been wounded in the grueling barrage of mortar and artillery. Yet on the orphanage property, only one building was damaged, and only one child was injured—not from any explosion or bullet, but from panic when a shell fragment rocked the building.

The penetrating odor of exploded gunpowder hung in the atmosphere, and the air tasted bitter. Smoke rose from what was left of the airport behind the Dowager's Boathouse. The orphanage grounds were littered with the shell belts, uniforms, and weapons of Kuomintang soldiers who had dashed over the Xing Long Bridge into the yard, frantically shedding everything that slowed their retreat.

Kenneth stooped over and picked up a shell belt. "The Communists will accuse us of helping the Kuomintang government if they find any of these weapons or uniforms on our property," Kenneth said gravely. "We must get rid of them immediately."

They collected all that was left behind by the soldiers, and then Kenneth and the boys buried the hardware. Laura set the girls to work pulling the Kuomintangs' wadded uniforms apart to be made over into quilts and gowns. The cloth was precious and easily disguised.

By December 18, the other airport was also in Communist hands, and the Kuomintang army backed up to a position about one mile from the city wall. The two armies positioned themselves for an extended siege of the city. Communist troops blocked the railways, occupied the suburbs, and took over the power plant that supplied Peking with electricity. The Kuomintang army leveled thousands of poor people's homes at the lines of defense just outside the city gates in order to provide their soldiers with a good line of fire. They chopped down valuable trees to create roadblocks and dug a vast honeycomb of ditches around the perimeter of Peking, denuding the countryside.

One hundred and fifty thousand Kuomintang soldiers moved into the city. Their commanders made little effort to find them food or shelter, leaving the soldiers to fend for themselves. The men moved into the city's public buildings. When that space was filled, they pushed their way into private homes. Food was scarce because of the siege, and the officers did not supply their men with regular rations. The soldiers ate whatever they could find or take.

Day by day, popular support for the Kuomintang leaked away. People began to feel that any soldiers would be better than the ones on their doorsteps, and any government would be better than the one they had. Finally, on January 22, 1949, General Fu Tso-yi, commander of the Kuomintang troops in Peking, announced that he had signed a peace agreement with the Communists. The first Communist troops marched through Peking's West Gate nine days later, on January 31, 1949, with loudspeakers blaring congratulations to the people for being liberated.

Gaily decorated trucks began touring the city streets, entertaining citizens with lively folk songs, dances, and Communist propaganda. Teams of students and political workers canvassed the neighborhoods and marketplaces, giving lectures on Communism and passing out leaflets. Children tagged after them through the frigid alleyways like a hundred re-enactments of the Pied Piper of Hamlin.

"Liberation" was the theme of the Communist takeover—"liberation from the Kuomintang reactionaries and the American imperialists." The coming of the Communists definitely did, in fact, bring a feeling of liberation to most people. The siege ended. The power shortages ceased. The early evening curfew was lifted. Food began flowing into the city marketplaces from the rural hinterlands, and all the soldiers moved out of the common people's homes. Only the rich were forced to continue putting up soldiers in their private residences.

Rich folk began having other sorts of problems, too. The Communists took over all the organizations and businesses of prominent Kuomintang leaders, with the promise of more takeovers in the near future for other wealthy people and those with close Kuomintang ties—like Kenneth Nieh's brother-in-law, the man who had rented out his compound to Canaan Home in 1937.

Ordinary workers and lower-ranking officials, however, felt reassured by the diplomatic way the Communists first took over government institutions, banks, and the media. "We've been living in the hills right along, and we know much less than you gentlemen about municipal government," General Yeh Chien-ying said in an informal speech to municipal government workers on the day that he assumed his new job as mayor of Peking. "Henceforth we must learn from you."

It was honeymoon time in Peking. Painful changes in everyday business operations began later, although it was obvious even at the start that the new regime intended to teach as well as learn.

In the countryside where Canaan Home was located, teams of Communist activists organized the poor in "speak bitterness" meetings. These events were designed to punish and sometimes kill middle-class villagers and Kuomintang supporters, then redistribute their land and property.

One cold afternoon in February, several cadres dropped by to look around the Canaan Home complex. A young female cadre wandered into the kitchen, where several girls were preparing the evening meal. Sixteen-year-old Foreign Doll was stirring a big pot of bubbling millet porridge.

"What are you doing?" the visitor asked.

"Preparing cereal for supper," Foreign Doll answered politely.

"Are you a Christian?" the woman asked next.

"Yes," Foreign Doll replied.

"I used to be a Christian, too," the cadre told her, "but not anymore. Why, if there were a God, you would not have to make cereal. It would all be prepared for you to eat."

Then she told the girls that they must all come to the Xing Long Bridge after supper for political study. "Right ideology produces right action," she said, and left to find her colleagues.

The girls had no idea what she was talking about. They showed up at the Xing Long Bridge after supper, though, along with the other children. All Chinese people in the Communist-controlled areas of China were assigned to a daily political study group for thought reform. The Canaan Home children were no exception. In these groups, specially trained young men and women painted an appealing picture of a future society in which there would be no more injustice, no more exploitation, no more corruption, and no more inequity. All the wealth and property of the enemy landlord class, these cadres taught, would be redistributed to the poor exploited peasants. Then, when the peasants had acquired control of the land, Mao's education would produce a new breed of people —right-thinking, incorruptible, loyal to the Party and and all of them serving each other unselfishly.

The cadres who gathered the Canaan Home children on the Xing Long Bridge were young, idealistic, and trained in this new thought. They had participated in study groups designed to replace old ways of thinking with the teaching of Chairman Mao. The neighborhood meetings they had been taught to conduct revolved around specific themes. If the theme of that night's meeting was "Americans are imperialists," for example, then each one in the group, from the schoolchild to the tottering grandfather, had to answer the questions correctly and repeat the theme:

"What are the Americans?" the cadres asked each one over and over.

"The Americans are imperialists" was to become each individual's conditioned response.

If someone in the group disagreed, it became the duty of the whole gathering to convince him. If he was slow to be convinced, the group berated and pressured him en masse until he changed his opinion. Most people quickly learned to avoid this ordeal by going along with the party line and by participating vigorously in group pressure tactics. Anyone who appeared to lack enthusiasm when the study group was browbeating another member was next in line for the same treatment.

Members of the group must criticize each other, too, and each individual must make self-criticisms—humble confessions of all their misdeeds, plus everything their ancestors had ever done wrong as well.

The Canaan Home children, however, did not follow the script. First, they seemed impervious to the cadres' theme ideas. Second, they were unwilling to berate or criticize each other, but instead kept bringing up some irritating nonsense about forgiveness. And worst, they kept raising unexpected difficulties that the cadres' training had not prepared them to anticipate.

For example, the cadres' plan during their first visit to Canaan Home was to discover what kinds of handicrafts the children were producing to support Canaan Home. Then they planned to point out to the children that the Niehs were exploiting them by forcing them to make those handicrafts. According to Chairman Mao, Western missionaries set up orphanages to make money for themselves through the sale of crafts. The Western imperialists said they used the money from their sales to buy food and clothing for the children, but really they just made a good name for themselves while lining their pockets with the products of the orphans' labor.

Unfortunately though, Canaan Home produced no handicrafts for sale. So the cadres had to be content that evening with giving a simple lesson on the definition of economic exploitation. It turned out to be a rather dull lesson, too, since the cadres could relate it to nothing in the children's daily experience.

"Economic exploitation is getting something which you yourself do not produce," they told the children. "If you hire people to work for you, for example, the income that you derive from them is exploitation, because they earn it, but you take it away from them."

The following night's meeting on the Xing Long Bridge produced no better results. In current Communist teaching, the United States had replaced Japan as the national symbol of imperialism. "The Americans are our enemies," the cadres told the children. "Americans are imperialists."

The children thought about their mama—her gentle touch, her laughing eyes, her loving ways. Some of them called up devastating memories of what their lives had been like before Mama drew them into the Canaan Home family.

Mama was an American. She was no enemy.

The Marines were Americans, too. The whole family had cheered that day the Marines dropped from the sky in their parachutes. After they came, the Japanese soldiers had to go away. When the family was hungry, the Marines had given Mama and Papa money to buy food. The Marines had played with them, too, and made them laugh and given them candy. Sweetness invaded their memories in a rush, remembering the Marines' candy. Besides all that, the men had bought everybody in the family a present for Christmas.

"Americans are our enemies? Americans are imperialists?" The teaching bounced off the children's young minds like a rubber ball on hard cement, leaving no imprint.

The next lesson, "There is no God," fared no better.

Where, the cadres wondered, *do these children come up with all those far-fetched stories about answers to prayer?*

The cadres were not about to give up, however. Their superiors were pressuring them to produce political results. So night after night, the indoctrination lessons continued on the cold Xing Long Bridge. And night after night, Laura prayed for her children's minds and spirits. She became so concerned about the nightly classes on the bridge that she was almost relieved when a cadre arrived one day and ordered the family to move out of the Dowager's Boathouse into the city. Now that the Boathouse complex was cleaned and repaired, the Communists wanted it.

"If we must move," Laura said, "then please find a place for us to go."

"That is your business," the cadre retorted. "Take care of it yourself."

Transition to New China

Excerpt from Florence Logan's letter to Becky Powers, December 10, 1984:

Now about Communist takeover: All during the Japanese occupation there was constant warfare between them and the Eighth Route Army. They were the patriotic Chinese fighting for their country. But after the Japanese were expelled, the Eighth Route revealed themselves to be Communists and were in constant struggle with the Nationalist (Kuomintang) troops. That was the situation we faced when we returned in 1947. Communications were constantly being cut—railroad tracks or bridges torn up, no trains; roads torn up, no trucks. Sometimes an airplane would come.

When the Nationalists (Kuomintang) finally gave up Paotingfu, the Communists came in like lambs, all sweetness and light, promising peace and happiness, etc. Then soon everyone had to register to detect any bad elements. People in places of responsibility were most severely attacked. But since I had refused to take any responsibility in the church, they couldn't find anything of which to accuse me. I lived with my Chinese colleagues, ate and dressed Chinese, we did our own work, no servants. I didn't leave the compound for if I had called on any friends they would have been under suspicion.

Rachel's memoir, translated from Chinese:

No matter how tired Mama was, every morning she gave us worship. She was a very hard worker. At night she couldn't go to bed early and her sleep was interrupted. Yet early in the morning, she led us in worship. At that time I didn't quite understand Mama. Now I know how deep Mama's love was for God. Mama had us grow up healthy in body and in spirit.

When the children grew up, Mama needed to look for jobs for them. Girls were usually sent to a Christian hospital to learn nursing. Some boys learned to drive trucks, some learned to fly airplanes, some learned to make shoes and stockings, some went out for further studies, and some learned typing. All were very good jobs.

We had a board of directors. Although I didn't quite understand what that was, it seems I was affected by it. Sometimes a lot of people came and had a meeting. They helped Mama take care of our life and our future. They loved God, and they were willing to help Mama take responsibility for us. Since Mama was an American, there were some Chinese customs she didn't know about. Having a board made things a lot better. Mama and all the members of this board of directors wanted us to have a happy life and good health and God's blessing. They loved us and took care of us also.

At the March 2006 reunion of orphans, Rachel said that before New China was born, Laura separated the Canaan Home children into three groups, planning to send them to the United States to be adopted. This photograph of older children taken at the Jade Fountain was the first group. They were all children Laura had raised from infancy. But when New China was born, the adoption plan had to be abandoned.

23.

Interrogation at the American School

The American School in Peking, 1949

A NUMBER OF BUILDINGS in the city had been vacated when the Communists took over. Of these, both the Peking American School and the College of Chinese Studies offered the Niehs their facilities to use for Canaan Home. Their owners wanted them occupied to prevent them from being confiscated.

The Niehs discussed the two options. The College of Chinese Studies was a spacious place, with plenty of room to spare for the children. In the past, they had always tried to move into a place with room to expand.

"But now," Kenneth pointed out, "if there is any extra room, the Party will assign cadres to move in with us. We can barely squeeze into the American School. Let us move the children there, where there will be no space for the cadres to put their beds."

So they borrowed sixteen army trucks, which had passed from the possession of the U.S. Marines to the Kuomintang to the Communists, and moved into the American School in March 1949.

A few days after the family settled into the new place, three cadres showed up at the gate and asked the boy on duty at the gatehouse to see

Happy Plum Flower. "We must have a place to stay while we do our work with your children," they told her. "We must move in here with you."

"There is no room for you," Laura said. "We are so cramped for sleeping quarters that some of the boys are sleeping on the floor."

The family was even more squeezed for space at the American School than they had anticipated because when they arrived they found that eleven orderlies from a nearby hospital had moved into the building while it was vacant.

"In that case, we will have to come at eight every morning and leave at night," the cadres said. "Where may we have our office?"

Laura showed them a room near the kitchenette where the older girls prepared the babies' formula. Then the cadres toured the American School building. They could see that Laura had told them the truth. The small room Laura showed them for their office was the only particle of available space.

The Communists intended to take over Canaan Home using the same strategies they were using to take over every office, factory, school, church, hospital, and local government in the Communist-controlled areas. They began by installing their own people within an organization. Then their cadres tried to set people in the group against one another until they lived in fear of each other and brought down their leadership themselves.

The cadres were courteous and friendly at first, then encouraged dissatisfaction. "What a nice garden you have here," a cadre would remark to a villager. "I notice your neighbors have chickens. Don't their chickens ever come over and get into your garden?"

Of course chickens get into other people's gardens. "You don't have to put up with that," the cadre would insist. "You should accuse them at the meeting tonight." So, under greater or lesser pressure, the villager would accuse his neighbor—and lose a friend.

People became isolated and afraid to confide their problems to anyone, because it was their neighbors' duty to inform on anyone saying anything critical about the new government. If they complained, they would be accused of being counter-revolutionary—that is, opposed to the revolution. Then they could be sentenced to a term of "education," or reform by labor. Husbands and wives grew guarded with each other because the cadres incited their study groups into browbeating wives to "help" their husbands confess. It was safer for wives if their husbands told them nothing. Talking in front of the children was also unsafe. The Communist Party gave children special rewards for informing on their parents.

In factories and offices, the cadres encouraged dissatisfied workers to accuse their bosses and fellow employees. They pressured orderlies and nurses' aides to accuse nurses and doctors. They coerced churchgoers to accuse their pastors and fellow members of the congregation. If someone refused to make accusations, that got him in trouble, too.

The cadres placed particular emphasis on finding ways to discredit people in positions of leadership. If the Party merely removed existing leaders, their followers would probably work against the cadres to bring the leaders back. Instead, the cadres worked to discover the weaknesses in an institution and gain the cooperation, one way or another, of dissatisfied or timid members. Then they aroused such fear and confusion and mutual distrust within the group, that people accused and destroyed their leadership themselves.

Thus, the cadres assigned to Canaan Home set out to discredit the Niehs and to wean the children from their parents to the Party. They began by questioning the teenage girls who were preparing formula in the kitchenette. "What does Mrs. Nieh think of us?" they asked the girls.

If they could discover any critical remarks Laura had made about them, they could accuse her of being counter-revolutionary.

"She thinks to boil the water, fix your tea, and bring it to you," Esther said. "That's what she thinks of you!"

After this unsatisfactory beginning, the cadres sent for all the kindergartners in a group. "Do you believe?" the cadres asked them.

"Yes," the little ones replied. "We DO believe in God."

The cadres shook their fingers at them and scolded. "You must not believe in God," they said. "You must not believe!"

When the session ended, they told the kindergartners to leave. "We will believe in God," the children announced, as they trooped out the door.

Then the cadres sent for all the older children to come stand before them, one at a time, to answer their questions. The days passed. It was a long procedure, and a fruitless one. None of the children said anything that pleased them.

"My own mother was blind," eight-year-old Miriam said. The diminutive girl stared straight into the eyes of the three cadres looming over her. "My mother could not take care of me, so Mama and Papa took me in."

"When I was a baby, my mother did not want me," 15-year-old Esther said, pleasant as always. "My mother threw me out the door and hurt my spine so that I was a little hunchback," she explained. "But a neighbor brought me to this orphanage, and Mama took me in. She cured my back." She paused, studying the cadres' frowning faces. Obviously they were not pleased, so she added helpfully, "So now I am straight and tall! I am strong and ready to help in the people's recovery!"

The older cadre's ears turned dusky rose. He dismissed Esther with a curt order to fetch her mother immediately.

"You are telling these children what to say!" he accused Laura.

He was wrong though. No one had given the children any instructions. Laura prayed for them, that was all.

It was the Canaan Home cadres' assignment to look for specific evidence for accusations to make against Happy Plum Flower. It would be easy, when the cadres were ready, to remove her husband from his position. He was a Kuomintang Party member, related by birth to a whole list of powerful Kuomintang Party officials, all of them by definition counter-revolutionaries. According to the Communists' bloodline theory of guilt, Nieh Shou Guang was guilty for the wrong doings of his parents, grandparents, and great-grandparents. All the misdeeds of the Nieh family could be pinned on him. And there were rumors about him. He behaved improperly with women, it was said, and they had been told to look carefully into his bookkeeping records for Canaan Home and any other business interests outside the orphanage. They were sure they would soon find something specific to prove that he had misused the orphanage to his own advantage.

Happy Plum Flower's case was more difficult. Of course she was an imperialist. All Americans were imperialists. It was just that, in her case, imperialism was hard to prove. She did not wear Western clothes or eat Western food or live in a fine house. She could not be accused of mistreating her servants because she had none. In fact, people said she acted like she was a servant herself.

Still they knew that if they searched hard enough, they would find evidence for her ulterior motives. Mao taught that all missionaries came to China with ulterior motives—not because they loved the Chinese people, as they claimed, but because they intended to manipulate people for their own political ends. In the setting of Canaan Home, this teaching seemed unconvincing, but eventually Mao would be proved right.

The cadres' biggest problem was that Happy Plum Flower was quietly popular with the people. She was well known inside the city and throughout the countryside for her dedication to helping the poor. Without specific accusations, the Communists could not discredit her. If only the children and teachers would cooperate by renouncing God and denouncing her! If only!

The cadres' frustration started showing. When their interrogations produced no results, they tried threats.

"Do you believe?" a cadre asked Samuel, who was on duty at the gatehouse.

"Yes, I believe in God," Samuel answered.

"What if I shoot you?" the cadre asked.

"That is all right," Samuel said. "Still you have not beheaded me." Being beheaded was a greater disgrace in China than being shot.

A few minutes later, two other cadres confronted Samuel's older brother Paul, who was a student home on holiday from the Tientsin Bible School. In Canaan Home, the older children were responsible for supervising the younger children and keeping them on task during family chore times. So that morning Paul had decided to check up on his little brothers to see if they were tidying their room like they were supposed to do.

A clamor of shouts and laughter reached his ears as he descended the stairway leading to their room. Not a bed was made. Clothes were strewn all over the floor, and the little boys were dancing around the room and holding wrestling matches on the beds and floor.

"Ungrateful children!" Paul scolded. "Can't you even take care of your room? Don't you know that Mama bathed you and changed your diapers when you were little, so that her hands were bleeding, and can't you do even this little bit of work to help her now?"

Two male cadres coming down the steps to the boys' dormitory overheard Paul's appeal. "So!" the older cadre roared furiously. "So YOU are the one causing all our trouble! YOU are the one who is making our work so difficult!"

The man shook his finger sternly at Paul. "Do you want us to report you to headquarters?" he demanded.

Paul thought quickly and held his head high. "Go ahead," he said. "I will go with you."

This was a safe reply, he thought. He had attended many indoctrination classes and knew that in the new regime, authority was given to young people.

The older man turned on his heel, and the two cadres stalked off up the stairs. Paul's younger brothers soberly set to work straightening their dormitory.

An hour later, when Laura checked on the sick children, she noticed that Deborah, who seemed to be suffering from a bad cold, could not focus her eyes properly. "We need to put on your warm *ta ao*," she told the child, drawing a red and black checked over-garment from a nearby cabinet. "You and I are going to the hospital."

At the gatehouse, Samuel hailed a rickshaw, and Laura helped Deborah into it. Then she wheeled her bicycle next to the driver to pedal along beside the rickshaw. It was a raw, windy day. Laura rearranged her scarf to protect her face from blowing dirt before she mounted her bicycle. Just as she started pedaling away, a strange bicycle pulled smoothly up alongside her. The cyclist slowed, then moved along just behind her and the rickshaw all the way to the hospital. Whenever Laura and the rickshaw driver made a turn, the cyclist turned, too.

So the Party has sent me an escort, Laura thought. She would have to get used to that.

The familiar outlines of Douw Memorial Hospital, with its handsome Chinese-style exterior and its glinting, green tile roof, came into view. Laura accompanied Deborah into the building, and they waited for the doctor. Big character accusation posters plastered the walls, and Laura felt sick to her stomach reading them. The placards blasted one of the finest missionary doctors at Douw.

How can people believe such obvious lies? she asked herself. *And how can he possibly carry on his work with this going on?* She shuddered, imagining how she would feel in the doctor's place.

Her old friend Dr. Henke had not, fortunately, been attacked yet, but Laura knew that he was having a difficult time anyway under the new regime. Along with the Chinese who worked in the hospital, he had to attend daily indoctrination classes. As an American, he was watched at all times. Whenever he talked to any of his Chinese friends or colleagues, the cadre assigned to watch him reported the encounter. Then, sometime later, the unfortunate Chinese he had spoken with would be taken aside and badgered with questions: "What did he say to you? What did you talk about?"

So now the fearful ones avoided him, and those who reached out to him in kindness were harassed. Laura thought it must make him feel like a leper—like he contaminated any Chinese he came into contact with.

Dr. Henke's wife and children had left China just before the worst of the fighting, so he was all by himself. This must be a lonely time for her old friend, with the Communists deliberately isolating him. It must be frustrating, too. She had heard that the new hospital director seriously hampered Dr. Henke's work. Surgery now had to be guaranteed 100% successful. If an upcoming operation was too complicated to risk the guarantee, he could not perform it.

The Communists had placed a former rickshaw driver in charge of Douw Hospital. The new director was illiterate. He had neither administration skills nor any knowledge of modern medicine. He was a loyal party member, though, which was all that mattered in the new China.

"It is better to be Red than expert," was the new slogan.

The lilting voice of a Chinese nurse broke into Laura's thoughts. The nurse directed her and Deborah into an examining room, where a new female doctor, a stranger to Laura, examined Deborah briefly, then wrote out a prescription for cold medication.

Laura was sure, though, that this was no simple cold.

"I was concerned about her eyes," Laura said diplomatically. "Did you notice how unfocused they are? And her neck is so stiff, she can't touch her chin to her chest."

The doctor turned back to Deborah and examined her over again. "Help her to hold very still," she told Laura. Then she poked a needle into the girl's spinal column, and drew out a bit of fluid.

Meningitis, Laura thought. *I was afraid of that.*

She arranged for Deborah to be admitted to the hospital, and the child stayed there for several weeks. One other girl from Canaan Home had to be admitted with meningitis a few days later as well. To Laura's relief, though, none of the other children came down with the disease. Both girls recovered completely.

Meanwhile, the interrogations continued.

American School Memories

RACHEL'S MEMOIR, TRANSLATED FROM CHINESE:

We moved again, but I don't know why. We moved to the American School in the city. There were only two stories in this building, but we had a basement. The boys lived in the basement. It was a smaller place than where we lived before, but it was a good place. When we moved to this place, our teachers changed. Those Christians who lived nearby taught us. Some of them were from Xiang Mountain. They were all Christian brothers and sisters of ours. They loved God very much, and it didn't bother them to go such a long distance from the city to teach us. They were Shi Jia Alley Christians from Wang Ming Dao's church.

It was by God's arrangement that we moved to the city near Wang Ming Dao's church. Whenever we were in the courtyard or in the different stories of the building, we could hear the singing and preaching. On Sundays these Christians worshipped at Wang Ming Dao's place, and in the afternoon they came to our place. On Sundays Mama also let us stand in line to go to Shi Jia Alley to listen to Mr. Wang's preaching. We liked it very much. We went there on Sunday and Wednesday nights at a small worship place.

Every night before we went to sleep, all of us knelt down and prayed. When we had meals, we prayed also. In the morning, we had morning worship. Although we did all that, we still couldn't guarantee that we wouldn't make mistakes.

FROM LAURA'S MEMOIRS, REGARDING THE ONGOING INTERROGATION:

While the children were witnessing, I was aware of the power of the Holy Spirit in our midst, such as I had never known before.

24.

The New Regime

Peking, at the American School, 1949

THE WEATHER warmed to planting time, while the Communists kept pressuring the children to renounce their faith and say something that the Party could use against the Niehs. The children, on their part, stuck to two or three simple assertions: when their own parents had been unable or unwilling to care for them, Mama and Papa had taken them in. They believed in the Christian God who sent his son Jesus to die for them. Because they had chosen to follow Jesus, his Spirit lived inside them, and they had eternal life.

The family missed having their garden in their new location that summer, but there were compensations. Their daily work load lessened because the American School was a modern building with central heating, indoor plumbing, and an up-to-date kitchen. Also, it was located only one block from the Peking Christian Tabernacle, so the children in middle school could easily attend Wang Ming Dao's church for Sunday morning service. The Niehs attended, too, in their own fashion. Wang Ming Dao used a loudspeaker to reach an overflow crowd that spilled over into the courtyard of his church building. The Niehs liked to sit inside the American School building by an open window, listening to him preach.

Canaan Home was so large, the family had their own Sunday School and worship services. On weekdays, a pastor gave daily Bible lessons in the school chapel. Every Sunday afternoon, Peking Christian Fellowship students and Christian middle school students taught Sunday School classes to the younger Canaan Home children.

New China's policy for dealing with the Christian faith was still ambiguous in 1949. Even though the Party sent a team of cadres into Canaan Home to indoctrinate the children in the tenets of atheism, they still allowed the orphanage to conduct daily chapel services. Also, even though the Party tried to pressure Wang Ming Dao to weave political messages into his sermons—and even though the Party sent spies into his services to try to find evidence for accusations against the church leadership—and yet the government still allowed Wang Ming Dao to preach.

During this first stage of the revolution, the Communists proclaimed religious freedom in official statements, while opposing religion in their propaganda. They said that religion was a "spiritual weapon of the exploiting classes for oppressing, enslaving, and exploiting the laboring peoples...."

Christians could claim the religious freedom which the new constitution promised, but students in particular paid a stiff price for doing so. Mandatory political study cells attacked Christian students for being uncooperative and superstitious. These groups constantly compelled them to discuss their beliefs and either deny or defend their faith.

The Canaan Home children were harder for the Party to manage than other school children because they were all part of one closely knit family. The younger children looked up to their big brothers and sisters, and the older children took care of the younger ones. Their teachers were part of the family, too. "Divide and conquer" was the Party's usual method for gaining control of schools and other institutions. Faced with this school where the teachers and students were strongly united, the cadres felt stymied.

Every day Laura thanked God for the family's staunch teaching staff. Several dedicated Christians had offered to join their educational team when they moved into the American School, and then a contributor donated money to be used to pay the teachers a small stipend. Never before had Canaan Home had such a large staff. For the upcoming fall classes, there were eight full-time instructors coming to teach the regular curriculum, plus four part-timers—two teaching English, one teaching Saturday music lessons, and one teaching a weekly art lesson in drawing and painting with watercolors. Ever since Pearl Harbor, the orphanage had been short-handed for staff. Now they had all the helpers they needed, and particularly good ones, too.

There were other causes for thanksgiving in daily prayers as well, the Niehs told Florence Logan when she visited them for lunch in late August 1949. Not only was the Niehs' staffing dilemma solved, but, as if to compensate for the extra troubles the revolution brought them, other concerns which had once caused constant complications now quietly cleared up.

"Ever since the Japanese came," Kenneth said, "cloth has been as precious as rubies. Even patches to mend the children's garments were not to be found." His dark eyes lit up with enthusiasm, and the usual rapid pace of his southern Chinese accent increased his speech to an almost incomprehensible staccato. "But now we have fine clothes in plenty! The Chinese church, the Western Christians, and the United Nations Relief and Rehabilitation Association have given us such an abundance that each of our children even has a change of clothing."

"We have plenty of food now, too." Laura said. "UNRRA gives us food, medication, and enough milk to supply it even to the older children. Not only that, we are able to give every child a daily dose of cod liver oil.

"Ugh!" Florence said. "How wonderful." Her lips puckered at a childhood memory, and she took a big bite of a crisp, juicy Peking pear to remind her mouth of better tastes.

Kenneth chuckled, and Laura's eyes crinkled shut in laughter. "The children who have been with us the longest talk the newcomers into taking it," she said.

Florence chewed her pear slowly, savoring the sight of her two old friends. Kenneth was still strong and youthful looking, although his black hair was thinning now, and his forehead seemed to be growing longer. Laura looked fragile though. Her summer gown hung loosely on her thin frame, her hair was streaked with gray, and the laugh lines around her eyes and mouth had deepened and lengthened into the wrinkles of approaching old age. And why not? She had turned 56 in February.

I wonder how they communicate? Florence thought. *In spite of their language differences they don't seem to have any trouble understanding each other.*

The Niehs' marriage seemed romantic and mysterious to Florence. She had never met a couple like them. Their union was not an arranged alliance, as in the Chinese tradition. Nor was it a love match, American style. Ten years ago, these two people had married for the sake of an orphanage full of children. Then a mutual concern for the children and a mutual respect and admiration for each other must have ripened into real love.

"How is your work going forward in Paotingfu?" Kenneth asked, interrupting Florence's reverie.

Florence told them. The stories were all too familiar now, unfortunately.

It was impossible for Florence to carry on these days as an itinerant evangelist. Anyone seen talking to her was taken aside and questioned repeatedly. So her work was limited to teaching in public meetings and trying to build up and encourage her Chinese colleagues, who could still travel—but with much more difficulty because the Communists kept close track of everyone these days through a system of registration. In order to come here to Peking to visit them, for example, Florence had to apply for a one-month travel permit.

Nowadays, if anyone wanted to move, or even if he just wanted to spend a night somewhere, he had to go to the police station to have his registration cancelled. Then, when he arrived in the new place, he had to register there. "If you stay the night where you're not registered," Florence said, "you're in big trouble."

Recently a woman from the country had come to stay with Florence and her colleagues for several days. When the Christians registered her according to the new regulations, they reported the number of days she expected to stay with them. The woman did not finish her shopping, though, so she stayed over another night. One hour after her registration expired, the police showed up. "To save the woman trouble, one of our girls assumed responsibility," Florence said. "So they arrested her."

Florence sighed, remembering how the girl's hands had trembled when she gathered up her things to leave with the police. "She had to write out a confession criticizing herself in every detail for anything she had ever done or thought that Chairman Mao would not approve. She had to analyze her class origins, too, going back three generations. She was supposed to denounce anyone in her family who was a bad element—her parents, her grandparents. The cadres made her write it over and over."

Florence traced the outline of a painted flower on her teacup with a thoughtful finger. "It was a frightening ordeal," she said.

The Niehs understood. The Communists put so much pressure on people making confessions that some of them broke down and made false confessions, or became so confused they could no longer tell the difference between fact and fiction. Sometimes the sessions ended in a beating, or a term in prison or labor camp for "re-education." And sometimes they ended in an execution. It was all part of the process of reforming people's thoughts and weeding out bad elements.

Kenneth stood. "It has been most enjoyable visiting with you again, Miss Logan," he said, "but I must make my farewell bow and ask you to excuse me."

As he shut the door behind him, Florence turned to Laura and asked in English, "Richie, do you remember the Wen family?"

"Of course," Laura said. The Wens were well-to-do members of the Presbyterian church in Paotingfu. "Have they been publicly accused?" she asked in concern.

"Yes, accused and brought before a people's court and struggled against," Florence said. Being "struggled against" meant being called to a public meeting where angry people screamed accusations and insults at you and beat you until you confessed whatever people wanted you to confess.

"Was anyone killed?" Laura asked in a small voice. More and more frequently people's confessons failed to satisfy the mob, and the group pressure tactics escalated out of control.

"No, they weren't killed, thank God—just driven out of their home with only the clothes on their backs. They were forced to beg from door to door," Florence said. "People aren't supposed to give them anything when that happens, you know. It's part of the punishment. It's supposed to humiliate them even more."

"How did they survive?" Laura asked.

"Well, people helped them secretly, and eventually they were assigned to live in a shed on their old property. Everything else they owned was redistributed, of course, as 'the fruits of struggle.' Now they sell bean cakes for a living."

Laura shook her head, remembering the gracious, cultured woman who was matriarch of the Wen clan. "Poor Mrs. Wen. She was such a dear."

"She says the family is happy now," Florence said. "She told me, 'We are so happy. Now that we have nothing, nobody envies us.'"

The two friends sat silent. Finally, Laura said, "Kenneth's family is in terrible trouble."

"I thought they would be," Florence said.

Local party leaders classified each person in the neighborhood or workplace according to the individual's economic, political, and social background. At the bottom of the scale came the "five black elements": landlords, rich peasants, rightists, bad elements, and counter-revolutionaries. A counter-revolutionary was anyone who opposed the revolution. All former Kuomintang government officials and former Kuomintang police and army officers were automatically considered to be counter-revolutionary—a definition which, along with the family's wealth, sealed the fate of many of Mr. Nieh's relatives. The Party sentenced people who were convicted of being a black element to prison, labor camp, or death.

Laura expelled a long shudder—an odd sound, something between a sob and a sigh. "Well, at least our children have a good political background. All their families were poor," she said.

"But they are connected to you, an American," Florence pointed out gently.

Tears gathered in Laura's eyes. "It's like a bad dream that won't go away, Florence," Laura said. She pulled a handkerchief from her pocket and dabbed her eyes. "I wake up, and the dream doesn't disappear. It gets worse."

She blew her nose and told Florence about the cadres' sessions with the children.

"Bear up, Richie," Florence said. "It's been over 28 years since we first came to China, and how many wars and disasters have we lived through since then? We'll live through this one, too, Lord willing."

"Of course," Laura said, dashing at her eyes with her handkerchief. Her mouth suddenly tilted into her wide, familiar smile, pushing her cheekbones into sharp relief.

She is too thin, Florence thought. *She is feeling the strain more than she realizes.*

Report from the American School

Laura's untitled memoirs:

When we moved into the American School, we were surprised to find eleven young men who called themselves medical students. From the time of our occupancy I asked them how long they planned to stay, and told them of our need to use the space which they were occupying. At last they did all leave. One day, while looking for a hospital in which to place a very ill patient—a little boy whom his father sent back to me after he had acquired a tubercular disease while rug weaving in a factory—I came across two of these so-called medical students who looked as though they were now orderlies. They seemed glad to see me and we engaged in a short conversation.

One evening as I was going out to the gate with them [the cadres], I noticed that the youngest was using a man's bicycle. I had thought that this was a young girl. The face was round, the hands were plump. I said, "It must be quite difficult for you to ride this man's bicycle." The other two, a man and a woman, began to laugh at what I said. It turned out that this was a young man from South China. The three of them wore the same kind of wadded garments and one could scarcely tell the men from the women. This was the only time that I saw them laugh all the time they were with us. I myself could hardly wait until I returned to my room where I laughed as I had not laughed for many months. What a mistake to infer that the young man was a girl!

25.

Hanging On

Peking, at the American School, 1949

DR. HENKE THOUGHT the same thing as Florence several months later when he came to the American School one bitter day in December, 1949. *She looks fragile,* he thought to himself when Laura greeted him in the school entry. Her welcome was as warm as ever, her smile as wide and spontaneous as always. There seemed to be a droop about her eyes, though, and a sense of exhaustion in her movements.

"Are you getting your sleep, Laura?" he asked.

"More than I ever used to, thank you," she replied. "We are not taking in any more children, you know. So we have no tiny babies needing nighttime feedings now. Sometimes I am up nights when children are sick, but the older children get up with the well babies now if they fuss at night."

She led him to the dining room, then stepped into the hallway and summoned the twins, Rachel and Rose Mary. She seemed to be giving them instructions.

I wonder what is going to happen to this family, Dr. Henke thought as he took a seat.

His responsibilities as the first missionary to return to the Presbyterian

Mission after World War II had acquainted him with the details of Laura's marital situation, and he figured that it was only a matter of time before the Communist Party found out what Laura's husband had done. The Party had access to the business records of the Presbyterian Church—their people had been quietly burrowing into the leadership structure of all the denominations for years. And although Laura had kept her husband's misdeeds private, she had been forthright whenever duty demanded it. She had reported the donation theft to the church, and she had sought medical attention from Presbyterian medical staff for the two girls her husband had taken advantage of. So eventually the Party would ferret out the scandal.

Dr. Henke was certain there had never been a repeat offense with any of the other girls. Laura strictly segregated the boys from the girls at the orphanage, keeping her husband safely quarantined with the boys. But Dr. Henke didn't really trust the man. He knew that Mr. Nieh had had an affair with one of the Canaan Home teachers—the woman had confessed it during the revival and then left—and there might be other things, things Laura didn't know about. He had heard that Mr. Nieh made improper remarks to the women staff sometimes, and he knew that people tried to protect Laura from gossip about her husband. No doubt about it, Nieh Shou Guang was a danger to Laura. When the Party found out about the girls or the embezzlement, they would try to implicate her. In New China, a wife could be accused and punished for something that her husband was solely responsible for.

Why had she married him? How could she make such a mistake?

Yet Abraham was the father of faith, and even so he had taken his wife's maid to be his concubine and produced Ishmael. And Jesus was betrayed by one of the disciples he chose himself...

People admired Laura. To them her life of faith seemed romantic and heroic. But in reality, the life of faith was an untidy affair.

He glanced over his shoulder and saw Laura entering the room. She was the picture of weariness and serenity mingled. "Excuse me for taking so long with the girls," she said.

Dr. Henke stood up and seated her courteously. "I'm leaving China, and I've come to say good-bye," he told her. "I've become a liability. I put the spotlight on the people I work with. It makes them a target."

Laura nodded. "I feel the same way," she said. "I don't think the cadres would be paying so much attention to the children if their mother wasn't American."

Rachel appeared then with the teapot and two sets of cups and saucers on a tray. Dr. Henke switched to Mandarin. "Rachel," he complimented her, "you look more like your mother every time I see you."

Rachel's oval face glowed, and an exact replica of Laura's wide smile stretched across her fair-skinned features. "You are most kind, Dr. Henke," she said, placing the tea items on the table. She bowed politely and walked away, taking the tray.

"It really is amazing how much she looks like you, Laura," the doctor said. "It's not only her physical appearance, it's her entire manner—the way she walks, the way she stands, the way she responds to people. Even your own daughter by birth, if you'd had one, might not necessarily look as much like you as Rachel does."

"People often tell me that," Laura said, pouring her friend's tea. She drew in a breath of the pungent jasmine steam rising from the teapot. "Rachel is a good girl," she said, "a blessing from God."

"You should be proud of all your teenage daughters," Dr. Henke said. "They are beautiful within and without. It won't be many years before you will be faced with some young men's parents on your doorstep with marriage proposals."

"The board will tell me what to do when that time comes," Laura said with a smile. "They are a wonderful help to me in those matters. Chinese customs are so different from American ways."

"The board keeps you from making mistakes," Dr. Henke agreed.

Dr. Henke asked about a number of the children by name, and Laura gave him an up-to-date report on each one. At one time or another the doctor had probably examined every child who entered Canaan Home.

Several of the children whose lives Dr. Henke had saved no longer lived at Canaan Home, Laura told him. Either they were working and living on their own, or they had returned to their families. "Now that the famine is over and economic conditions are better," Laura explained, "many of the children's parents are coming back for them."

Laura did not tell Dr. Henke how relieved she felt whenever another parent showed up at the gate to reclaim a child, but the doctor understood. These children, at least, would now be free from the glare of the spotlight trained on Canaan Home.

One of the young Communists assigned to Canaan Home strolled past the door and glanced in. He paused a moment, staring at the doctor, and then he moved on. *The authorities have probably informed the cadres here that I was coming to the orphanage, and why,* Dr. Henke thought.

These cadres, they knew so much about people...and at the same time, they knew so little....

They hated the Christian doctrine of original sin—that we live in a fallen world where people's innate selfishness and weakness undermine every good thing people try to do. To them the teaching was worse than insulting. It was unpatriotic, treasonous. These people were intoxicated with their own goodness, full of glee and righteous indignation as they went around exposing the misdeeds of wrongdoers. They really believed that enlightenment was all it took to make themselves incorruptible.

Dr. Henke sighed and stood up. "I must go now, Laura," he said. "Thank you for tea."

She saw him to the door. "Give my love to Jessie Mae and the children when you get home," Laura said.

Dr. Henke opened the door, and a frigid wind blasted their bodies like pummeling fists. The doctor braced himself against the wind and departed, shoving the door closed behind him. A feeling of loss covered Laura like an icy, weighted quilt. She wiped a rim of tears from her eyes and went upstairs to the girls' dormitory.

The teenagers were undressing the younger girls for bed and overseeing their nighttime washing-up routine. From the doorway, Laura could see Foreign Doll bending to lift Tabitha out of bed. Tabitha's childish arms reached around her sister's neck in a weak embrace. Her swollen head lolled sideways, smacking her helper smartly on the nose. Laura rushed forward as Foreign Doll staggered back.

Tabitha was 19 years old now. Every year her body remained skinny and toddler-sized, while her head continued to swell larger and grow heavier. She was lightweight except for her wobbling head, which unbalanced the load when someone carried her, making her an unwieldy burden.

"Try to support her head like this, against your shoulder," Laura instructed. Tabitha nestled close to Laura and smiled so hugely that her eyes disappeared into the puffy folds of her face. "Mama!" she said happily.

Laura hugged her close. "I'll take Tabitha to the toilet tonight," Laura told Foreign Doll. "Go help the other girls get the little ones ready for bed."

She carried Tabitha to the bathroom and steadied her daughter on the toilet, kneeling next to the commode with her right arm supporting Tabitha's frail back and shoulders. Tabitha leaned her giant head sideways, resting it against her mother's cheek. In her sweet soprano, she began to sing: "Abide with me: fast falls the eventide; The darkness deepens, Lord, with me abide...."

A fierce protectiveness welled up inside Laura, followed almost immediately by a sense of overwhelming weakness. For a moment she felt as limp as the day she learned her mother had died. *What kind of future can Tabitha have in New China?* she wondered.

Tabitha was useless to the revolution. Laura had noticed the cadres' looks of disgust whenever they glanced Tabitha's way. They could neither see nor appreciate the valiant spirit trapped inside this young woman's deformed, unresponsive body.

"When other helpers fail and comforts flee," Tabitha warbled, "Help of the helpless, O abide with me...."

Laura hugged her misshapen daughter's shoulders as Tabitha sat there, propped upon the toilet. They sang the hymn together.

The days passed by, sharp and bitter in the raw North China December. The boys decorated the large auditorium for Christmas, and Chinese friends threw a big Christmas party for the children, with candy, a gift for each child, and shadow pictures for entertainment.

On Christmas day the older boys made up plays and acted them out for the younger children. Then on December 28, the Niehs went with the older children to hear Christian students from Yenching University sing Handel's *Messiah.* The soaring strains of the glorious composition always lifted Laura's spirit. Tonight though, gazing at the earnest, familiar faces of the students who had attended the prayer conferences at the Dowager's Boat House in 1947 and 1948, she was as moved by the performers as the performance. This indeed was a sacrifice of praise.

Many of these students had had relatives killed or imprisoned by the new regime. As believers, they were under continual attack in mandatory political study groups, where they had to study the works of Chairman Mao, write out self-criticisms, and submit to intensive, hostile questioning. Special political meetings and study groups took so much of their time outside of classes, they had little time for anything else. They paid a high price to practice Handel's music, and they would pay another high price for their courage in performing it.

There were two national Christian student organizations in China: the Young Men's Christian Association (YMCA) and the China Inter-Varsity Fellowship (CIVF). The Peking Christian Student Fellowship at Yenching University was part of the CIVF.

The two organizations represented two sides of the debate between liberal and orthodox theologians that had been raging during Laura's two years at the Biblical Seminary in New York in 1926–1928. The YMCA had become theologically liberal, emphasizing a distrust of the supernatural and an activist social gospel—salvation through human good works. This had made it easy for Communist students to infiltrate and take over the organization before the the birth of New China. They simply joined the group's many discussions on social problems, spread propaganda, then rose to prominence and took over positions of leadership.

To avoid being taken over from within like the YMCA, CIVF encouraged students to do their part to relieve people's suffering as individuals instead of as a group effort. Then they deliberately restricted student activities on campus to Bible studies and prayer meetings. Communist students felt out of place in Bible studies and prayer meetings, so it was hard for them to develop enough prominence in the group to assume leadership roles. In this way, CIVF was able to maintain its central, orthodox Christian teachings. It emphasized each individual's need for a transformation of the heart, a fundamental change which was impossible to bring about by manipulating people's environment, but would happen only through the power of the Spirit of God when individuals invited Jesus into their lives.

A month after their concert, members of the Peking Christian Student Fellowship sent representatives to Canaan Home every night for two weeks to sing, preach, and give their testimonies to the children. Seated beside Kenneth in the American School auditorium, Laura listened to their words with a lump rising in her throat. She wondered what their future held.

Later, during the dark days of the year 1950, Laura often encouraged herself by recalling the faces and the words of these young students, resting her mind and spirit on the memory of their stirring songs and fearless witness.

Reports from New China

1988 INTERVIEW WITH DANIEL TSAI, WHO WAS 14 YEARS OLD AT THE TIME OF THE CONCERT:

The students sang the Messiah *in the American Congregational Church, not far from the orphanage near Yenching University. The church is open now under the Three-Self church [the official Communist-controlled church in China].*

I liked that music and wanted to buy a copy, but in high school I didn't have much money. So I saved my lunch money to buy a copy of Handel's Messiah. *It took about two weeks without eating lunch to save enough money.*

During the time of the Cultural Revolution [dated approximately 1966 to 1976], the Red Guard burned most of the copies of Handel's Messiah *in China. Then after that, the Three-Self church wanted to reprint the* Messiah *but they couldn't find any copies. They asked many, many people for a copy. Even the man who had translated it into Chinese didn't have a copy. My aunt was a Bible woman who worked in the church. The government had sent her to the countryside to do labor. They [Three-Self church officials] asked her, and she told them I had one. They borrowed it and never returned it to me.*

RACHEL'S MEMOIR, TRANSLATED FROM CHINESE:

At this time, because conditions were improving, some of the parents wanted to take their children back. Mama was very happy and willing for them to take those children back. Several children left, both older and younger. There were three brothers, all taken back by their parents. Then the youngest boy developed a lung disease because his parents made carpets at home. So they sent this child back to Canaan Home, and Mama immediately gave him treatment. Mama was a very kind person, and she loved children.

26.

Censored Letters, Censored Thoughts

Peking, at the American School, 1950

IN THE EARLY SPRING of 1950, Laura sat down at the dining room table to compose a cautious newsletter to the supporters of the China Children's Fund. Laura wanted to send Canaan Home's supporters as much information about the family as possible. Yet she also had to be careful to avoid sending any information that a Communist censor could twist into an accusation against Canaan Home staff. All mail going outside the country was now opened, censored, and harvested for any remark that could be used as evidence against people.

The government also intercepted, translated, and studied Laura's incoming mail before they delivered it. In her dresser she had several letters from the U.S. that had obviously been tampered with before she received them.

Laura wanted to be true to Jesus in her newsletter, acknowledging all that God had done to provide for the family during these hard times. Yet she must phrase her testimony with care. The Communists labeled any mention of Christ's second coming, for example, or any reference to the darkness of society as "reactionary" or "counter-revolutionary."

So, as the strident winds of March blasted dirt against her window,

Laura began scratching out a long letter: "For a number of years we have received help for our Chinese children from their sponsors in America. At this time when there is so much distress, the Lord Jesus cares for His orphan children and every child has received according to his needs. Our Lord has showered multiple blessings upon us. We thank our Heavenly Father for His gracious love, in that we have received His protecting care." She gave no explanation why the family needed God's protecting care, but instead described His multiple blessings, like the comfortable new home in the American School, their large teaching staff, Wang Ming Dao's preaching, and the university students' evangelistic meetings.

She gave no explanation why the family had moved, or why the American School building was available. She made no comment on the bravery of Wang Ming Dao and the Christian students. She gave no hint of the cadres' presence at the home. Nor did she mention the children's political indoctrination classes. In fact, she eliminated all references to the new government.

She did not tell the people back home how ecstatically the youth of China sang and danced in the streets to celebrate their savior Mao Tse Tung, who had rid China of the hated foreign powers, who was even now rescuing the country from all her economic and social woes, and who would surely restore her to her ancient glory. Nor did Laura mention the way that the Chinese Communist Party was re-organizing all of China from the inside out into a vast spy system.

Nowadays, whenever Laura visited her few remaining Western friends at the Presbyterian Mission compound, she had to register her name with the gatekeeper and tell him whom she had come to see. He kept the Party informed of her visit. All the workers on the mission grounds had to report any strangers or unusual activities they noticed inside the compound.

Now whenever she or Kenneth visited local businesses to find employment for an older Canaan Home orphan on the verge of independence, the workers there had to inform their Party secretary later about every detail of the visit. Whenever the Niehs made a trip to the market, the Party knew which shops they visited and what purchases they made at each one.

Laura's American friends and supporters would have been astonished to learn how thoroughly the Party controlled its citizens through an interlocking, three-part system using the workplace, the home, and the "small group," or political study group.

People no longer had any choice where they worked. All jobs were assigned, and every workplace kept a dossier on each employee containing information about his education, work record, and any political charges ever made against him. It also included the Party's evaluation of him, as well as his class background going back three generations. Everyone in the workplace was required to give reports to the Party secretary on their fellow workers and all visitors.

The street committee kept track of people in their homes. A street committee representative in each neighborhood had the right to come inside and search his neighbors' houses anytime he wanted to. When anybody had visitors, the representative usually came over to find out who they were and question them. If people refused to cooperate, he called in the police.

People's mandatory political study groups used information gathered from the workplace and the street committee to keep individuals in line through indoctrination, self-criticism, isolation, and increasingly violent struggle sessions.

The campaign against corruption and the land reform movement had degenerated into a reign of terror. All someone had to do to enrich himself was think up a righteous-sounding accusation against a neighbor who had more than he did. Revenge became simple, too—no matter how petty the offense.

The Communist Party politicized all relationships and deliberately tried to destroy family ties. Party leaders ridiculed family loyalty and parental authority. "You are a child of the Revolution," they taught Chinese children, "not a child of your parents." The only loyalty allowed was loyalty to Chairman Mao and the Communist Party. The Party gave special rewards to children who—out of rebellion, ambition, idealism, or fear—publicly accused one or both of their parents. Some children who lost their parents in this way committed suicide afterwards.

By the spring of 1950, the Suppression of Counter-Revolutionaries

Campaign was also well under way, targeting everyone who opposed or hindered the revolution, especially all former Kuomintang government officials or army and police officers as well as all "imperialists." An imperialist was any Westerner who remained loyal to his own country or any Chinese with Western connections who failed to cooperate fully with the new regime.

Millions of people were being imprisoned or executed throughout China.

Of course, all of this was too dangerous to describe in a letter home. So Laura reported what she could write safely and thanked the sponsors. "Our school as one body joins in thanking our sponsors for spending heart and time upon us. They have greatly helped us and our hearts are very happy." Then Laura arranged to have the letter typed, mimeographed, and mailed.

It was the last newsletter she mailed from China.

The pouring rains of summertime brought the Korean War, which made everything worse. People had to work more hours to help China prepare for war. In addition, they had to spend more time in their political study groups—usually two hours or more after work every night and another hour before work each morning. Everyone lacked sleep, which added to the pressure of self-criticism sessions and people's trials.

"More and more people are being admitted to the hospital because they attempted suicide," Dr. Lewis told Laura when she and Kenneth came to dinner once. Dr. Lewis was a Presbyterian missionary doctor at Douw Hospital.

During the summer and fall of 1950, big posters began appearing on the walls of shops and compounds throughout Peking: "Down with America!" "Oppose America, Aid Korea!" "Kill the Paper Tiger!" "Drive America out of Korea!"

Mrs. Jenness, one of the few Presbyterian missionaries left in North China, was publicly accused in a people's court and "struggled against." Mrs. Jenness was a widow who directed the Presbyterian school for girls in Shuntefu, where Dr. Henke had once worked. The Communists arrested her and placed her on trial for the wrongdoings of all the Presbyterian missionaries who had ever worked at the Shuntefu station. They forced her to kneel on a table for twelve hours while an angry mob shoved, slapped, and spat on her, shouting accusations and insults.

The cadres accused Dr. Henke of bungling an operation so badly that the patient died, and they held Mrs. Jenness accountable for the wrongful death. They charged that before Mrs. Jenness' husband had died in 1940, he ran over somebody's chicken. If the chicken had lived, it would have laid so many eggs, and the eggs in turn would have hatched so many chickens, until finally, by the time that Mrs. Jenness' accusers had properly analyzed and calculated that chicken's total value, Mrs. Jenness now owed the chicken's owner a million Chinese dollars.

And so it went.

After the twelve-hour ordeal, the cadres shoved Mrs. Jenness off the table and led her home, exhausted and shaking. They placed her under house arrest. The next morning one of her jailers coldly informed her that the cadres in Shuntefu had received an order from Peking during the night directing them not to kill foreigners. So instead of executing her, he said, the Party was giving her three days to leave the country.

At about this same time, several male cadres moved their bedrolls and personal belongings into the American School, taking up permanent residence inside Canaan Home. The intruders scrutinized the Niehs' every move and eavesdropped on their conversations. They tried to coerce the children to report anything the Niehs said when the Communists were unable to hear them.

It took pressure off the children if they could answer all the cadres' questions freely, with nothing to hide. So Laura and Kenneth's communication dwindled to workday details and surface matters. Whenever they had to communicate something important, they tried to find a safe way to manage it—like talking softly as they rode their bicycles closely together on a mutual errand.

Laura noticed that the animated expressions of the people of Peking had disappeared. All the faces she passed in the streets these days were now wiped blank. Chitchat died away. Free expression remained only for the old men's pet crickets, chirruping loudly in their tiny cages.

The situation in Presbyterian and other denominational churches became too painful to talk about—if anyone dared risk the danger of discussing it. Too often these churches had failed to become strong and self-sufficient, depending instead on missionaries to oversee national workers and supply workers' salaries. This meant that denominational pastors and church leaders had many Western ties, leaving them defenseless against accusations of being imperialistic and counter-revolutionary. The Party threatened them with imprisonment or death unless they included political messages in their sermons and replaced Bible studies and prayer meetings with political discussions and accusation meetings.

The faith of certain pastors was weak or nonexistent. Some of these were "rice Christians" who had joined the church for material gain. Others were modern materialists who believed liberal theological doctrines that rejected the possibility of supernatural events and cast doubt on the reliability of scripture. They made decisions and lived their daily lives without reference to God. So although they were Christians in name—and although they believed the label—they lived as practicing atheists. When they came under political pressure, it was simple and natural for them to become political atheists as well. They quickly fell into line, doing whatever they thought would please the government.

Denominational pastors whose faith was sound faced a cruel dilemma. If they refused to cooperate and were sent to prison, what would happen to their congregations? Perhaps it was best, some of them agonized, to compromise in a few areas in order to remain alive to guide their troubled flocks. Those who refused to compromise were usually killed or imprisoned. Others disappeared.

The government appointed Reverend Wu Yuo-tsong to remodel the Chinese church and purify it from all imperialistic influence. Wu set up the "Three-Self Patriotic Movement" to serve as a liaison between the church and the state and to coerce the church to cooperate with Communism. He declared that the progressive (pro-Communist) elements in the church must purge out the reactionary elements (such as conservative Christians) and remove the poison of imperialistic doctrine which, he claimed, permeated all aspects of church life, from its hymns to its theology.

Indigenous pastors like Wang Ming Dao who had no formal ties to the West were harder for the government to control. Wang Ming Dao insisted that the issue facing the church under Communism was not political, but doctrinal. If the church compromised the basic doctrines and practices of the faith and allowed an atheistic government to be in control, he maintained, then the church in China would cease to be part of the true church of Jesus Christ.

Wang Ming Dao preached that "in the Scriptures there is nothing but the bare truth of God without any 'imperialistic poison.'...We must go on believing and preaching it. Nobody can interfere with us and nobody can forbid us to do it. We are willing to pay any price to preserve the Word of God, and we are equally willing to sacrifice anything in order to preach the Word of God."

Throughout China, missionaries were arrested, placed on trial, imprisoned or placed under house arrest, and deported. Some died. Many others, like Dr. Henke, applied for exit visas and left voluntarily.

Under pressure, the Presbyterian and other denominational Chinese churches joined the Three-Self Patriotic Movement. In the fall of 1950, they issued the Shanghai Manifesto, which implied breaking all ties with foreigners as quickly as possible. After that, most of the remaining missionaries began to make arrangements to leave China in order to spare their Chinese friends embarrassment and persecution. Florence Logan reluctantly moved from her home in the countryside onto the Presbyterian Mission compound in Paotingfu and applied for an exit visa. She waited there for three months, unable to work or associate with her Chinese colleagues, while the government investigated her.

The Communist Party dealt with each missionary separately. In Laura's case, they could find no believable evidence to support any of their categories of accusation. Everyone knew that Happy Plum Flower ate the food of the poorest Chinese, and that she refused no task, however menial or degrading, in order to care for a poor child or a destitute neighbor. Furthermore, she had no formal tie to any particular Western religious organization. Although many Western organizations sent money to

Canaan Home, so did many indigenous Chinese organizations, such as Wang Ming Dao's church. Also, the board that set policy for the orphanage was, except for Happy Plum Flower, entirely Chinese. Besides all that, she apparently never talked about other people behind their backs, so they could not get anyone to turn against her by repeating something bad she had said about them.

As autumn hardened into winter, the cadres assigned to Canaan Home sent for Laura again and again, questioning, criticizing, and sometimes shouting. "You have turned these Chinese children into little Americans!" they accused her. "Why are you making trouble for your children with your stubbornness? Do you want them to be put on trial in the future as counter-revolutionaries?"

The cadres assigned Kenneth to a study group. Every night for two hours and again every morning for one hour, he had to meet with his group to study the works of Lenin and Marx and to withstand the unrelenting pressure of his fellow classmates' accusations. He looked exhausted. His tall frame drooped. The dark pouches beneath his eyes made them seem to sag downward, accentuating the conspicuous lines deepening about his nose and mouth. And his eyes held fear.

The cadres continued to allow the children to come and go freely to their parents, but they forced the teachers to stop associating with either of the Niehs unless it was absolutely necessary for their work. They also forbade Laura and Kenneth to speak privately with each other anymore. In addition, the government cut off all money and supplies sent to the orphanage from the China Children's Fund and other overseas supporters. It was New China's policy to foster complete national independence from foreign assistance, but to Laura the sudden cut-off felt like one more government attempt to wean the family from God to the Communist Party.

They are trying to bring us so low that we will have to appeal to them for help, Laura thought. *But I will appeal only to my Heavenly Father. He will take care of our needs.*

The orphanage still had plenty of the powdered food that the U.S. Marines had left behind. People had donated most of their supply, partly just to get rid of it. Now that so many Westerners had left, members of

Canaan Home were about the only people left in Peking who would eat it. So the family still had enough to eat, and they were able to sell the empty food containers at a high enough price to supply cash for other needs.

Unfortunately, there was no extra cash or supplies for the Niehs to help the older orphans make a gradual transition to full independence outside the orphanage like other families could do. Once the orphans left home, they were completely on their own financially.

Laura's gravest concern was not food or money, but the thought of what the cadres might be saying to the children behind closed doors. The Communists were intensifying their campaign against the Niehs and their staff. They were trying to get one or two of the children to crack and accuse Kenneth publicly. The cadres mocked the children's loyalty to their parents. They told the children that revolutionaries should not show personal affection.

How much longer will it be before one of the children gives way under the pressure? Laura wondered.

They were only children after all. They had their jealousies, their disagreements, their bouts of self-pity, and, of course, their fears and their insecurities. The cadres were trained to manipulate all these human tendencies. How long could the children stand up to them?

The orphans working and going to school outside the orphanage were under even greater pressure. Like all the other students and workers in Peking, they attended mandatory political study groups twice a day to find out how to take their place in New China. Their new teachers based all their instruction on the assumption that people on their own are inherently good, but society causes them to think and do what is wrong. Therefore, in order to make the nation just and prosperous for all, the government must mend society with right policies, train people to think rightly, and weed out all those who are too contaminated to allow the new society to work. Once the Communist Party accomplished these goals, all of society would become enlightened and virtuous.

Given the assumption, the plan made good sense.

Poverty, the study groups learned, was caused by injustice and exploitation. If you were poor, it was because someone somewhere had cheated you. Therefore it was everyone's duty under the new government to expose the cheaters, remove or reform these bad elements, and provide just restitution. Then there would be prosperity for all.

Some of these ideas resonated with Gate of Righteousness. Because the orphans attending schools outside Canaan Home received no extra help from their family, they were poorer than any other students. The orphan students lived on meager stipends and food allowances from the government, and at some schools the food allowance was inadequate. Those orphans went hungry. By now Gate of Righteousness knew that these poverty-stricken orphans had, in actual fact, been cheated, just as the cadres taught.

Even before New China was born, he had talked with his brother Silas, Mama's scribe, to find out if Silas knew anything about the rumors Gate of Righteousness had heard about Nieh Shou Guang. When Silas told his brother what he knew—and the amount of money Nieh Shou Guang had embezzled during their mother's Pearl Harbor arrest—the young man's world splintered.

How could a Christian like his father steal food from the mouths of hungry children? And how could a good God allow such a man to get away with it?

Vivid memories of the famine years flooded his mind—the days of searching for wild plants and edible leaves for food, the sleepless nights hearing his little brothers crying with hunger and cold...And to think that the children had never needed to suffer that way...that the Presbyterians had given the family enough money to buy food and coal for the duration of the famine...and their father had stolen it all—all!

As the civil war continued to unfold and New China came to birth, Gate of Righteousness continued to search for information. What, exactly, had Nieh Shou Guang done with the money...and what else had he done?

Gate of Righteousness found that there were people who were willing to help him investigate, and eventually he learned the reason why his mother had sent all the older girls in Canaan Home to Tientsin during the famine. The revelation made him sick with disillusionment and rage.

He was a tender-hearted young man, deeply loyal to his siblings at the orphanage, with a strong sense of right and wrong. He revered his mother, who had saved their lives time and again and never let them down. Nieh Shou Guang had betrayed every single member of his family, and Gate of Righteousness wanted justice.

There had been no possibility of justice from either Japanese or Kuomintang Party officials. The Presbyterian Church had helped his mother over and over again, but they had been powerless to seek or provide justice. Now, though, the new government was urging people to cleanse their corrupt society by publicly accusing evildoers. The Communists were offering justice for all, and the more Gate of Righteousness learned about his father, the more he began to feel that he should turn to them.

Mama had encouraged the family to forgive their father when they were children—innocent, ignorant children who did not know what the man had done. Mama thought Papa had repented and changed. But what about that affair he had had with the teacher in 1947? And what about the other things people said about him? Mama was too pure of heart, too willing to believe Nieh Shou Guang's fine words. Papa had deceived her. He was deceiving her still.

Gate of Righteousness started gathering his brothers outside the orphanage to tell them what he had learned. The information devastated and disillusioned them. While they were still sorting out these revelations, Gate of Righteousness went to the Communist Party with his information. With government encouragement, he published an article in the daily newspaper accusing his father of stealing money from the orphanage and he documented the charge.

The Canaan Home orphans in 1950 in front of their new home at the American School in Peking. Mr. Nieh is in the middle, the tallest person in the back row. Laura stands beside him, her face half hidden.

More New China Reports

INTERVIEWS WITH FLORENCE LOGAN, JANUARY 28, 1985 AND JUNE 3, 1987:

You had to go along as an automaton, just doing what you were told and saying what they [the Communists] wanted you to say. Then you got along well. Any deviation, and you were in for big trouble.

Laura's poverty was her greatest protection really. They couldn't accuse her of mistreating servants, and things like that. She was a servant herself. [So] in one way Laura's way of life gave the Communists no grounds for their usual accusations against foreigners. In another way it made her more vulnerable, for the Communists could not endure to have anyone else recognized as doing good. All good had to come from the Communist Party. Laura was a rival, so she had to go.

27.

Day of Decision

Peking, at the American School, 1950-1951

AT NIGHT, after evening prayers with the girls, Laura knelt beside her bed and prayed. She read and re-read the psalms, converting the anguish of the psalmists into her own prayers.

> *Be merciful to me, O God, for man would swallow me up,*
> *Fighting all day he oppresses me.*
> *My enemies would hound me all day*
> *For there are many who fight against me, O Most High.*
> *Whenever I am afraid, I will trust in You.*
> *In God (I will praise His word),*
> *In God I have put my trust,*
> *I will not fear.*
> *What can man do to me?* (Psalm 56:1-4)

Afterward she was not sure exactly when she understood what she would probably have to do. Perhaps the realization dawned with Tabitha's unexpected death.

• • •

One cold winter morning, Rose Mary sprinted down the hall toward Laura's room shouting, "Mama! Come quick! Tabitha fell!"

Laura raced to the girls' dormitory. A knot of girlish forms gathered around a still body sprawled upon the hardwood floor. The little girls were crying, and the older ones were trying to calm them through their own tears.

The girl in charge of Tabitha this month had lost her balance and dropped Tabitha when she tried to pick her up to take her to the bathroom. Tabitha was still breathing, but her pulse was faint, and she was unconscious. Tenderly Laura gathered up the tiny body and placed Tabitha back into bed. Then she covered her up warmly with an extra quilt.

For three days Tabitha remained in a restless coma, moaning and keeping her sisters awake at night. The family kept her clean and warm, and Laura made constant visits to the child's bedside day and night. Tabitha never regained consciousness, though, and after three days, she died.

Laura instructed one of the older girls to wash Tabitha's body, comb her hair, and dress her in a fresh, clean gown. Then Laura gathered up a soft wool blanket that a dear friend had given her a dozen years before as a wedding gift. Through all the years of starvation, occupation, and civil war, Laura had treasured this blanket and kept it special. Now she carried it to the dormitory and wrapped its softness carefully around Tabitha's childish form. Then she prayed with the girls and sent them to their classes.

For a long time she stood by the bed, gazing at Tabitha's body, filled with an odd mixture of sorrow and relief.

Tabitha was safe now. The cadres could neither neglect nor abuse her. They had no power to hurt this little one now. "I will see you in Heaven, Tabitha," Laura murmured, stroking the soft wool bundle.

There is nothing I can do for Tabitha anymore, she thought, *and there is nothing I can do for her brothers and sisters any longer here either. I am a danger to them now. Just by staying on, I keep the government's spotlight focused on them. Maybe the only one I can possibly do anything to help is Kenneth.*

Although the cadres refused to allow Kenneth to speak to Laura anymore, they did not place the couple under house arrest. So they could still meet and talk on occasion, like the times each of them received a dinner invitation from their friends at the Presbyterian mission. They just had to be sure that each traveled to the friend's home separately. Laura figured that the Communists separated them within their own residence to harass and intimidate them.

They were isolated both inside and outside the home. It was dangerous for anyone to be linked publicly with an American. Every day in Peking a half dozen or more public rallies were staged in various parts of the city to demonstrate against the Korean War and China's chief enemy, the United States. Some of the rallies were gigantic, and they frequently turned ugly. People began shouting just to prevent being accused of a lack of enthusiasm. Then the mob spirit took over, and they started killing. Sometimes the shouts of the demonstrators were so loud, Laura could hear them inside the building, even with the windows shut against the bitter Peking cold.

Wang Ming Dao and his wife came openly to Canaan Home to visit the Niehs anyway, ignoring their danger. They told the Niehs that Chinese Christians in Peking were aware of the situation at Canaan Home and were praying. Laura hoped the Wangs' courageous show of friendship would not get them arrested or killed. It comforted her to hear that their Chinese friends were concerned about the family, even in the middle of the Christians' own deep troubles. For the sake of her dear friends, she no longer visited or greeted them in public. If one of them spoke to her on the street, they could be accused of being an American spy—a capital offense. The danger was so great that Susie Dean, the grown, adopted Chinese daughter of the orphanage's American music teacher, was afraid to speak to her own parents. The Communists forbade her to visit them.

Finally the inevitable day arrived. In February 1951, the government tried one last time to bring Laura into line. The three cadres assigned to Canaan Home sent for her, and when she appeared before them, she found a fourth man waiting in the room as well. He was a squat, swarthy fellow with a flat nose and broad cheeks. He seemed to be the one in charge.

"Mrs. Nieh, I am Comrade Lao," he began in a tone of grave respect.

"The Chinese Communist Party has sent me to tell you that we have known about you for a long time. We know that you have lived in China for over twenty years and that you have done much good. You have saved the lives of many Chinese children."

The room felt oppressive—stuffy, laced with body odor. Laura felt wary. She noticed that the other three cadres were watching her closely.

"I am honored by your kind words," Laura said.

Comrade Lao nodded approval. "As you know, Mrs. Nieh," he said, "there is a new government in China, and the Chinese Communist Party must now be taking over all the hospitals, schools, and orphanages which were founded by foreigners." He paused, eyeing her reaction. Laura forced her face to remain calm.

"You will be happy to hear, however, that we wish to make an exception of this institution," he went on. "The Communist Party hopes that you will stay here in Peking and continue as head of this orphanage."

Again he paused. He seemed to be waiting for Laura to say something.

"The Party is most kind," she murmured.

Comrade Lao nodded again. His mouth turned upward at both corners, but the smile failed to reach his eyes. "If you wish to remain here, however," he said, "it is the Party's decision that you must change the old methods in two ways."

Here it comes, Laura thought.

"First," Comrade Lao said, emphasizing his words carefully, "you must give up Jesus. You must no longer mention Jesus or use Jesus to educate the children. It is best for them to give up their faith in God now because the Chinese Communist Party is atheistic."

For a moment Laura felt as if a big hand had jammed a pillow over her face. She drew a deep breath to clear the smothery feeling.

"Secondly," the man continued, "you must change your thinking about your country and the American president, Truman. You must make a public announcement that America is the ultra-imperialist country, always invading other countries. You must recognize and admit that Truman is the Head of War."

Laura said nothing. She willed her hands to remain in a relaxed position by her sides and sent up an inarticulate prayer for help.

"If you will accept these two conditions," the party official said, "then the Chinese Communist Party will allow you to remain head of this orphanage, and we will honor you as a living Dr. Norman Bethune."

Norman Bethune was a Red Army hero, a Canadian who died serving the army's guerrilla bases. Communists extolled him as a model of absolute selflessness.

For a full minute, Laura kept silent, considering her reply. In the stillness she could hear her children singing their mealtime hymn of thanks. At last she smiled at the Party official. "It is a great honor," she said, "to hear that the Communist Party has noticed and approved of the work I have done with Chinese children."

Comrade Lao's mouth turned up at both corners again. The four Communists waited.

"But as to your two conditions," Laura said, "I cannot lie and say there is no God. I can give up almost anything for my children, but I cannot give up Jesus.

"And as to Truman, it is hard for me to get American newspapers to read anything about him. Whether or not Truman is the Head of War, I would have no way of knowing. I cannot lie to you about this, and I cannot say bad things about a person behind his back."

She cleared her throat to hide the sudden tremor in her voice. "I love the Chinese children," she finished in a steady tone. "I also love Jesus. And I also love my country."

Mr. Lao's eyes narrowed to slits, and his dark skin turned dusky rose. "Spy! American spy!" he shouted. "I know what you are doing! You are feeding these Chinese children with superstitions! You are turning these Chinese children into American imperialist spies!" Spit exploded from his mouth as he shouted, shooting across the room like tiny, furious bullets.

Then they were all yelling at her.

Something inside Laura hardened and turned to steel. She kept her eyes fixed on Mr. Lao and stood her ground, as unmoving and patient as a statue. The yelling gradually died, and Mr. Lao's color faded from dusky rose to a dark tan. "You are making a very serious mistake, Mrs. Nieh," he said in a harsh tone. "If you love your husband and your children, you can still save their future. Think carefully."

Laura made no reply. She felt she could not trust her voice. There was a long silence.

"Since you are so stubborn," Mr. Lao finally said, "the Party will now appoint a new director to replace you and your husband as head of Canaan Home."

He waited, but still she said nothing.

"You may go," he said.

The youngest cadre opened the door, and Laura stepped into the hall. Nineteen-year-old Foreign Doll came hurrying toward her, apparently running an errand for one of the staff. Her usual lively smile was gone. Her lips trembled, and her eyes held fear. Perhaps she had heard the shouting.

"Don't be afraid, Darling," Laura said. "God will help us."

Foreign Doll bowed politely. She passed on, and suddenly, in Laura's mind, she could see her daughter once again as a tiny, fluffy-headed three-year-old, tearing through the courtyard shouting, "Mama! A great worm! A great long worm! Come see!"

Laura smiled, remembering the innocent description. She felt her eyes fill with tears. *She is innocent still,* Laura thought, *but now she is facing a danger much worse than the snake. And this time I cannot protect my little daughter with a stove poker.*

Anguish poured through her like a fire. "I thought I was ready and willing to die for You, Jesus," she whispered, "but I never thought I would have to die a death like this one."

She made her way to her bedroom, dressed warmly, and pedaled her bicycle to the British Embassy. "I need your help," she told the official there, "to apply for my exit visa."

Dr. Chang's Report

Letter to Becky Powers from Dr. Chang Yu-Ming, August 22, 1987:

While we were thinking of our old and beloved friends and co-workers in our risen Lord Jesus Christ, Mr. and Mrs. Laura Richards Nieh, your letter arrived at our hand. Both my wife and I knew the Niehs and brother Wang Ming Dao, who married us February 3, 1954 at the Peking Christian Tabernacle. My wife was a graduate from Yenching University, from 1947 to 1951. [At] all Christian student summer conferences in Peking at the Canaan Home Orphanage at "Ching-Lung-Chiao" to the west of the Summer Palace of Peking, we were there. Just on the very eve of Mrs. Nieh's departure, I was on the way to the West Mountains to see my aunt (my uncle was killed by the Communists). We met on the street of "Hai-Tian" which is close to Yenching University. We had a ten-minute talk on the street. She informed me that her situation was from bad to worse. She was forced to leave immediately, and she asked me to pray for her.

28.

Mama, Good-bye

Peking, 1951

HE WAS KIND, so very kind.

He answered her questions, made arrangements, and told her which papers she needed, what procedures she must follow. Her status as an American citizen was unquestioned, he assured her. The 1924 law, which revoked the citizenship of Americans who married Chinese, had been canceled. Unfortunately, the Chinese government did have legal grounds to detain her as the wife of a Chinese citizen, he said, but the British Embassy would do everything in their power to help her obtain an exit visa.

He seemed so anxious to help that she wished she could ask him all her questions. There were a few she must keep to herself though. She would have to wait until she reached Hong Kong to find out the requirements Kenneth must meet to emigrate to the U.S., for example. It would be too dangerous to ask questions about that in Peking.

She left the Embassy and pedaled her way slowly through the winding lanes of the city, stopping her bicycle outside the compound walls at 5 Fang Chia Hutung, where she had moved with the children when they left from the Russian Retreat Place.

A stark winter sun shone in a massive dome of blue heaven. Its rays glinted golden on the amber roofs of the city, making up in light and brilliance what it lacked in warmth. Laura's fingers and toes tingled with cold. Her thoughts chilled, too, at the sight of accusation posters decorating the high gray walls of her old home.

The cadres had executed its owner, her former landlord. How much longer would it be before new posters would be going up to denounce his brother-in-law, Kenneth?

She pushed her bicycle next door to the gates of Pearl's family compound. Pearl had met and married a young Christian man in Shanghai. Then her uncle had sent them to the U.S. to handle the American side of his import-export business. Pearl's parents had written their daughter in America warning her not to come back to Peking, even though Pearl's mother lay dying in the hospital.

Such dear, dear people. They would probably never in this life see their daughter again, yet Laura must not visit to comfort them. She dared not endanger yet another loved one with the contamination of her presence.

Laura gripped the handlebars of her bicycle with all her strength and wished she could go to some utterly private place to scream. Surely Jesus had felt this angry, too, sometimes. He had flailed the moneychangers from the temple with a whip once, and overturned their tables of cash. Oh, for such a whip! Oh, for the satisfaction of justice, the splendid righting of wrong!

Jesus had righted wrongs on the cross though, too, and there He had used no whip. He had given Himself up to death. He absorbed wickedness into Himself and refused to return evil for evil. In life He met every sin with virtue, every wrong with a right. He countered hatred with love, selfish ambition with relinquishment, the abuse of power with sacrifice and loving service.

Yet He had screamed, hadn't He? On the cross?

"My God! My God!" He had bellowed. "My God, why have You forsaken me?"

The anguish ripping from His throat had been for her, for Kenneth, for the children, and yes, even for these hardhearted, foolish atheists.

A teardrop trickled down her cheek and landed on her metal handlebar, where it froze. Laura stared at it curiously. Why wasn't it red? It should be blood.

It didn't seem right that she should feel such pain and see no blood. She should be bleeding from the eyes, the ears, the mouth. She should be hemorrhaging through the *hutongs* of Peking, trailing heart, liver, intestines through the dust behind her.

With a sigh, Laura mounted her bicycle and resumed her weary way home. "Lord Jesus," she prayed, "if only You might send a Christian mother to take my place, I should be grateful. It would ease my heart if You should send a fine Christian woman like Miss Cho to oversee this work and care for these little ones."

At the gate house to the American School, Samuel greeted her in a cheerful, husky rumble. How manly and grown up he sounded these days! Such a fine, responsible young man he had become.

Samuel had been the first baby boy she had taken in who survived. He had been two years old when the crippled beggar crawled up the steps to beg a home with the family. He had been three when she nursed him through the measles and pneumonia epidemics, that time she nearly died from coal gas poisoning. He had been less than four years old during the Japanese assault and the bandit invasion. As a young boy, he had survived the deadly famine years of the Japanese occupation. As a young teenager he had dodged mortar shells to run errands for the family when they were trapped in the center of the final battle for Peking.

Samuel should have died years ago, many times over. Naturally speaking, he should never have survived to age 18. Miracle upon miracle had preserved him—and all the other children as well.

The nerve of these people! Taking over, putting themselves in charge of such treasure—God's treasure! How could they be so arrogant?

The Communists gave her little trouble once she applied to leave the country. The government issued her an exit visa without difficulty, and the cadres at Canaan Home even threw a farewell party for her with all the children.

Laura filled out her paperwork. She turned her Brownie Kodak camera in for inspection to obtain a permit to take it out of the country. The Chinese director of the YMCA offered to sell her bicycle for her. He sold it for more than she had paid for it and bought her a train ticket to Tientsin. Several people gave her money to help pay her passage home.

When Laura visited Dr. Lewis and his family to tell them she was going, Kenneth joined her there. The Lewises would realize later that her farewell had been his as well. She dared not endanger Rebecca Tsai's Chinese in-laws by visiting the Tsai family at home to say her good-byes, so her friend Ivy Gordan invited the Niehs and Tsais to her home for a farewell dinner for Laura. Rebecca Tsai was the American woman married to a Chinese translator who had tried to discourage Laura from marrying Kenneth back in 1939. Mr. and Mrs. Tsai and their three children were close friends of the Wangs and active members of the Peking Christian Tabernacle. They did much to support Canaan Home along with the rest of the congregation. The Canaan Home children were especially fond of the Tsais' middle child Ruth who had given up her summer vacation to teach the Canaan Home children Bible lessons during the family's first summer at the American School.

Laura wondered what would happen to the three Tsai children under the new regime. All their lives, Becky, Ruth, and Daniel had been taunted and persecuted for being half-American. The church had been their one place of acceptance. Now an anti-American government was trying to take over the church. Would the Tsais survive the growing violence against people with American ties? Even without American ties, how much longer would a staunch Christian leader like Mr. Tsai remain free?

She had to trust that God would provide for the Tsais, just as He would provide for her children. More than likely, He would provide for each, at times, through the other.

During Laura's brief opportunities to communicate privately with her husband, she and Kenneth devised a simple plan of escape for him. Laura would sail to Hong Kong and wait for him there. Kenneth would travel south to Canton and then attempt to sneak across the border to meet her. Kenneth thought that he was a marked man, that the government wanted to kill him. They would probably make no move, though, until Laura was out of the country. So he would drop out of sight as soon as she boarded the train for Tientsin.

She had to offer him an escape. Kenneth had betrayed the family. That was true. But he had tried to make amends. Few people realized all that he had done for them.It was also true that Kenneth had not been a good husband. But she had to ask herself, had she been a good wife? Always she had put the children ahead of him; always she had focused on them first. It had to be so. The orphans' lives were at stake. Kenneth had been too young to really understand what he was doing when he offered to marry her, and she had misjudged his maturity. And she had refused to bear his children....Perhaps in America, if she could give Kenneth her full attention without the children, perhaps they could start over and the marriage could work.

For she was sure that Kenneth loved her. He loved the children, too. It must be so, for why else would he have stayed with them? He could have returned to his clan, married another woman, and moved on to a comfortable life with servants and special privileges. There had been nothing at Canaan Home for him except the crushing burden of 100 plus orphans and her love.

As soon as the older boys found out that Laura was going to leave, they held a meeting to plan ways to take care of their younger brothers in the future. Then they met with Laura to let her know about their plans. *Bless their hearts,* Laura thought, looking around her at the earnest faces of the teenage boys. *They are trying so hard to lessen my burden.*

A stiff March wind shook the windows of the classroom where they were meeting, shutting out the sunlight with a yellow curtain of Gobi grime. Laura strained her eyes in the dimness to fix the youthful forms and faces of the boys in her memory forever.

"If the younger ones become ill," Samuel began, "we can try to find a place for them."

Zechariah, now grown into a handsome, sturdily built young man, sat still as a stairstep directly across from her, staring at his cloth shoes. Beside him sat Titus, a crippled boy who got around on crutches. Titus had developed a habit of playing an imaginary piano whenever he felt nervous. Today he was performing fugues in the air while Samuel talked.

"We can help them find jobs, too, when they are ready to work," Samuel continued. "We can help them in many ways."

Then the room filled with the sounds of fresh young baritones, basses, and tenors offering ideas. A stab of grief pierced her. She and Kenneth would never see the promise of their sons' young manhood fulfilled. No careers to follow. No accomplishments to praise. No young wives to admire. No grandchildren to spoil.

Her tongue tasted salt, and she realized that a tear had trickled into her mouth. Titus quit playing imaginary fugues and began using his fingers to rub his eyes instead. All the boys appeared to be waiting for her to say something.

"My dear children, I am very sad to be leaving you," she began, "but you have your motherland, and I have my motherland. Even though I must go now to my own motherland, it encourages my heart that you are making plans to be of help to the younger children. I hope after I leave, that all of you will love each other and take good care of each other."

She pulled out her handkerchief to wipe the tears trickling down her cheeks, and she noticed that some of the boys' faces were crumpling into tears, too. She took a deep breath to compose herself. This last message to her sons was important. All their lives they would remember their mother's final words to them.

"The government is calling up young men to be soldiers in this war, and perhaps it may be one day that I will hear that one of you has died in the war," she said. "Hearing this would make me very sad, but it would not make me feel as sad as hearing that you have turned away from Jesus. For me, the saddest thing in my life would be hearing that you have stopped believing in Jesus."

All the boys were crying hard now, sniffling into handkerchiefs or wiping their faces on the sleeves of their padded jackets. Laura could barely see them through her own tears. "Good-bye," she finished, with her voice cracking. "Good-bye. I will see you in Heaven."

Then they all cried together. The boys came up to her for individual good-byes and asked if they could write to her in America. She had to say no. It would be too dangerous.

It was no easier with Rachel the next day. The young woman asked if she could help Laura pack, and Laura agreed. It seemed a good way for the two of them to spend a couple last moments together.

They gathered up the few possessions Laura planned to take along—her Brownie camera, documents, photographs, watercolors the children had painted, Florence Logan's pamphlet about Canaan Home, copies of the circular letters she had sent supporters (a couple letters, she noticed, had never been mailed due to the war with Japan), as well as a modest wardrobe of Western clothing that missionary friends had passed along to her when they returned to the U.S. on furlough.

"Mama," Rachel said in a tentative voice as she smoothed and folded a long-sleeved flowered dress, "you will be lonely in America without one of your children. Please take me with you."

Laura could not speak.

Rachel's words rushed on: "Everyone says I look like you, Mama. *I look like you!* I could be your daughter in America, and no one could say I was not your child. Please take me with you."

Laura cleared her throat and tried to speak normally around the lump. "No, Darling, I can't."

Rachel straightened from her task, her eyes dark wells of anguish. Her wide mouth trembled. "Why, Mama?" she whispered.

"I don't have the proper documents," Laura said.

She hugged her daughter, and they wept together.

The night before Laura left Peking, she walked to the Peking Christian Tabernacle to say a last good-bye to friends at the Wangs' church. Kenneth was there. The two of them broke down completely, in such pain they could not talk. All they could do was cry out to God while their friends sobbed alongside them.

By morning, Laura was numb. An invisible curtain seemed to hang between her and the rest of the world. Sound seemed muffled. Everything looked remote and unreal. She felt lazy, too. Pushing back her covers was an effort.

She willed her thin frame out of bed, then forced her hands to cover it with the outdated Western clothes. She picked up her small suitcase and a couple parcels. She compelled her legs to carry her down the hall. Passing the girls' dormitory, she noticed that it was empty except for one teenager who lay on a bed sobbing, with the covers pulled over her head.

Laura had slept in late. The family was up, and the children were in their classes. She had insisted that the school day be carried on as usual, with no final gathering of children and staff for a last farewell. Two of the teachers and a few of the children disobeyed orders, though. They came out to the entry, weeping. She walled herself up in the numbness.

Kenneth waited for her in the entry, and the Communist director who had come that morning to take over Canaan Home stepped up next to him. The woman seemed small and far away, as if Laura were looking at her through the wrong end of a telescope. The new director thrust out her palm to shake hands with Laura.

Laura heard her own voice saying something and watched her hand give the woman's a mechanical shake. Then she picked up her suitcase and walked out the door. She felt she could no longer shed a tear.

Laura Richards Nieh in 1957, at the age of 64, six years after the Communist government forced her to leave mainland China and her adopted Canaan Home children.

Rachel's Final Memories

Excerpt from Rachel's memoirs, written 38 years after her mother left China, translated from Chinese:

In the morning of the day she left, Mama wouldn't let any of us say good-bye to her. Why not?

I think Mama was afraid she would break down if all the children came around to say good-bye. She was afraid it would be too hard for us to see our mother leave and never come back again. Mama loved us and let us have classes as usual.

I was sitting beside the window by coincidence, paying no attention to the class. So I saw how terrible Mama looked when she left, taking only a few very simple packages. She went out of the gate with Papa, and I cried and cried. I missed my mother. I thought, I will never ever see Mama again in my whole life. *Then I had another thought:* I must believe God very much. That way, after I die, I will go to Heaven and meet Mama again. *After that I stopped crying.*

Mama didn't let us say good-bye to her, but through the window I saw Mrs. Wang Ming Dao and some of the other members of the board of directors coming toward her. So when Mama went out the gate, she was not alone. When I saw God's believers leaving with her, I felt consoled. I said in my heart, Mama, good-bye.

Deep in my heart I know that if Mama hadn't come to China, I wouldn't exist—and probably not only me, but also many other people besides me as well. I thank God that I was born in a very poor family, and then God took me out and sent me to Canaan Home Orphanage. I came to a very rich place.

The most valuable thing in my life was that Mama brought God's love to me when I was young. She led me to know the God Jesus. It was Jesus who led Mama to come to China and raise up so many poor children so that we could grow up to adulthood. Our mother spent a lot of hard times with us, and finally we found happiness.

None of the orphans will forget Mama and her love. She planted all these seeds, and now I must depend on God for strength to do the work of harvesting the fruit. Later I will go to Heaven and meet Mama there.

Mama left us forever. When she went away, she said nothing to any of the children. Usually when she went out, she would tell us to take good care of the younger ones, take good care of the house, and so on. This time, though, when we needed her last words to us, Mama kept silent. Was it because Mama didn't want to speak to us?

No. Her heart had broken. What could she say to us?

Mama, we understand. You can go in peace.

Just like that, she left us forever.

29.

Miss Richards Returns

United States and China, 1951-1981

So many people were disappearing. Would Happy Plum Flower disappear, too?

Chinese Christians thought the government might be planning to detain her once she was away from Peking where people knew her. It would be so simple for them to arrest her somewhere on her solitary journey between Peking and Hong Kong, to take her away and kill her. Who would know? Who would try to stop them?

Happy Plum Flower was a vulnerable mama hen fluttering from her nest to draw attention away from her brood of chicks. The Christians held their breath, and, as best they could, they closed ranks around her.

On the morning of Happy Plum Flower's departure, Wang Ming Dao's wife, a couple of the older Canaan Home boys, and several members of the orphanage board accompanied both the Niehs to the railway station. Then Mrs. Wang boarded the train with Happy Plum Flower and escorted her all the way to Tientsin. It was an astonishing act of bravery. It could have meant a death sentence for Mrs. Wang.

To everyone's relief, neither woman was arrested.

Two of the older Canaan Home boys met the women's train in Tientsin. Their mother appeared dazed when she greeted them, and then the customs office swallowed her up. After that, there was nothing more to do but pray and hope and wait for news.

Nieh Shou Guang dropped out of sight. He never returned to Canaan Home. No one knew where he went after he said good-bye to his wife at the railroad station. Through posters and newspaper articles, the government denounced him as a counter-revolutionary and an imperialist spy, accusing him of stealing money from the orphanage. Some of the newspaper articles were written by Gate of Righteousness.

Meanwhile, Laura settled down at the Lutheran Guest House in Hong Kong. She devoted herself to caring for a sick missionary while she waited for Kenneth to escape to her side. She hunted for work, too, hoping to find a way to earn enough money to stay as long as necessary. The expense of her room and board at the guest house was minimal, but so was her supply of funds. Chinese customs officials had kept most of the money her friends had given her for her passage home. Of the $200 she carried into customs with her, the cadres gave her back only $20.

For five months she waited in Hong Kong with no job, no husband, and no word. Finally, when her Uncle Edward Russell in Ohio sent money for her passage home, Laura returned to America by ship. Night after night as she sailed, the children visited her dreams. One night the toddlers came to her. The next night, the kindergartners thronged her pillow. Every night she dreamed of a different child or a different group of children. The dreams comforted her.

Laura was 58 years old when she returned to the United States in 1951, and she lived another 30 years. For the first 16 years, until she grew too frail to take care of anyone but herself, Laura spent her days quietly caring for the sick, the dying, the troubled, and the dispossessed. And for almost all of the rest of her life, except for one brief interlude, Laura lived in a kind of secret suspense, ever alert for news from China, yet covering her past from the world to protect her loved ones behind the Bamboo Curtain.

Most of Laura's relatives had been mortified when they learned that Laura had married a Chinese. They were quietly relieved when no embarrassing Chinese husband arrived with Laura on the boat from China.

Her friends were excited to see her again. They wanted to hear all about her adventures during World War II and the ongoing Chinese revolution. She should write a book about her experiences, they told her.

The thought made Laura cringe. Americans had no concept of the danger that even a chance remark could bring to the people she loved. For the sake of her children, former Canaan Home staff, and all her dear Chinese friends still living on the mainland, she refused to talk about what had happened in China. Almost anything she said could be twisted and used against them in a people's court. An innocent story or a simple word of praise could sentence someone she loved to a term of hard labor or to death. When a reporter from her hometown newspaper interviewed Laura soon after she returned home, she told many stories about the early days of the orphanage, but she refused to discuss any events since the birth of New China. Even if there had been no danger, though, Laura was by nature a private person. Her grief was too raw and her private life too complicated for her to tell her story to strangers. Writing a book was out of the question.

She traveled to Washington D.C. in 1952 to ask her Ohio representatives and senators to grant her husband special immigration status through congressional action. She filled out all the necessary paperwork. While she was on the East Coast, she made a side trip to New York to visit Pearl, whose husband was working in her extended family's import-export business. The young couple had a small son, and Pearl was learning how to cook and sew for her family.

"Guess what, Pearl?" Laura said. "When I left China, the children were still wearing the over-garments you gave them!"

"Still?" Pearl asked. "It's been fourteen years since we made them."

"The children just outgrow them and pass them down to the younger ones," Laura said.

She settled in Ohio to nurse her ailing 85-year-old uncle, Edward Russell. Then, when his health temporarily improved after a few months, she decided to work as a nurse in a local hospital. She filled out her job application under the name of Miss Laura Richards and asked her friends to call her by her maiden name.

Several years passed, one after another. She worked for a year in a pediatric ward in Ohio, then nursed her Uncle Edward for several months in his final illness. After that, she moved to California to nurse her old friend Dr. Maud Mackey, the physician who had been in charge of the women's hospital in Paotingfu during Laura's first missionary term. Laura took care of her terminally ill friend for three years, until the doctor's niece placed her in a nursing home. She died not long afterward, in 1957. Laura was probably still with Dr. Mackey when friends in China were finally able to send her word about what had happened to her husband and to the children of Canaan Home.

After Kenneth made several unsuccessful escape attempts from Canton, he was captured, imprisoned for three years, and, finally, executed. She had been a widow since 1954. As for the younger children still in the orphanage, the government moved half of them into a government boarding school with children who had been indoctrinated to the government's satisfaction. The government then moved 50 indoctrinated children into Canaan Home, thus attempting to dissolve the Canaan Home children's close family support system. By the time Laura heard this news, many of the leaders of the Peking Christian Tabernacle, including the Wangs, had been sent to prison.

When Dr. Mackey died in 1957, Laura was 64 and nearing retirement age. She had spent her life caring for others. She had no savings, no property, no investments. She had not worked long enough in the U.S. to qualify for social security payments. She had no children near to take her into their homes and support her.

She seemed unconcerned about it, though. She decided to take the gospel overseas once more under Go-Ye Fellowship, which sponsored missionary candidates even when they were past the usual mandatory retirement age decreed by other mission societies. Laura wanted to work with children again, so she took a year of training with Child Evangelism Fellowship. Then she sailed to the Philippines at the age of 65. Unfortunately, after only a couple years in the Philippines, Laura contracted hepatitis, and doctors advised her not to remain overseas. So in 1961 Laura reluctantly made plans to return to the United States.

While in the Philippines, Laura had kept up a correspondence with Miss R. Celestia Churchill, the founder of the Mary Martha Home. Miss Churchill began the Home in Los Angeles in 1921 to provide a safe refuge for women and girls who were unemployed or homeless. Miss Churchill invited Laura to come to the Mary Martha Home when she returned from the Philippines.

There Laura slowly recovered and gradually assumed more responsibilities. Visiting friends were astonished to find her at times scrubbing the floor on hands and knees at age 70 and beyond. She did whatever was needed.

In 1966, at the age of 81, Miss Churchill suffered a major stroke. Her ministry had to be closed, and the Mary Martha Home, located in an historic old mansion at 632 Brittania Street, was put up for sale. Laura was 74 years old when she helped find new homes for the women staying there and served as one of the caretakers for the property for a year until it was sold.

Fortunately, Laura learned that she qualified for social security benefits as a veteran of World War I. Her stipend was not enough to live on, though, and she had become too old and frail to work for a living. She had no idea where she might go next or how she might live.

Then, quite unexpectedly, through the help of a friend, a bequest, and the sale of the Mary Martha Home, she and Miss Churchill were able to move into the Hollenbeck Home, a beautiful retirement center in Los Angeles. It was a well-kept place, with lovely flower gardens and a bird sanctuary. Most of the people living there were wealthy.

Laura lived at the Hollenbeck Home from March 1967 until she died on April 22, 1981, at the age of 88. To the end of her life she remained "Miss Richards," a quiet, cheerful spinster who entertained a variety of well-traveled visitors and kept her ears open for any news from mainland China. The news she gleaned was meager. Bits of detail escaped from behind the Bamboo Curtain and were pieced together over many years into a story puzzle, full of gaps and unanswered questions.

After Laura left China in 1951, the Peking Christian Tabernacle struggled on against intense opposition. Wang Ming Dao refused to join the Three-Self Patriotic Movement (TSPM) because its leadership was theologically liberal and because he believed his church should not be part of a political movement. In 1954 the TSPM, working closely with Communist government officials, ordered all Protestant churches and Christian organizations in Peking to come to a meeting to accuse Wang Ming Dao. At the meeting they tried unsuccessfully to pressure a majority to agree to demand his imprisonment or death. To counter the national "Accuse Wang Ming Dao" campaign, students from the Peking Christian Student Fellowship started a "Stop Persecuting Wang Ming Dao" campaign.

Meanwhile, the pastor held doggedly on course, preaching the gospel, warning against false teachers, and teaching Christians how to live out the moral principles of Christianity in everyday life. When no printer dared to publish him any longer, the pastor set the type for his materials himself and continued to publish his magazine and booklets on his own small hand-turned press.

In 1955 the government arrested Wang Ming Dao, his wife, and many of the leaders of the Peking Christian Tabernacle. The Communists subjected the pastor to intense brainwashing techniques, with at least two cadres in his prison cell with him at all times. After a year, he suffered a mental breakdown, signed a confession regarding his "imperialism," and was released from prison along with his wife and other church leaders. Broken in mind and body, he wandered through his house murmuring, "I am Peter," referring to the disciple who denied Jesus.

A year later, after Wang Ming Dao had recovered his health, he went to authorities and retracted his confession. As a result, he and his wife were arrested and imprisoned a second time. A number of Christian leaders from his church were also arrested or re-arrested and sentenced to labor camps as well. These included Rebecca Tsai's husband, her eldest daughter Becky, and her son-in-law—her daughter Ruth's husband. Also arrested and sentenced were a number of leaders from the Peking Christian Student Fellowship—many of the same students who had ministered to the Canaan Home orphans and used the Dowager's Boathouse facilities for their 1947 and 1948 summer prayer conferences. The government singled out those members of the Peking Christian Tabernacle who escaped arrest to be struggled against and criticized in their units of work.

By the time Laura sailed for the Philippines in 1958, few orthodox Christians attended the institutional church in China anymore. They felt it was pointless. If they went to church, they would be pressured to criticize and accuse their fellow believers instead of loving, supporting, and having fellowship with each other. Also, the TSPM reported to Christians' work units whatever they said and to whomever they talked in church. Their superiors then called those believers in for criticism. So Christians met by twos and threes in their own homes for fellowship and worship, when they dared to meet at all.

As church attendance dropped and one political campaign followed another, all the rural churches and most of the city churches closed down. Of the 64 Protestant churches in Peking before the birth of New China, only four remained open by late 1958. The Christian church in China was pushed almost entirely underground.

Laura's loved ones in China suffered economic hardships along with political ones. The Great Leap Forward, Mao's disastrous economic modernization campaign of 1958-1960, brought about several years of famine, resulting in the deaths of an estimated 30 million people or more.

As news leaked out from behind the Bamboo Curtain, Laura sometimes remembered her final words to the older boys: "The saddest thing in my life would be hearing that you have turned away from the Lord Jesus. I hope that all of you will continue to believe in Jesus."

Were her children persevering under trial? Were her children somehow remaining faithful to Jesus? She could only pray and hope as news from the mainland grew worse.

During Laura's years at Hollenbeck Home, a chaotic civil war rose up and engulfed the People's Republic of China. The Cultural Revolution, commonly dated 1966 to 1976, began when Mao Tse Tung combined a purge of his political rivals with a fresh campaign to develop revolutionary fervor within the new generation born under Communism. At first he encouraged youthful Red Guards to attack their teachers, mobbing and ransacking their homes, beating and humiliating them in public, and burning everything that represented "The Four Olds"—old ideas, old thoughts, old habits, old customs. They destroyed books, records, music, fine art—anything that they declared to be bourgeois or feudal.

Then, drunk with power, the Red Guards turned their attention to other elements of society. They targeted religious believers and intellectuals first. Then people started settling personal accounts, manipulating mobs against fellow workers and neighbors to take revenge over petty offenses and personal jealousies. Tens of thousands were beaten to death. Families shattered as parents were murdered or marched off to "re-education camps." The victims' children were left to fend for themselves, stigmatized and abandoned, because their relatives refused to take them in for fear of the mobs. Factions developed among the Red Guards, and these cliques then turned on each other. Civil war spread.

No one emerged from the decade untouched, including the Red Guard. Businesses and factories closed. The government transported 17 million urban youth to rural areas to do manual labor—the greatest forced movement of a population known to history. Schools were either closed down or in chaos for a decade. A generation lost their opportunity to become well-trained or even educated at all. Business, industry, medicine, science—all suffered not only from the scarcity of well-trained workers, but from the ignorance of ill-trained ones.

To all outward appearances, the church in China vanished. The few church buildings that had remained open were closed down early in the Cultural Revolution, and the TSPM stopped functioning. (The single exceptions were two church buildings in Peking which the government reserved for foreign diplomats and which no Chinese were allowed to attend.) A treasure store of Bibles, hymnals, and Christian study materials went up in flames during the rampages of the Red Guard.

Many Christians were betrayed. Rebellious teenagers turned in their Christian parents. Weak believers gave away Christian brothers and sisters. Red Guards paraded Christians through towns and villages in dunce caps and shamed them in other public displays. They were abused, ridiculed, and spat on by neighbors and co-workers. Many were exiled to the countryside and condemned to forced labor. Others were imprisoned in "re-education camps," where guards and inmates joined forces against them, devising cruel forms of mental and physical torture.

Under this fearful pressure, some Christians recanted their faith, had nervous breakdowns, or committed suicide. Still others grew bold. *What more can we lose than we have lost already?* they reasoned. They took advantage of people's growing disillusionment with the government to share their faith with close friends and trusted relatives. They brought a message of hope to shattered victims of the Cultural Revolution. They also tried to restore believers who had fallen away or whose faith had weakened. Miracles occurred. Signs and wonders stunned the belief system of Party cadres and entire villages. Converts multiplied, and private house church meetings flourished in rural areas. These groups had no formal relationship with the government and were considered illegal.

After Richard Nixon's visit to China in 1972, political conditions between the United States and China changed enough for Laura's old friend, Mrs. Rebecca Tsai, to apply for immigration to the United States as an American citizen. She returned in 1974 at the age of 82 and began working through diplomatic channels to obtain immigration visas for her surviving family members.

Both Mrs. Tsai's husband and the Tsais' son-in-law (Ruth's husband) had died in prison, Laura learned. Ruth had been left a widow to raise two children. The Tsais' older daughter, Becky, had also been imprisoned. The Communist government denied Mrs. Tsai's son, Daniel, permission to continue his college education and assigned the young Christian intellectual to do farm labor in the countryside.

Mrs. Tsai had not seen her oldest daughter Becky for 16 years. Becky had completed her 15-year prison term, but in effect, she remained in prison still. She had suffered a fate common to prisoners in the Chinese gulag. In New China, people needed government permission to move from one locality to another and had to remain in job assignments given to them. When Becky's prison term ended, the Cultural Revolution was still going on. People in positions of responsibility were afraid to make any decisions, especially decisions that could be criticized and bring them to the attention of the Red Guard. So Becky's application to live and work in Peking near her family was turned down. Instead the government "re-assigned" her to continue living and working in the same labor camp where she had lived and worked as a prisoner for 15 years. Becky's application to travel to Peking to visit her 82-year-old mother before she left the country was also denied.

Mrs. Tsai brought Laura a few bits of news from the Canaan Home children. Many of the former orphans had married and now had families of their own. They were scattered all over China. Grace and Gloria worked for a daycare facility in Peking—sometimes they visited the Tsai family. Before Daniel Tsai had been sent to the countryside, he attended school with Zechariah. Their whole class got in trouble, Mrs. Tsai said, because Zechariah refused so vehemently to denounce Wang Ming Dao when a school official pressured the class to accuse the pastor. For a time, the crippled boy Titus had come regularly to Mrs. Tsai for English lessons. Rachel still looked and acted just like Laura.

In 1976, two years after Mrs. Tsai's return to America, the Cultural Revolution ended with the deaths of Mao Tse Tung and Zhou Enlai and the arrest of the Gang of Four, a group of four high officials who were prominent in the Cultural Revolution and the power struggle connected with it. Faced with a shattered economy and a cynical, disillusioned populace, Mao's successor Deng Xiaoping turned his back on Mao's policies of isolationism and national self-sufficiency. In 1978 he opened the door for Chinese students to study overseas and allowed a more open press and freer contact with foreigners. After concluding that the socialist economic system had failed, head officials under his leadership began instituting economic reform under a free market system.

Deng also restored limited freedom of religion in 1978. In rural areas, Christians who had been meeting in secret began to meet more openly. Itinerant Christian workers began traveling from village to village to build up believers and evangelize. House church leaders began to be much more open about their activities. Western Christians became increasingly aware that the church in China had not only survived more than two decades of brutal persecution, but had flourished and increased. Western believers stepped up efforts to smuggle Bibles and other Christian materials into the hands of Chinese Christians. The Far East Broadcasting Company dictated scripture portions over the air waves so believers could copy the Bible by hand. When the ban on listening to foreign radio stations lifted, a flood of hundreds, then thousands, of letters began pouring into the Far East Broadcasting Company, evidence that their Bible teaching and dictating programs were reaching many grateful listeners.

Deng allowed several churches in large cities to re-open in 1979, and these churches were so packed with young and old that new services had to be created. Chinese people emerged from the ordeal of the Cultural Revolution with their faith shattered in the dream of achieving paradise through a political system. As a result, millions embraced Christianity. TSPM leadership struggled to re-establish itself and exert government control over a Christian church that had increased to tens of millions in the countryside.

Laura lived long enough to hear about this astonishing revival and about the 1978 release from prison of her courageous friend, Mrs. Wang Ming Dao. Mrs. Wang had spent 20 years in prison, where she had become blind, a victim of untreated glaucoma. Two years later, her husband was released as well.

Undated photograph with a notation identifying Orpha Gould (left) and Laura Richards in Florida. Orpha and Laura served together as Red Cross nurses in the U.S. and France during World War I. They attended language school in Peking together in 1921 and remained close friends the rest of their lives. Orpha took over the care of the orphanage briefly in 1937 when Laura was recovering from burns suffered during a near-fatal coal gas poisoning accident.

After the Break-Up of Canaan Home

ROBERT CERLING INTERVIEW, 1987, DESCRIBING LAURA, WHOM HE FIRST MET IN 1952:

Laura was small. She was a real quiet, gentle kind of person and always seemed to be very self-effacing, wanting to take a back seat. She never pushed herself forward. She was real considerate of people. She had such a soft voice. Although she was very subdued, you didn't get the idea that she was quiet because of a lack of strength. I think it was the experiences she'd gone through that made her quiet.

Laura was very observant and had a sharp sense of humor that was never caustic or sarcastic. It was merry. You always had a feeling that she was about ready to laugh—a kind of twinkle in her eye and a smile.

DANIEL TSAI INTERVIEWS, JULY 1988 AND JULY 1990:

Many of the orphans kept their family names and had Bible names for their given names. One boy, Daniel, changed totally to another name to please the Communists. [Zechariah] said he should not have done that. [Zechariah] said you shouldn't change your name just for fear of the Communists. The children's names marked them. If the Communists looked at their names, they knew they were Christian. Many of those boys and girls never changed their names.

I was sent to the countryside to do farm labor because of my background—being Christian and having an American mother. I was accused of being a spy—a CIA man—all the time because of my mother. I thought, If I am a spy, I wish the CIA would pay me. *Some of the orphans were accused of the same thing because of Mrs. Nieh.*

The believers survived. Christians met together—two or three, not a whole group. I got together with [Zechariah], my friend. We would share and talk. Sometimes we could sing some hymns and pray.

I had a teacher who had graduated from Asbury College in Kentucky. All the time, he had an English Bible class. When people [cadres] came to them [members of the Bible class], they said, "We are learning English." The Communists thought he was teaching English to some people. They couldn't tell what the books were.

Ruth Tsai interview, July 12, 1988:

The ones [former orphans] that dared to get in touch with me, they had everything to lose by doing it. That means they still really loved the Lord.

Like me, the orphans had a foreign mother. Those I know of never complained that they suffered because of that. They didn't count it as a burden or something bad. One of them quoted to me Psalm 27:10, "My parents have forsaken me, but the Lord received me." Through whom? Through Laura's love, the woman said. It was [Grace] or [Gloria] who said this to me.

It's easy to say, "I still believe in Jesus" and then they kill you. That's easy [to endure]. It's the long torturing that is hard. Some thought it was too difficult. In their hearts, they still believed. Some became pro-Communist. There is always a Judas. Still, many of them remained faithful.

From a letter from Rachel, March 2001,
in which she reported that for several years the orphans have been gathering for an annual reunion on Mother's Day:

One time we had 24 of us gathered together in remembrance of Mother's love, care, sacrifice, and hard work. The most important part is to pray that the Lord will lead us all to His presence. We sing, pray, read the Bible, and encourage one another. We have each other's mailing addresses, so we can visit. May we be God's children forever for His love never leaves us.

Florence Logan (left) and Laura Richards in 1976 when Laura was 83 years old. Florence Logan and Laura became close friends during their first missionary term. They attended language school together in 1921 and then were both assigned to serve the mission in Paotingfu. Florence tried to discourage Laura from resigning as a Presbyterian missionary in 1929 in order to found the Canaan Home orphanage. Once Laura made her decision, though, Florence gave her full support, visiting Laura when she was able and writing newsletters for her.

Pearl Wei with her husband Peter and their four children in the 1950s. As a teenager Pearl volunteered to help at the orphanage. She cut the children's hair, took them to Sunday School, and made a special trip to Tientsin to persuade her wealthy relatives to donate funds for winter clothing. After graduating from normal college, Pearl taught at the orphanage for one year in 1942. Her family risked their lives to help Laura escape Japanese imprisonment in 1943. A few years later, Pearl married and emigrated with her husband to the U.S. Laura often visited them after she returned to the States in 1951.

What Happened to the Canaan Home Orphans?

THE POLITICAL CHANGES shaking China scattered the orphans like lambs without a shepherd. China Central Government officials at the highest levels of the Party adopted several of the smartest, best looking younger orphans. These children disappeared into heavily guarded palatial homes, cut off from contact with ordinary people. None of the other orphans ever heard from them again. The cadres divided the rest of the younger orphans—those in middle school and younger—into two groups. They sent one group to live in a fully indoctrinated government boarding school, and then mixed a large number of successfully indoctrinated orphans from a different orphanage into the group remaining at the Canaan Home facility.

All their lives the Canaan Home orphans had been taught to give thanks to God before eating meals. But now when they closed their eyes to offer grace, the other children stole their food. At Canaan Home the orphans had been taught to be kind, follow the rules and, when necessary, appeal to adults for justice. In their new living situations, they were taunted, bullied, and persecuted by the other children but unprotected by the adults. They had no idea how to stand up for themselves.

Neither did the older children. Although they had believed the Canaan Home staff when the adults told them that Laura saved their lives, they had still lived with the tunnel vision of children, unaware of most of the problems their mother confronted and with only a childish understanding of the faith with which she faced seemingly impossible situations. "We were too young then," Rachel explained. "We didn't understand much and didn't really care about what was going on."

The older orphans went to work or passed exams to attend public high school as boarding students or go to nursing school, college, and other kinds of advanced training. Like young adults everywhere, they needed to venture into the world from a place of security—a place where they could return for encouragement, comfort, advice, acceptance, and healing when necessary. The takeover of Canaan Home destroyed their secure home base, and Laura's departure orphaned them all over again. Where could they turn when petty officials arbitrarily reduced their inadequate government stipends and food allowances? What could they do when people took advantage of them? They were poor and powerless, without clan connections in a clan-based society in which people compartmentalize their lives on the basis of *guanxi*, or relationship. In general, people treat you well if you are family, friend, colleague, or guest. Otherwise, they act as if you don't exist or don't matter.

With their mother gone, the older orphans had only one refuge, one place where they could gather and reconnect with each other—Wang Ming Dao's church. The Christians there were concerned about them and tried to help them. But the members of the Peking Christian Tabernacle were a beleaguered people, watched and criticized in their neighborhoods and workplaces. Even at church, believers were unsafe. Covert government agents attended services and, as happened in all churches, some people with responsibilities in the church began secretly cooperating with the Communist Party.

The new government wanted to silence Wang Ming Dao, but it was difficult. They could not plausibly accuse him of being imperialistic because his church was indigenous and self-supporting, with no financial ties to Western churches. He refused to join organizations outside his church, Western or otherwise, and although he had welcomed foreign missionaries, he had rarely invited them to preach. Chinese Christians admired him for courageously refusing to allow the Japanese to mix their politics with the gospel message during the Japanese occupation. Under threat of death, he had refused to join the Japan-sponsored North China Church Union, place a picture of the Japanese emperor in his church, or print Japanese slogans in his quarterly magazine. Now he could declare himself consistent when he refused the new government's demand that he join the Three Self Patriotic Movement (TSPM), include Communist propaganda in his publications, and place a picture of Mao Tse Tung in the Peking Christian Tabernacle. Wang Ming Dao was a threat to the new government. He vigorously refuted Communist charges against the gospel, and his magazine and booklets influenced Christian believers in every corner of China.

In 2006, the orphans said they thought the government targeted their father politically because the Communist Party hoped to discredit Wang Ming Dao through his association with Nieh Shou Guang. Otherwise, Mr. Nieh was too insignificant for the government to expend the effort needed to pull together what now looks like a nationally orchestrated campaign against him. For where did Gate of Righteousness get all the bad reports that he passed to other orphans and published in the *Peking Daily*? Silas gave him details about Mr. Nieh's embezzlement of orphanage funds in 1941, but where did the young man's other information come from? Gate of Righteousness charged his father with a long list of evil deeds besides the violation of his two older sisters and the embezzlement. Most of these accusations cannot be proved or disproved today, and it is hard to believe that some of them could have been substantiated even at the time.

With what people know now about how the Communist government operated, it seems likely that secret Communists in churches associated with the orphanage formed relationships with the two young men and passed along information…and possibly disinformation. Mistrust is a poison. Once it enters people's thinking, it ripens into gullibility, making them willing to believe bad things with little or no evidence. Once the older orphans learned that their father had in fact stolen orphanage funds and violated their two sisters, their trust was shattered, and they were susceptible to believing any other accusation against him.

Gate of Righteousness and Silas were young, idealistic, and furious for justice. When they told the older children what they had learned about their father, the orphans were devastated. How could their father do such things? Rape their sisters? Steal money when they were hungry? Hurt Mama? (How they missed her every single day!) And then for him to turn around and preach the Word of God! The amount of money Mr. Nieh had stolen was huge. (The orphans say it was the equivalent of over 1.8 million dollars in today's currency.) With that much money, the orphans reasoned, the family could have survived the famine without suffering from cold and hunger. Maybe there could have been money left over to give them a better start in life as young adults, so they wouldn't have to be so desperately poor and hungry still.

The government offered just restitution—the recovery and return of money and goods—to people who had been cheated if they would publicly accuse and denounce the wrongdoers. Gate of Righteousness and Silas believed the government's offer, and they encouraged the orphans to join them in publicly protesting Nieh Shou Guang's misdeeds. Several groups of orphans did so, both before and after the government informed them that it had arrested their father and put him in prison. One of the older girls from Tientsen also protested, charging that Nieh Shou Guang had raped her. It was unheard of for a young woman to admit voluntarily in public that she had been raped because it guaranteed a life of social stigma and it cut off her chances to marry. It was interesting that the young woman's protest in Tientsen was immediately linked into the Peking campaign and publicized there to lend weight to the case against Nieh Shou Guang. Some time after these protests, the orphans learned that their father had died in prison. At the reunion in 2006, they said they no longer remember when or how this information came to them. Laura herself indicated that Nieh Shou Guang was shot in 1954.

Before Laura left China, the *Peking Daily* published one or two of the articles that Gate of Righteousness wrote accusing his father. The Communists probably made sure Laura knew about it. Otherwise she might have remained unaware of the articles. She did not read Chinese newspapers herself, and the orphans believe that for years people had shielded her from information or gossip about Mr. Nieh's activities. Laura was greatly respected and greatly loved. People near her shrank from adding to her burden or her pain. Today there is no way to know all that Mr. Nieh actually did or did not do, nor is there any way to know how much Laura knew. She seemed, though, to be genuinely hopeful that her husband could come to the United States.

At a reunion in 2006, the orphans discussed the reasons why Gate of Righteousness had been so zealous in condemning his father and persuading the other orphans to denounce him publicly. Some of them thought perhaps he wanted to become a member of the Communist Party, but Obadiah said that was out of character. Gate of Righteousness had no political ambitions, and he never betrayed anyone to curry favor with the Party. He was a kind man who loved and protected his brothers and sisters, and he took personal risks to stay in touch and to stand up for them through the years despite the dangers of various political campaigns. His actions probably flowed out of a strong sense of right and wrong and a fierce loyalty to his brother and sister orphans. His father's sins genuinely disillusioned him, and he lost his childhood faith. When he was dying of stomach cancer in the 1980s, a pastor visited him and reminded him of the gospel. Gate of Righteousness countered the message with stories about his father's hypocrisy, and he died refusing the pastor's pleas to put his faith in Jesus.

There was never any government restitution. In 1955, the government arrested Wang Ming Dao and closed the Peking Christian Tabernacle. The young adult orphans were pushed to the margins of society and, with their gathering place gone, they began losing contact with each other. The family network fragmented. Emotionally and spiritually, the orphans drifted.

"From the time Mother left until the time of my marriage in1961, I led quite an unpleasant life," Rachel said. "It was entirely different from Canaan Home. I felt very uneasy. It seemed I roamed from place to place."

When Laura left China, her children believed Jesus with a child's faith that was all tied into their trust in their parents. Like all homegrown Christian children, they either had to lapse into adult unbelief or else come into faith all over again with an adult ability to reason and an adult understanding. They needed to find their own personal reasons for crying out to God and choosing or refusing to recognize and experience His guidance and provision. They needed to mature into a relationship with Jesus that was fully independent of their relationship to their parents.

For the orphans, this process had to take place without the benefit of Bibles or regular teaching and counsel from church leaders, most of whom were now in prison. In addition, the revelations about their father's betrayal deeply wounded them. How could they ever forgive? Yet without forgiving, how could they ever heal?

Government job assignments scattered them throughout China. Under the circumstances, many of the orphans wound up marrying unbelievers, which made fellowship with other believers even more dangerous or simply impossible.

In America, we take freedom for granted. It's hard for us to imagine what it would have been like to live in China when the orphans were launching their careers and raising their families. Ruth Tsai tried to explain once by telling me a story about her mother's return to the U.S. at the age of 82 after having lived under Chinese Communist rule for 25 years. "When she first arrived in the free world," Ruth said, "people must have thought she was half crazy because whenever she would refer to the Lord, instead of saying God or the Lord, she used her index finger and pointed upward to Heaven.

"In China, it was too dangerous to mention God, not just for herself, but for the person she was communicating with. Five minutes later the police might come along and ask, 'What did you say to her? Did you mention Jesus? What is your thought?' It's best if you don't answer a word. But if they torture you, you have to say something. You think, *If I say that, Maybe they will arrest her, or maybe they will arrest her daughter.* You're afraid to speak and afraid not to speak."

In general, the orphans' background of poverty and lack of political affiliation helped them. The government assigned them safe political class identities as workers and clerks, which protected them during the early campaigns against capitalists, bourgeois rightists, counter-revolutionaries, and (the worst of identities) underground spies, especially if they changed the telltale Christian names that Laura had given them.

But during the approximate ten-year period of the Cultural Revolution, the hunt for enemies escalated until it overwhelmed the social system. More and more people were accused and attacked verbally and physically in public meetings. If they survived, the humiliating treatment continued regularly year after year. One to two million people died at the hands of mobs and Red Guards, and a similar number were permanently disabled. Millions more were exiled to remote provinces or sent to labor camps (where more millions died), or they were forced to become farmers and miners.

Mobs not only beat people to death on the streets, they attacked the victims' children and other relatives. And once individuals were accused, everyone ostracized them. Co-workers and neighbors pressured their spouses to divorce them and their relatives to shun them. Teachers, students, and neighbors mocked and persecuted their children, because children were automatically assigned the new political identity of their parent and suffered the same social stigma. There was nothing parents or children could do to erase a bad identity. The pressure and the terror became so great that relatives of political victims started refusing to take in their own homeless grandchildren, nieces, and nephews for fear of social retaliation. Victims and their families felt shamed and hopeless. And in each fresh round of attack, many of those who had escaped the last round desperately tried to divert attention away from themselves by scrutinizing old records and finding new victims to accuse.

During this time, the Red Guards labeled a number of the orphans as an underground spies and sent them to labor camps because they had been raised in a Christian orphanage and their mother was an American. One of these was Zechariah, who wrote two memoirs for this book. He lost his job as engineer at a factory, spent six months in a concentration camp, and then was exiled with his whole family to work as farmers. His children were refused the opportunity to go to high school and college. After four years, he was able to return to his engineering position (where he probably had to work alongside some of the same people who had accused and banished him).

Samuel, the first surviving boy in the orphanage, also received a spy identity and reportedly committed suicide. What actually happened is hard to say. There were many genuine suicides during the Cultural Revolution, but there are also a number of documented cases in which Red Guards either forced people to commit suicide or covered up murders by reporting them as suicides. Samuel's ordeal led to trouble for one of the older orphans, Obadiah, who had left the orphanage during the Japanese occupation. Not realizing that Samuel had died, Obadiah tried to visit him. This brought Obadiah to the attention of his work unit. His co-workers investigated him, discovered his tie to Canaan Home, labeled him a spy, and sent him to labor camp.

In the early days of the Cultural Revolution, the hospital where Mercy worked found out that she was a Christian who had been raised by an American mother. They sent her family to an undesirable assignment in Gansu, one of China's most impoverished provinces, but fortunately they did not change her worker identity. The family's life there was strenuous and harsh. Mercy had to be separated from her husband and two children for two to three months at a time while she hiked up and down mountains with her medical team to provide medical care to remote villagers. The children's non-Christian father was kept occupied all day and into the nights with political meetings and his work as chief engineer of a power plant. After the first year or so, the older son had to attend a boarding school far away from the family.

So, from about the age of nine, Mercy's daughter had to take over the family cooking and housework. The little girl had to start a fire in the outdoor coal stove each day and keep the fire going while she cooked the family meals. She cleaned house and washed the family clothes by hand. Each month she sorted through one ton of coal delivered to the yard and made coal balls from the coal dust. During grade school, she hiked three miles round trip to school every day. During middle school, the round trip was eight miles and over a mountain.

Yet in the midst of hardship, the remoteness of the province shielded the family. In Gansu, people did not know their background. They were able to retain their safe worker identity and weather the Cultural Revolution in relative peace. Years later when the family was able to return to Beijing —and when they learned details of what had happened to friends and family during their absence—Mercy realized that their exile, which had seemed like such a disaster, had really been God's protection for her family.

As the years passed, each of the orphans experienced their own spiritual journey; each had their own story. Like the Hebrew children, the Canaan Home adults wandered in a dangerous wilderness for many years. For some of them, faith died. Others learned to trust God and take hold of their spiritual heritage. "Those who are still Christians have forgiven Mr. Nieh." Mercy's daughter said. "Their forgiveness is deeper than I can describe."

Although the family network in general fragmented, individual orphans tried to stay in touch with each other as best they could through visits, letters, and phone calls. One would be in touch with two or three others, and one of those others might know how to contact somebody else. Titus and Gate of Righteousness made it their mission to find and reconnect the links of family chain. So, in time, after the Cultural Revolution, the Canaan Home adults began gathering for occasional reunions. After the TSPM churches reopened, a number of the orphans began trying to attend the same church on Sundays so they could visit with each other after the service.

I first published the Canaan Home story in 2010 as *Laura's Children: the hidden story of a Chinese orphanage.* At that time, the orphans remained scattered across China. The whereabouts of most were unknown because the older orphans lost touch with their youngest siblings when the government divided the orphanage. In 2010, the youngest orphan in contact with the others was 65. She had been eight years old when Laura left in 1951. Most of the other orphans who were still in touch with each other were in their 70s and 80s. It was difficult for them to get together. They were poor, with too little money to pay taxi fares, and it was, and is, hard for the elderly to manage the rough and tumble of China's public transportation system. (Rachel's twin sister Rose Mary died in 1986, at the age of 55, when she was accidentally pushed out of an overcrowded bus.) Still, they tried to gather at least once a year to honor their mother's memory. Mostly they wrote and telephoned each other.

Today, 20 years later, we have lost touch with all of them. We believe that they have all died. They can no longer be threatened, no longer harassed, no longer abused.

When Laura left China in 1951, the number of Protestant Christians in China was estimated to be a 700,000 to one million. Despite the deaths of many believers during the next half-century of persecution, the official government estimate in 2001 was 25 million Protestants. However, *U.S. News & World Reports* reported in 2001 that because most of the church remained underground in groups unregistered by the government, expert observers agreed that the true number of Protestant believers could be 90 million. In addition, the news magazine reported that there were five million Roman Catholic believers attending authorized churches, plus another ten million Roman Catholics meeting underground.

That was 25 years ago. Today, accurate statistics remain impossible to find, given the need of many Christians for secrecy. But even if one accepts only official government statistics, the growth rate of Christianity in atheistic China is astonishing.

So how many Christians are there today in China?

Only God knows.

But since 2010, the government has been increasingly and aggressively trying to bring the Christian church into line with official Chinese Communist doctrine—removing crosses from church buildings, forcing churches to close, even bulldozing their buildings. Police impose heavy fines, harass, arrest, and even imprison pastors and church leaders, especially those in the underground church.

It appears that the Communist Party has given up their attempt to wipe out Christianity through public shaming, violence, and death and is focusing instead on pressuring the church to rewrite the Bible and reshape fundamental Christian doctrines to conform to Communist doctrines. In other words, to syncretize Christianity with Communism.

Breaking news and up-to-date information about the Chinese branch of the Christian family can be found at www.chinasource.com.

Today the saga of Laura Richards and the Canaan Home orphans continues, but after decades of research and discovery, and now the probable deaths of the orphans who stayed in touch with each other, it is time for me to bring the story to a close.

Some readers will want to know more details about the sources of information and editorial decisions I made writing this history. Did these crazy accounts of answered prayer really happen, or did I just make them up? Did the Communist Party really offer to make Laura Richards a "living Dr. Norman Bethune?" Or is that just drama for effect?

So, for the historian and for the curious, I am publishing Endnotes along with stories about individual orphans and their families at www.beckypowers.com.

—Becky Cerling Powers - Vinton, Texas - August 2025

My Quest for the Canaan Home Story

When I was a little girl, my mother used to tell my brothers and sister and me romantic, tragic stories about her cousin, Laura Richards. Mom told us that Laura's mother had died when Laura was young, so her father remarried. And when Mom was little her relatives recalled that Laura's stepmother made the little girl work too hard, and Mom had thought that was just like the stepmothers in fairy tales. When Laura grew up, she served as a Red Cross nurse in World War I, and then in 1921—the same year my mother was born—she sailed off to China to be a missionary, and none of the family could understand why she had gone off like that.

In China, Mom told us, lots of people didn't want baby girls, so they drowned them in the river. Laura started an orphanage to save some of the baby girls that people didn't want, and when war came, she saved the lives of Chinese boy orphans, too. After a few years, Laura met a Chinese Christian named Mr. Nieh who wanted to help her raise her children, so she married him even though in those days people didn't think a white woman should marry a Chinese man. Mom's family in America were so angry and upset when they found out, they wouldn't talk about it, but by the time that happened, my mother was older and she secretly thought it was all right. Then, Mom said, the Communists took over China, and they made Laura leave all her children behind and come back to America.

Mom said that Mr. Nieh tried to escape to Hong Kong to go with Laura to America, but he was arrested and put in prison and executed.

I was four years old in 1951 when Laura returned to the United States. She used to visit my family every year or two until she became too old and frail to travel anymore. We all enjoyed her visits, although Laura appeared neither romantic nor tragic, like my mother's stories about her. She looked too ordinary to seem romantic, and she was too cheerful to seem tragic. She was quiet and self-effacing—much more interested in hearing our stories than in telling any of her own. In fact, she never told us anything about her experiences in China unless we asked, and even then she said little. Mom told us that Laura could not talk much about her story because she needed to protect her family and friends in China. The Communists could take something she said or published and twist it to put her loved ones in prison or labor camps. So I grew up feeling very curious about Laura and her mysterious Chinese husband.

When I married in 1970 and started raising my own family, I corresponded with Laura, and she helped shape my spiritual journey. Once I wrote her a long letter asking her advice for coping with the task of raising my two small children. All that Laura wrote back was one sentence: "I have found I must be completely dependent upon Him in order to receive His blessing."

This hurt my pride, because I saw myself as a mature Christian leader in the church, and Laura seemed to be implying that I had missed something basic. As I prayed and pondered her words, though, I gradually began to realize that whenever I felt threatened, my automatic response was to start assessing my own resources and scheming some kind of solution. It dawned on me that my real trust was in myself. So I prayed to God to teach me to turn to Him instead, like Laura said. In a stumbling way, my praying, my thinking, and my whole spiritual experience began to change.

Soon after sending me her one sentence response, Laura mailed me a copy of *Something More,* by Catherine Marshall, a book which apparently expressed many of Laura's own conclusions. This book also influenced my personal spiritual journey.

And all the more I wondered what Laura's day-to-day experience had

Laura Richards at about age four with her Auntie Maude, age 14. Maude Russell Eberhardt was the younger sister of Laura's mother, Cora Delle Russell Richards. Maude was also the author's maternal grandmother. Maude's parents raised Laura's little brother Edwin after the children's mother died when Laura was nine and Edwin was a baby five months old.

been in China. I stayed alert for news of the Chinese church and wondered whether Laura's children were surviving the persecution I read about. If so, how? Had they become Communists? Had they remained Christians? I knew it was too dangerous for Laura to try to make contact and find out. I tried to remember to pray for them.

Time passed and then suddenly, for a few months in the spring of 1976, it began to look like Laura's story might finally be told. Jean Cerling Allen, my father's sister in California, had heard about "The Laura Mystery" from my mother. Intrigued, she began visiting Laura at the retirement center in California. Aunt Jean had a knack for drawing out people's stories, and Laura began telling a few of hers. Then one day Jean asked Laura if she would let Jean write the story of her life and the adventures of Canaan Home.

It was March 1976, exactly 25 years since Laura had last seen her children. By now she had heard a little about the secret house-church movement in China, and she had heard good news about some of her children's faith from her old friend, Mrs. Rebecca Tsai. This news must have eased Laura's long grief. In any case, for the first time in a quarter century, Laura finally agreed to tell her story to a writer—under one condition. She refused to answer any questions that touched on politics. To Jean's surprise, this condition included a refusal to give any information whatsoever about Laura's late husband, Mr. Nieh.

After Jean and Laura set to work, Laura began having second thoughts. Mao was still in power. The political situation in China was still volatile. No one ever knew what Mao would do next, but even if he died, things might become no better. Without doubt, there would be a struggle for power. In China, when people in power felt threatened, they looked for scapegoats, and Christians were traditional scapegoats.

Laura wondered if it might still be too dangerous to publish her experiences. Even if she never mentioned politically sensitive subjects, simply telling the early story of Canaan Home might turn the government's spotlight back on people associated with the orphanage. The Communists kept records of everyone's whereabouts. They could track down former Canaan Home orphans, board members, and staff. Was writing her story worth that risk to them?

Besides that, she was exhausted. Talking to Jean was stimulating, but her body paid a price for the excitement. Years of famine during World War II and the hepatitis she contracted in the Philippines had damaged her digestive system.

So she told Jean she had changed her mind. She didn't feel well enough to continue the project and she also thought that telling her story was still too dangerous for her children.

Jean was disappointed. She filed away her notes, hoping that Laura would change her mind, unaware that her sessions with Laura had stimulated so many memories that Laura was writing them down and giving them to her friend Fern Nelson to type. Miss Nelson filed Laura's memoirs away along with the old newsletters from China that Laura also gave her. Miss Nelson re-typed two of these old newsletters at Laura's request and mailed them to some of Laura's friends and relatives. These were letters that Laura had never mailed from China because of the Japanese occupation.

Five years later, in 1981, Laura died at the age of 88, and the next year Jean also died unexpectedly of cancer at the age of 55. My mom wrote to Miss Nelson asking if there were any more old newsletters from China like the two Laura had mailed her. So Miss Nelson re-typed several more of the newsletters for her, and my mother made copies for me. Then my cousin found and mailed us Jean's folder of notes and materials.

The stories in this pooled collection amazed and inspired me so much that in 1983 I decided to try to find out all I could about Laura's story. I began researching the history and cultural traditions of China to understand the context of the stories, and I began writing, phoning, and visiting any of Laura's old friends and colleagues that I could locate. Over the next few years, I made several trips from Texas to California to interview people who had known Laura, like Florence Logan and members of the Tsai family. The Tsais had immigrated to the U.S., and they were still in contact with Wang Ming Dao and his wife, both recently released from prison in China. The Tsais wrote to the Wangs on my behalf, asking them to contact the former orphans for me. As a result, in 1990, Rachel and Zechariah sent me memoirs of their experiences growing up in Canaan

Home. Unfortunately, while I was assimilating the orphans' material into the story timeline, Wang Ming Dao and his wife both died. This meant that I lost my only source of contact with the orphans.

During all this time I was meeting deadlines, writing for the *El Paso Times*, and homeschooling, so my progress writing the Canaan Home story was slow. I was able to write quite a bit of it, but there were important gaps. I knew my readers would want to know what happened to the orphans after Laura left them, and they would also want to know more about her husband, Mr. Nieh. In the two orphans' memoirs, they said nothing about their own lives after 1951, and they focused all their stories and comments on their relationship with Laura, their mother. They said little or nothing about their father, which puzzled me. Most of the scanty information I had about Mr. Nieh came from Florence Logan, who admired him and thought he had made important contributions to the welfare of the orphanage. I doubt she knew about the scandal. A couple other missionaries who had lived closer to Laura's situation in Peking seemed critical of Mr. Nieh, but they gave me no clear reasons why when I asked. So I wrote the parts of the story about Mr. Nieh from Miss Logan's perspective. And I prayed that somehow, some way, I could reconnect with the orphans—although that seemed impossible.

In 1994 I flew 1,500 miles from El Paso to Chicago to attend a five-day writers' conference at a Bible college. The day before the conference ended, I sat down at lunch next to a Chinese woman, who said she was from Beijing. "Beijing!" I said. "I am writing a story about an orphanage in Beijing." After explaining the story, I asked her if she had ever heard of Wang Ming Dao.

"Why yes!" the woman said. "He was my parents' pastor."

This young woman was attending summer school at the Bible College, and the summer school students usually ate in the cafeteria at a different time than the writers' conference attendees. I felt that it was by God's hand that I had met this lady, and we arranged to meet again. At lunch the next day my new friend told me that after meeting me, she had discovered that her parents knew Laura and Mr. Nieh. They had been part of the group of students that attended the prayer conferences in 1947 and 1948 on the orphanage grounds. Her parents were visiting her at the time, and she brought me to meet them in her dormitory room. We all began to cry, we were so moved by the marvel of our meeting. Her parents told me they might be able to contact some of Laura's children for me, and they agreed to carry packets of photographs and letters back to China.

I heard nothing more for three years. Then the daughter of one of the orphans faxed me using the fax number that I had included with the packets of photographs. Finally I was in touch with the orphans again. That Christmas, they sent me a Christmas card with a photograph of one of their reunions. When I saw it, I burst into tears. Here they were, the children themselves, now white-haired grandparents.

It took me a lot of time to gain any information from the orphans. All our correspondence had to wait for translation, each way, and because of personal circumstances or problems with mail delivery, we sometimes did not hear from one another for a year or more at a time. I learned that the orphans were gathering annually to worship together and to commemorate their mother's love and faith. I specifically asked them to tell me about Mr. Nieh and about their lives after Laura left China. They wrote me a few stories about what happened immediately after Laura left, but they ignored my questions about Mr. Nieh. Their reluctance to talk about him puzzled me. Finally, 22 years after I first started collecting information about Laura's story, I decided I had all the material I would be able to get, and it was time to self-publish what I knew about the story.

The manuscript was in the hands of a book designer in September 2005 when I received surprise news from the Tsais. Sherry[1], the daughter of one of the orphans, had phoned them, looking for me. Sherry had become a Christian, married an American believer, and moved to the United States. Ever since she was a child, she had longed to know the story of Canaan Home. When she learned that I had written the story, she wanted to contact me. I phoned her, and we became friends over the phone.

Sherry began to translate my manuscript. At first she was excited and happy to read the story, but then she grew troubled. Sherry had grown

1 "Sherry" uses a pseudonym to protect relatives and to avoid political backlash traveling inside China.

up with an orphan mother, an orphan aunt, and orphan visitors, so she had heard many stories, and she knew how deeply Mr. Nieh's betrayal had wounded the orphans. Although she realized they had forgiven him, she also felt that they would be uncomfortable to read the story as it was written, with Mr. Nieh portrayed as a hero who gave up his life for the children of Canaan Home. Naturally, when she told me about the things she believed about Mr. Nieh, I was troubled, too. Her accusations were serious, too serious for me even to mention unless the orphans verified them directly.

I wrote to Rachel, asking her about the accusations. She wrote back confirming some details, but she also said the orphans would prefer not to mention Mr. Nieh. They felt that his actions unfairly tarnished their mother's reputation. She said they wished I could just write the story without Mr. Nieh in it.

I wrote Rachel that although I could understand why the orphans would prefer not to include their father in the story, I felt it was impossible to leave him out. Laura's story, I explained, was not primarily about Laura. The story was really about the loving faithfulness of Jehovah God, the God whom Laura trusted. While writing the story, I had made meticulous notes documenting all the anecdotes and answers to prayer woven into the storyline. I planned to publish this documentation in the book or on a website, because I wanted people to understand that Laura's story was historical, not something I made up. Mr. Nieh was part of that history, and I felt that leaving him out would be dishonest.

I reminded Rachel that Jesus once said, "Do you bring in a lamp to put it under a bowl or a bed? Instead don't you put it on its stand? For whatever is hidden is meant to be disclosed, and whatever is concealed is meant to be brought out into the open." My task as a writer, I explained, was to be a lamp, showing what was there. And that was this: Laura wanted so much to be close to Jesus that she prayed that she could share in the sufferings of Christ. So God allowed her to walk very, very close to Jesus and she DID share in His sufferings. She healed the sick, she fed the poor, she gave up everything to identify with the sorrows and sufferings of the people…and then, like Jesus, she was betrayed.

American Christians think the life of faith is romantic, creating a nice, beautiful picture. In reality, though, the life of faith is messy. It's messy because we live in a fallen, sinful world, and Satan, working through the sinful twist in our nature, undermines every good thing we try to do. Jesus said that the kingdom of God is like a man who sowed good seeds in his field. An enemy came when it was dark and sowed weeds among the wheat. When all the seeds ripened, the man's servants came and said, "Look at all the weeds! How did this happen? We sowed good seeds but now here are all these weeds." The master explained that an enemy had sowed evil seed among the good. The servants asked, "Should we root up these weeds?" But the master said no, because the roots of the good plants were now entangled with the roots of the weeds. If the servants pulled up the weeds, they would also be pulling up and destroying good plants. The master said that weeds and wheat must grow together until the time of harvest. Then they could be sorted and separated.

To me, I told Rachel, it looked like this same thing happened at Canaan Home. Laura planted good seeds, but the enemy came in a dark time and planted something evil. God works through natural means. Once Laura married Mr. Nieh, he was the natural means for the children's protection during the occupation. If he had been uprooted from Canaan Home too soon, much good would have been uprooted with him.

In our own lives it is the same way. Good and bad mix together and we must trust God to know the right time to separate them.

What Mr. Nieh did was not Laura's fault. Laura made a difficult decision to marry Mr. Nieh during wartime, for the sake of the children. It appears that when Mr. Nieh offered to marry her, he was sincere. He made a grand gesture, and he could have lived up to it. He could have chosen differently.

Just before Jesus was arrested and crucified, He said, "The Son of Man will go as it has been decreed, but woe to that man who betrays Him." Betrayal and murder are so much a part of our fallen, sinful world that it was inevitable for God's Son to be betrayed and killed. If Judas hadn't chosen to betray Jesus, the crucifixion would still have happened. But woe to Judas! He was the one who chose to let it happen through him.

In the same way, as long as Laura was trying to follow Jesus absolutely, then she was going to suffer in the ways that He suffered. She, too, was going to be betrayed. But woe to the one who betrayed her!

In my letter to Rachel, I said that some of the people who read Laura's story will be inspired to try to live like Laura did. Therefore, they need to see the big picture of her story so that they won't be shocked into quitting when evil things happen. Seeing the big picture can help them to stand firm.

My communication with Rachel about this matter took a number of months because of translation delays and the slowness of the postal service. While this was going on, Sherry's office assigned Sherry to travel to China for her work. Generously she invited me to come along with her to Beijing to meet her parents and the orphans. While we were en route, the orphans discussed the letter I wrote to Rachel about Mr. Nieh, and they agreed that they would tell me what they knew about their father.

So I had a wonderful reunion with a small group of former orphans in March 2006. I brought along Laura's old box camera to give them, as well as many old photographs. We ate a meal together and rejoiced. The orphans identified many people for me in the photographs, and they told so many stories to Sherry to translate for me that Sherry could hardly keep up. They spoke honestly about Mr. Nieh and described their memories of his departure and return and how they learned later what he had done.

From their memories, Laura emerged for me as a very human person. Although she had an extraordinary faith, she was an ordinary woman, shaped by her past and struggling to figure out what to make of her present circumstances. Her grasp of the Chinese language was poor, and she approached her tasks with the blinders of turn-of-the-century Midwestern American culture. She made many mistakes. For example, she did not realize that to Chinese in the 1930s, she and Mr. Nieh were behaving improperly when they—an unmarried man and an unmarried woman—stayed up late at night alone together working on orphanage accounts. Also, Laura had no knowledge of lactose intolerance and did not realize that milk products give many Asian people stomach aches. So when some of the children refused to eat or drink milk products, she scolded them for being ungrateful for the food they were given. Nor was she aware that apparently healthy older children who wet their beds may have a medical problem. One of the women at the reunion laughed and said, "I wet the bed! I was the one who had to run!" Laura used to discipline her for wetting the bed by making her run laps.

But whether right or wrong in her decisions and her discipline, Laura loved her children with every beat of her heart. She did everything that she could with the understanding that she possessed. She saved her children's lives and showed them how to endure hard times with grace and a generous spirit. Laura demonstrated that a life lived in faith is worth living, no matter what circumstances bring. Her life brought glory to God, and it brought life and hope and strength to her children and the people around her. No matter what she was going through, she held onto God and she experienced His faithfulness.

At the end of Laura's life, when she was writing her memoirs and describing the day that she saw her children for the last time, she ended her account by quoting this old hymn:

> Though the rain may fall and the wind be blowing,
> And cold and chill is the wintry blast;
> Though the cloudy sky is still cloudier growing,
> And the dead leaves tell that the summer has passed;
> My face I hold to the stormy heaven,
> My heart is as calm as the summer sea,
> Glad to receive what my God has given,
> Whate'er it be.
> When I feel the cold, I can say, "He sends it,"
> And His winds blow blessing, I surely know;
> For I've never a want but that He attends it;
> And my heart beats warm, though the winds may blow.

—Becky Cerling Powers
Vinton, Texas

Epilogue

Exiled to Gansu Province

By Sherry Lucas as told to Becky Cerling Powers

INTRODUCTION

The Cultural Revolution *(1966-1976) produced a reign of terror in China under Mao Tse Tung, commonly known as Chairman Mao. Chairman Mao was a founding father of the People's Republic of China from its inception in 1949 until his death in 1976. Though there were other leaders of New China, some of them working behind the scenes, most people saw Chairman Mao as China's savior, and the founding father. During the Cultural Revolution, Mao attempted to purge China of his political rivals and eradicate the country of traditional Chinese culture and remaining vestiges of capitalism. With his encouragement, Chinese young people formed Red Guard groups around the country. The Red Guards attacked teachers, intellectuals, and religious believers of all persuasions. Under the guise of revolutionary fervor, they changed the cultural and physical landscape. They destroyed books, music, and fine art. They razed temples and palaces and tore down the wall that surrounded Beijing. They wiped out ancient treasures in museums.*

The Red Guards were also enticed to murder thousands of Chinese citizens, manipulating mobs to turn against fellow workers and neighbors. They sent hundreds of thousands more to "re-education camps." At these camps, they forced citizens to endure political re-education training and perform hard labor, often without adequate nutrition. Relatives and neighbors, afraid of potential repercussions if they cared for the victims' children, simply abandoned them. Factions developed within the Red Guards and civil war tore the country apart.

Businesses, factories, and schools closed. Near the end of the Revolution, the government transported 17 million urban young people to the rural areas to do manual labor. Every major segment of society—business, industry, medicine, science, and on—suffered not only because of the scarcity of workers but because of badly trained workers.

Sherry Lucas was born in Beijing, China in 1962, four years before the Cultural Revolution began there and then spread throughout China. Her essay begins when she was seven years old, the year her family was exiled to Gansu Province.

• • •

I used to get so angry with our children when they wasted food that my husband Barry must have thought *This lady has to be crazy!!* But when I was growing up in Gansu Province in China, I knew children who were so hungry, they tied a rope around their stomach so they could sleep in spite of their hunger pains.

My family was exiled to the impoverished province of Gansu in 1969 during the early part of the Cultural Revolution. The Cultural Revolution was a power struggle among China's top leaders. In 1966, Mao Tse Tung began encouraging young Red Guards (being young and simple minded) to attack authority figures. The Red Guards mobbed and ransacked people's homes, beat and humiliated people in public, and burned everything that represented "The Four Olds"—old ideas, old thoughts, old habits, old customs. Then they started attacking religious believers and intellectuals. As the Revolution spread, people began manipulating mobs to get personal revenge against fellow workers and neighbors, or they accused other people out of fear, to distract attention from themselves. Tens of thousands were beaten to death and hundreds of thousands were sent to labor camps for "re-education."

In those days the government determined people's job and residence assignments. My mother was working as a nurse for a famous hospital in Beijing. Vice-Chairman Lin Biao (the official next to Mao's rank) wanted to test his power, so he issued a policy that the country's Medical and Health focal point shall be in rural areas. In response to his policy, all the big hospitals (Beijing, Shanghai, etc.) had to send some of their doctors and nurses to work in the countryside. Mom's hospital chose to send her. They wouldn't say why.

Technically my mom should have gone to the countryside, and my dad should have stayed in Beijing. Families were being separated that way all over China. But the hospital pulled a dirty trick and sent a delegation to my daddy's factory.

Before New China was born, he co-owned that factory. He engineered the very first movie projector in China. His brothers were good at working with their hands, so their uncle invested the money to start that factory. When New China was born, the government took over the factory and assigned the three brothers to work there. My father was chief of engineering, and people in the Cultural Revolution hated those with power. So, the factory was glad when the hospital delegation came. They said, "We support you, we can send him to Gansu, too."

My mom cried every day. My dad was depressed. My 12-year-old brother begged my parents to leave him with relatives. But he was a troublemaker, and no relatives wanted him. My family knew it was exile, they understood that we might never be allowed to come back. But I was only seven years old and to me it sounded like taking a vacation. I was excited, the only one who was happy.

The government sent my father to a coal power plant and gave him a two-bedroom apartment for our family to live in. He was in charge of engineering for the power plant. There were no hospital facilities, so my mom's medical staff occupied a big Buddhist temple in the local area. Her medical team had to travel for three months at a time visiting farmers in remote mountain villages. They had to hike on foot and wade through mountain streams in their bare feet.

So, Mom was gone most of the time. My daddy went to work early and came home late because after work he had to attend political meetings. I cried and cried in bed because I was just seven years old and had no experience being separated from my parents.

Gansu was the poorest of the poor provinces. Our new home was remote. There were few telephones. People didn't even have bicycles. I had to walk three miles round trip every day to elementary school. Gansu is in the middle west of China. Winters are very, very cold.

My school in Beijing had a different graduation time from the school in Gansu, so I ended up getting into middle school half a year early. I was the youngest—tall, but mentally just a little kid. The rural students who boarded at the school were even older than the urban students at the same grade level. The middle school was four miles away, so the round trip every day was eight miles, and I had to climb a mountain both ways. On the way to my school, the local authorities executed a man who murdered his wife. I didn't see the execution, but I was terrified, afraid to go past that spot.

My dad never learned to cook. He couldn't take care of himself. So, I started cooking at a young age. It was hard. I had to build a fire, keep it going, and cook everything from scratch. My older brother had to go to boarding school in another county, so by age nine I was cooking, making coal fires, cleaning the house, and washing clothes by hand when I came home from school. The coal dealer would dump a whole truckload of coal in the yard, and I had to gather the coal, sort it, sift it, and make coal balls. By nighttime, I was so tired I could hardly move.

I was a little girl. There was no one to take care of me. Life for me was tough, but I didn't know about the different life other people had. So, I was happy. I raised pets—a sheep, a cow, and some chickens. And I had food—food enough to share.

The government treated farmers differently from city people. My family's identity was urban, but 90% of my class had a farmer identity. With an urban identity we could get government food coupons like flour, cooking oil, and meat. Farmers were supposed to be self-sufficient, though, so there was no way their families could get extra food. Since my family got the government coupons and both my parents worked for a salary, I was a rich girl compared to the other kids.

Every day I packed my lunch box solid. I pushed and pushed to get all the food inside, as much as I could bring to school. Then I shared with my classmates. Sometimes the teachers volunteered to share my lunch. I felt honored. Those kids loved me and hated me. They loved me because they could have some of my lunch. They hated me because I had so much. I was young and didn't understand their attitude.

Rural Communist leaders still cared about their kids' education. So, they could send their children to school as boarders. The farming kids went home once a week to bring back steamed buns and bread to eat at school for the week. In the winter, the bread was OK, but in the summer, it went bad. It got stringy and turned gray. The kids just broke the bread and let the sun dry it so it wouldn't stink. It was all they had to eat. Even if the bread turned green, they would still eat it.

In high school I took an agricultural equipment class and joined the tractor team, because the high school was preparing the students to be farmers in the future. We went to villages to plow farmers' fields. We'd work the whole day. By nighttime when we came back from the field my eyes would be full of stars, and when we had a chance to eat, we were like wolves. We'd fight for the food. I could eat seven bowls of noodles, I was so ravenous.

Wherever we went, the school found a farmer for us to live with. The farmers lived in such poor conditions. To build a house, they would dig a hole in the side of the mountain. They made bricks from mud, and when the mud dried, they used the bricks to build a wall with a door and a bed—a hollow platform for sleeping, with the wood oven at one end. So, the family lived in a tunnel. Everyone slept in that one big mud bed, the women on one side, the men on the other. They would fight for one blanket. There were fleas. It was an education. I saw kids who were really poor, really hungry—and I saw that I had great privilege.

My parents were very worried about me, because I chose the class for driving and repairing tractors instead of taking academic subjects. But after half a year, I had enough. Thank goodness, in the late 1970s, Vice Premier Deng took over China after Mao. Then schools started to shift to academics again. When the school picked the best students to prepare them for college, I was one of them.

The teen years were a dangerous time for me. I grew up like a wild child, with my parents gone, no one taking care of me. I could have gone wrong. But I had a dream: there were two paths before me. One path was being a good girl, doing what was right. The other path ended up in jail. There was no hope for the other path. Then I woke up. After that I would remind myself, I must go on the right path. I was terrified by those two paths. I knew nothing about God back then. It was illegal to talk about God. But today I believe God helped me through that dream.

All this time the Cultural Revolution was going on. The whole country was brainwashed. Everything had to be Mao's way. Everyone must bow their heads, follow, and never ever complain openly about the government. Even in my own home, if I expressed a different opinion than Mao's thought, my parents shut me up: "Don't say anything! You'll get in trouble!"

Everything depended on your identity. If you had a good identity like farmer or worker, nobody was likely to bother you. But if you had a bad identity, you were persecuted. In most of the mandatory political meetings, they pulled out the people with bad identities, and everyone forced them to confess to everyone else in the room. The meeting couldn't be over until they satisfied everyone. It happened to them over and over, sometimes daily, sometimes weekly, no matter what position they held.

My schoolteacher was a really good person. Yet they made her stand on the platform to confess her sins to all the students. Poor lady, at every meeting she had to confess: what she did wrong, what her parents did wrong, how her family treated the farmer badly, because the farmer had nothing to eat, but she and her family could eat white flour noodles. She had to say how bad those things were, and on and on....

People might have a good reputation, and then suddenly be persecuted. Their critics shamed them by writing accusations saying how evil they were in big characters with a big brush on sheets of newspaper. Their accusers papered their house with the signs every day. Their children were too ashamed to come out of the house. Their persecutors put a huge newspaper hat on them, then made them kneel down and confess their sins to an entire school or factory or an entire neighborhood. Everywhere they went other people pointed their fingers at them. People with bad identities felt hopeless, faced with endless confession meetings where they were verbally and physically attacked. Children carried their parents' identity—they didn't do anything, but they inherited a bad identity. So, they felt helpless, because there was no way to erase a bad identity.

Fortunately, the violent stage of the Revolution was over by the time I was in high school. I never saw people being beaten to death like my older brother did. I did attend meetings though, and write slogans. Being a Red Guard was expected. If you wanted to be considered a good child, you joined. We knew nothing. We were just simple-minded kids.

The vice-principal at my school was against the teachers with bad identities. So once, to humiliate the chemistry teacher, the vice principal told me "I think you're a good candidate to teach the chemistry class." I struggled with that. Could I do it? He talked to me about it a couple of times. Finally, one day I told the chemistry teacher in front of the class, "You don't need to teach. I'm going to teach."

He stared at me. He was speechless. So, I just took over.

Since I needed to teach, I studied hard. I got a good response from the students. After a month, though, I used up all my knowledge. So, I told the teacher, "You can go back to teach the class," without any apology. How foolish I was! However, I was thankful for that opportunity to teach. I found out I could really study and remember things.

After Mao Tse Tung died in 1976, the Cultural Revolution ended, and the country began gradually recovering. My father's factory decided to let my father come back to work for them again, so in 1979, after ten years in Gansu, he and I were able to come back to Beijing. It took my mother another year to be allowed to come back, and it took my brother even longer. Many doctors and nurses who moved to the countryside under Lin Biao's order are still in the rural areas today. No one gave them a chance to return. Now they are too old to work, and their children married local people. Their families became the bottom of society in China.

One day after my mother returned to Beijing, she found out why the hospital exiled her to Gansu. Our apartment was next door to the hospital's former director. She assumed that my mother knew why she was exiled and carelessly referred to the reason: Mom was raised in Canaan Home, a Christian orphanage run by an American, Laura Richards. Mao Tse Tung taught that all religions were evil and that America was China's enemy. So, the hospital chose my mom for exile because she was raised Christian and her adoptive mother was American.

All the time we were in Gansu, my mom complained and said it was not fair that we were sent there. But when the former director told why she was sent, Mom realized that exile was God's way to protect us. Our lives were hard in Gansu, but no one knew our background. No one knew how my mother was raised. No one knew that my father used to own the factory in Beijing. So, we had a peaceful time. I didn't get persecuted or mocked in school.

If we had stayed in Beijing, who knows what might have happened? Really bad things happened to our relatives who remained living there. Some of the other Canaan Home orphans were given the identity of being a foreign spy because their adoptive mother was American. A spy identity is the worst political identity. Some orphans were sent to labor camps or remote places to work as farmers because of that identity.

My mom took English classes at Canaan Home, and she taught me some English. I decided to learn English, so I studied hard and eventually used my language skills to get a job at an international trading company.

In Gansu I was a little girl who cooked and cleaned for my dad, and he spoiled me. He used to give me a whole month's wages, so I could go on a trip. But when I became a young adult, he suddenly turned against me.

Today I understand my dad better. New China's politics and the Cultural Revolution ruined his chances to fulfill his dreams. The government took over his family business, and he had to work in his own factory, where he was treated badly and sent to Gansu. So, his heart was bitter. He put all his hopes and expectations in me, using me to fulfill his dreams. But I was strong-willed and had my own ideas. When I showed disrespect for his way or made decisions he disagreed with, it hurt him.

My dad's bitterness pushed us apart and caused me to make a terrible mistake. He treated me so badly that I left home and lived in a little room by myself. I wanted someone to love me. I wanted to leave that little room and have my own family. So, I married a worker, a mold maker.

There was a huge gap between us socially. My friends left me, and his friends felt uncomfortable. My career took off, my salary was much more than his, and the gap grew bigger and bigger. Husbands don't like a wife to be too strong, too talented. It causes too much pressure on them. My husband had a terrible temper. He used abuse to control me and after our son was born, he used our son to control me. Once when we took our son to visit his parents, we got into an argument, and he beat me in front of his parents. That is when I promised myself, *Someday I'll leave.* Eventually I did, but in the meantime, I was miserable.

I traveled a lot inside China and internationally because of my work. Travel was my escape. I loved money, power, position—and I got them through my job. But deep inside of me, there was big hole. I couldn't fill it up, I needed something much more, but I couldn't explain it. In my mind I knew there must be a God, that evolution couldn't cause the universe. There's the sky, stars, sun, and moon. On the earth, there are animals, seasons, sowing and harvest times…, everything arranged perfectly. It is impossible that these things happened just by evolution or through a big explosion.

So, I started searching for spiritual answers. Who is God? How is this God related to me? I went to some Mideast countries many times. People from Egypt gave me some Muslim tracts to read. But every time, after only reading one or two sentences, I went to sleep. So I never read them. Now I know it was God preventing me from reading such things. Plus, when I saw how the men treated women there, I said to them, "I will never be a Muslim. See how you guys treat your women! I am too modern. I love to wear miniskirts too much to be a Muslim woman."

But deep in my heart, I still asked, who is the true God? Is it my choice to choose who is my God, so as to comfort myself and to meet my desire? Or is He supreme above everything? Who is in Control?

In the early 1995, I was given the honor to represent our company at an international trade show in Germany. I started to gather samples for the show. However, I couldn't find a particular product that I was sure would have a good market in the West. I searched the whole country continually for over a month. Finally, I found out that another trading company had a sample of the product I was looking for.

In my mind I wanted to cheat that trading company, so I told them

I would get resources through them if they just sent me the product's brochure. They agreed. But I found out they were very smart people. They scratched out all the supplier's contact information when they sent the brochure to me. I had no way to find the supplier. My frustration built up and up. By that time, I had spent about two months searching with no result.

Then one night I had a vivid dream, with a telephone number displayed in front of my eyes. When I woke up, I knew immediately that the number in the dream was the supplier's phone number. So, I wasted no time and called the number right away. Yes, it was the supplier's phone number! How had it happened?

I didn't know that it was God preparing me and turning me in a new direction. Instead of thanking God—for I truly had no knowledge of God anyway—I called all thirteen of the professional staff who reported to me, and I said to them, "Listen, I got the sixth sense! I got the supplier's contact through a dream!" I could see my staff did not believe me, but no one dared to contradict me. Nor could they deny that I got the phone number supernaturally.

In Germany at the international trade show I attended, I met a white-haired German who spoke perfect Mandarin. He gave me a Chinese translation of the Bible. That was my very first Bible. I treated it like a treasure, because it truly caused my life's turning point. It took me over the next two years to finish reading it. I had so many questions, and I couldn't find the answers. Like, why did this God repeatedly punish His own chosen people? Wasn't it enough to punish them once?

Some of the stories, however, were familiar even though I was just reading them for the first time. I realized that my mom had told me some of the stories when I was a child. But she always disguised the names of the Bible characters. For example, instead of saying "Abraham," but she would say "a grandfather."

In 1996, I started working for an America company in China. One time three of us traveled by air from Mianyang, Sichuan to Shanghai. The flight should have lasted an hour and a half. About five minutes after the plane took off, a flight attendant, looking very alarmed, started walking back and forth along the middle of the plane. Then two pilots walked to the middle and checked both wings on each side of plane. They looked even more serious.

Soon, the flight attendant made an announcement, "The plane has some mechanical issues. Both wings of the plane can't be opened to reduce speed for landing. Therefore, we will have to fly continually until all the fuel is exhausted."

Suddenly the entire plane filled with loud noises, crying, and shouting. I don't know what happened to me. My entire being turned numb. I could hear noises, but I felt I was in another zone. My co-worker on the right, who was a Christian, prayed aloud to his God. The colleague on my left hand, who was Buddhist, looked very scared and didn't know what to do. I was seated in the middle seat, like the living dead.

A couple of hours later, our plane rushed high speed into the airport, touching and bumping a couple of times on the ground, but safely landing in a Shanghai emergency runway. All the people hugged and cherished each other, giving praise. Suddenly, I lost control. I was crying like a baby. It was the first time I realized that I am sinful, I am so small, where is this God who would save a proud, cold-hearted person like me?

After this flight, my American Christian co-worker and I had to continue traveling by car, but the Buddhist co-worker left us and went to Malaysia. On the way to Changzhou from Shanghai, the American Christian said, "God told me to pray for you...." And he also prayed for me in tongues. Then, I knew that the Christian God is the true God who loves me, a sinner, and He saved me.

We prayed, we talked, and we worshipped God together. I felt love, peace, and joy fill my heart, the love, the joy, the peace which I never had before but deeply desired since so long ago.

People think it was a tragedy for me that my family was rejected and exiled because of my mother's religious upbringing. In some ways it was. The civil war affected the quality of my education. My schools were poor, and my teachers lacked authority to insist on strong academic standards. The war also deprived me of a modern urban lifestyle. My peers in Beijing had more opportunities and much better material possessions than I. Most important, the war robbed me of my parents' presence and guidance when I was young, and it caused my bad first marriage decision. Still, I think my experiences growing up made me more mature and gave me a stronger character. I thank God for that.

. . .

After several years, I married that American Christian. We were together twenty-five years until his death. Life has never been the same. Today I've found my life purpose. Whatever I chased before—money, power, position—what used to my "gods"—never filled the deep desires of my heart.

For life is precious and its purpose is to reflect God's image. Nothing can replace the Maker's desire. I live for HIM now, to testify that God, through His redemptive plan, made the way for us to have an eternal life. He, God, has never wanted to pour out His wrath upon His creations for their sins. But He is a righteous God; sin must be punished. So, He allowed His begotten Son, Jesus, to be crucified and die, taking all the punishment to fulfill the requirement of payment for sin. Jesus is the only way. He is the truth.

Tracing back to my life, I can see God has never left me nor forsaken me. Rather, He has longed for me to know Him as I searched for Him. He has drawn me to know His truth in my daily life and tells me He has prepared a life, an abundant life, with the free gift of salvation for me and for everyone who dares to believe.

What amazing grace!

ABOUT THE AUTHOR

Sherry Lucas is a retired Subsea Engineering Quality Assurance Leader for a global company in Houston, Texas. She is also the Chinese translator for *Forbidden Orphanage Outside the Forbidden City* (titled in Chinese *Faith Journey: Laura Richards and the Orphans of Canaan Home in China*), which tells the true story of her adoptive American grandmother's efforts to save the lives of more than 200 Beijing-area children through famine and war from 1929 to 1951.

Acknowledgments

WITHOUT THE INSIGHT, labor, and kindness of four remarkable women, this story could not have been told.

Florence Logan was the first writer to recognize the importance of recording the Canaan Home story. The pamphlet and letters she wrote for Laura in China as the tale was unfolding were critical source materials—as was Miss Logan herself. She patiently and extensively answered my many questions by letter, phone, and in person, giving me essential background information about local customs; political, social, and historical conditions; the Presbyterian mission and the Presbyterian church in China. She read through all her old letters and journals, then culled out, typed, and sent me every sentence that referred to Laura. She gave me photographs and primary-source documents that I could have obtained nowhere else. Finally, she read through the manuscript in its various stages, correcting my mistakes and misunderstandings and making helpful suggestions. She vetted all of the storyline except the hidden story of Mr. Nieh's disgrace and those portions of chapters 1, 2, 16, and 29 that I rewrote after she died and I met the orphans in China.

My aunt, Jean Cerling Allen, was the second writer to take up the task of telling Canaan Home's story. Although Aunt Jean was my father's sister and not related to Laura, she used to visit Laura at Hollenbeck Home. Laura agreed to tell Aunt Jean her story in March 1976 except for the political parts. After the two women set to work, though, Laura had second

This book could not have been written without the assistance that Laura's close friend Florence Logan gave me so generously and cheerfully. Miss Logan died in 1997 at the age of 100.

thoughts and decided it might still be dangerous for the orphans and former Canaan Home staff for her to publish her experiences. So, to Aunt Jean's great disappointment, Laura ended the collaboration. Consequently Aunt Jean only gathered material, organized data, and wrote it down. Nevertheless, her contributions during this brief period were absolutely critical to the final project. In most families, Aunt Jean's hard work would have been lost after she died, though. But her daughter, my conscientious cousin Janet Allen Decker, found Aunt Jean's irreplaceable collection and sent it to my mother. Mom sent it to me.

Fern Nelson, secretary of Go-Ye Fellowship, faithfully visited Laura at Hollenbeck Home and encouraged her to write down the memories that the discontinued book project stirred up. She re-typed Laura's fragile collection of Canaan Home newsletters, and she typed and preserved Laura's ongoing memoir project. She mailed Laura's Christmas newsletters and updated Laura's address list. She gave me addresses from this list, leading me to many of my richest sources of eyewitness accounts. She also lent me James Leynse's *Beauty for Ashes,* a book which was invaluable to my research and which I probably would have been unable to find in those days, before Amazon made it easy to find out-of-print books.

In addition, I thank two other collectors of Laura's memorabilia. Laura's brother Harold R. Richards passed along family photographs and a scant collection of fragments from Laura's early letters. He also enthusiastically answered my questions about his childhood, his family, and his memories of Laura's life. My mother also gave me family photographs, passed along materials that Harold and others gave her, wrote down her own memories of Laura, and gave me extended interviews about Laura's family background. My mother's love for Laura and her intense interest in learning Laura's story led to the writing of this book.

I also thank those who wrote personal memoirs and/or allowed me to interview them by letter, phone, or in person: my father, Bob Cerling; Dr. Chang Yu-Ming; John Detrick; Laura's nephew, Edward Eberhardt; Chaplain Harold Flood; Dr. Henke's wife, Jessie Mae Henke; Annie Kartozian; Dr. Rolfe Lewis; Pearl Wei; and, of course, the former orphans and the Tsai family members, all of whose real names have been withheld.

I am grateful to those who supplied specialized information: Dr. Craig Cameron, Dr. Frank Cormia, Lois Hermann, Linsey Ponzio, Charlie Wasson, and Jerry Worley.

David H. Adeney, Dr. Chang Yu-Ming, the Tsai family, Pastor and Mrs. Wang Ming Dao, and a Chinese family whose name cannot be published all generously provided information and services that connected me to the former orphans. Sherry Lucas, whose mother and aunt were Canaan Home orphans, took me with her to China to meet her family and arranged an unforgettable reunion with some of the former orphans. She translated interviews and also made phone calls to China to verify details and obtain additional information. Timothy Lee and Martin Yee helped translate correspondence with former orphans. Others eased my way through different forms of help: Ken and Pi Kuei Lee, Lupe Casillas-Lowenberg, Jan and Gordan Robertstad, Bill and Karen Tinsman, Barney and Moni Field, Bill McConnell and Betsy Madsen.

I am grateful to my friend and editor Lee Byrd, who steered this project back on track after it bogged down. Her suggestions for restructuring and rewriting were invaluable, and she helped me figure out how to use primary documents effectively as part of the whole story, sandwiching them between chapters.

Finally, I thank my family: thanks to our sons Erik and Matt for their support; thanks to our daughter Jessica for reading the manuscript in various stages and offering excellent editing suggestions; and thanks to my husband Dennis for his long patience with this project, for providing software and computer equipment, and for encouraging me, at a critical point, to complete it instead of going out and getting a "real" job.

I thank my Heavenly Father for all these people. But above all, I thank Him for allowing me to gather the hidden strands of this story and weave them together during the child-raising, prime years of my life when I most needed to be challenged by Laura's wisdom and practical example.

"Great is the LORD, and greatly to be praised;
And His greatness is unsearchable.
One generation shall praise Your works to another,
And shall declare Your mighty acts."

—Psalm 145:3-4

Sources

INTERVIEWS

(All interviews are by Becky Cerling Powers unless otherwise indicated)

Cerling, Bob, Jan. 15, 1985

Cerling, Laura Jane Eberhardt (Laura's first cousin); daily interviews over a one-week period July 1985; also Dec. 30, 1985

Chang, Dr. Yu-Ming, Fall of 1987 and July 26, 1992

Cormia, Dr. Frank, June 21, 1988

Eberhardt, Edward, Jan. 6, 1985

Henke, Jessie Mae, interview in Duarte, California, July 15, 1988

Logan, Florence, June 1984, Jan. 1985, June 3, 1987, July 1988

Lucas, Sherry, Sept. 26, 2005; Jan. 23, 2006; Feb. 17, 2006; March 13, 15, & 18, 2006; May 10, 2006; Oct. 4 & 23, 2006; July 2, 2006

"Mercy," telephone interview by Sherry Lucas, March 6, 2007

"Obadiah," telephone interview by Sherry Lucas, March 6, 2007

Ponzio, Linsey, July 10, 11, & 27, 2000

Reunion of ten former orphans in China in March of 2006

Richards, Harold R., Jan. 26, 1985

Richards, Laura, two or three interviews by Jean Cerling Allen, Spring of 1976

The Tsai Family (Mrs. Rebecca Tsai, her two daughters Becky and Ruth, and her son Daniel), July 12, 1988; July 2, 1990

Tsai, Ruth, July 14, 1988; May 6, 1990; Aug. 3, 1999; Sept. 2, 2001; Sept. 27, 2005; Jan. 23, 2006; June 10, 2006; April 23, 2007

Wasson, Charlie, June 7, 1988

Wei, Pearl, June 1984; Feb. 10, 1985; June 28, 1986

Worley, Jerry, May 8, 1988

"Zechariah" telephone interview, March 22, 2006, with Sherry Lucas translating

LETTERS

"Abraham" (former Canaan Home orphan) to B. C. P., May 18, 1999 and Feb. 19, 2001

Allen, Jean Cerling to Laura Jane Eberhardt Cerling, June 28, 1976

Adeney, David H. to B. C. P., undated, received Summer of 1986

Cameron, Dr. Craig to B. C. P., Dec. 4, 2003

Cerling, Laura Jane Eberhardt to Jean Cerling Allen, March 17, 1976 and Aug. 4, 1976

Chang, Dr. Yu-Ming to B. C. P., Aug. 22, 1987

Detrick, John to B. C. P., July 9, 1984 and Aug. 11, 1984

Flood, Harold D., to Jean Cerling Allen, Nov. 23, 1976; to B. C. P., Sept. 3, 1987

Gui, Ni Heu (second secretary of the Embassy of the People's Republic of China) to Laura Jane Eberhardt Cerling, June 1989

Henke, Jessie Mae to B. C. P., 1984; Oct. 22, 1984; and July 11, 1989

Kartozian, Annie to B. C. P., July 1, 1984

Lewis, Dr. Rolfe to B. C. P., March 6, 1985

Logan, Florence to her U.S. supporters, Spring of 1921 and Sept. 22, 1928; to B. C. P., June 24, 1984; July 4, 1984; Dec. 10, 1984; Jan. 12, 1985; Jan. 28, 1985; Aug. 9, 1985; Sept. 19, 1985; July 26, 1986; July 12, 1987; Oct. 22, 1987; July 27, 1987; July 31, 1987; Aug. 8, 1987; Aug. 19, 1987; Sept. 2, 1987; Oct. 1, 1987; Aug. 4, 1988; Dec. 14, 1988; July 14, 1990; Aug. 15, 1992; Oct. 30, 1992; May 20, 1993; July 27, 1987; and July 31, 1987. In these last two letters, Miss Logan typed excerpts from old letters and journal entries dated: June 7, 1929; Sept. 9, 1929; May 11, 1932; Aug. 31, 1932; Oct. 5, 1937; Aug. 11, 1940; Aug. 13, 1940; Aug. 18, 1940; Aug. 21, 1940; June 8, 1941; Aug. 3, 1941; Aug. 10, 1941; Aug. 17, 1941; Aug. 19, 1941; Aug. 31, 1941; Oct. 17, 1941; Nov. 8, 1946; Dec. 1, 1946; Aug. 24, 1949; Sept. 1, 1949; Sept. 3, 1941; Sept. 17, 1949; and Apr. 14, 1951

Lucas, Sherry to B.C.P., March 6, 2007

Nelson, Fern to B. C. P., March 3, 1983; Oct. 27, 1987; and June 28, 1984

Pottinger, Elsie to B. C. P., March 22, 1984

"Rachel" (former orphan) to B. C. P., March 13, 2001; September 14, 2003; April 23, 2004; Oct. 19, 2004; Jan. 7, 2005; Dec. 1, 2005; March 31, 2006; July 23, 2006; Aug. 7, 2006; Dec. 4, 2006; Jan. 7, 2007

Richards, Dick, to B. C. P., Feb. 8, 1988

Richards, Harold R., to B. C. P., June 27, 1984; July 13, 1984; Oct. 2, 1984; Sept. 23, 1984; Jan. 17, 1985

Richards, Laura, to Harold Richards, Feb. 23, 1929; to American supporters, Fall (probably Sept.), 1930 (fragment); June 20, 1931 (fragment); Nov. 12, 1930; June 8, 1931; Dec. 6, 1931; Jan. 18, 1934; Dec. 17, 1936; Aug. 20, 1937; "The Men in Black," undated, late Fall of 1937; Jan. 24, 1938; Jan. 1947; "Canaan Children's Home News Letter," Spring of 1950

Shih, Margaret, to B. C. P., Aug. 24, 1984

"Sun, Ma Lia" (daughter of a former orphan), to B. C. P., April 22,1997 and Dec. 25, 1997

"Titus" (former Canaan Home orphan) to "Ruth Tsai," Sept. 12, 1988

"Tsai, Ruth" to B. C. P., Dec. 10, 1984; Oct. 23, 1988; March 16, 1990; and March 29, 2001
Wang, C. H. Stephen to B. C. P., Aug. 17, 1987
Wei, Pearl to B. C. P., May 13, 1983
Wei, Peter to B. C. P. on behalf of Pearl Wei, Dec. 11, 1984

UNPUBLISHED MEMOIRS

Flood, Harold D., "My Cherished Contact with Laura Richards," Nov. 5, 1976
"Zechariah" (former Canaan Home orphan), "The Memory of Our Dear Mother Laura May Richards," 1988; untitled memoir, Aug. 2001
Nelson, Fern, "Precious in the Sight of the Lord is the Death of His Saints," May 1981
Richards, Laura, "My Own Testimony," 1957; "Old Temple Building"; "The Dowager's Boat House"; "Moving From the Dowager's Boat House to the American School"; "Short Stories"; and about 20 additional untitled pages all written from 1976 possibly to 1980
"Rachel" (former Canaan Home orphan), untitled, 1989

MISCELLANEOUS

Go-Ye Fellowship records—Laura's application form dated 1958 and her medical report for a visa application to the Philippines, dated Sept. 19, 1957
Logan, Florence—notations for numerous photographs, including the only three known photographs of Mr. Nieh
Logan, Lorna—journal entry June 8, 1938
Richards, Harold R.—marginal comments and reminiscences on first drafts of the manuscript in 1984 and 1985

BIBLIOGRAPHY

Adeney, David H. *China: The Church's Long March.* Ventura, CA: Regal Books, 1985.
Adeney, David H. *Christian Students Face the Revolution.* Inter Varsity Press, 1973.
Arlington, L. C. and Lewisohn, William. *In Search of Old Peking, City of Palaces and Temples.* Shanghai, China: North China Daily News, 1935.
Barnett, A. Doak. *China on the Eve of Communist Takeover.* Frederick A. Praeger, Inc., 1963.
Bianco, Lucien; translated from the French by Murel Bell. *Origins of the Chinese Revolution* 1915-1949. Stanford, CA: Stanford University Press, 1971.
Bloodworth, Dennis. *The Chinese Looking Glass.* Farrar, Straus and Giroux, 1966, 1967.
Butterfield, Fox. *China: Alive in the Bitter Sea.* New York: Bantam Books, 1982.
Chan, Gilbert F. and Etzold, Thomas H. *China in the 1920s: Nationalism and Revolution.* New York: New Viewpoints, A Division of Franklin Watts, 1976.
Chang, Yu-Ming with Greene, Lee. *Sowing Seeds of Faith: The Story of a House Church in*

China. Enumclaw, WA: Pleasant Word, 2004.

Chao, Jonathan, interviewer, and Richard Van Houten, ed. *Wise as Serpents Harmless as Doves: Christians in China Tell Their Story.* Pasadena: William Carey Library, Hong Kong: Chinese Church Research Center, 1988.

Cheng, Nien. *Life and Death in Shanghai.* New York: Grove Press, 1986.

Cheung, Stephen. *Refining Fire.* Community Christian Ministries, 1993.

Ch'i, Hsi-Sheng. *Warlord Politics in China* 1916-1928. Stanford, CA: Stanford University Press, 1976.

Chow, Ching-li. *Journey in Tears: Memory of a Girlhood in China.* McGraw Hill, Inc., English translation, 1978.

Franck, Harry A. *Wandering in Northern China.* New York: Grosset & Dunlap Publishers, 1923.

Fry, Varian. *War in China: America's Role in the Far East.* Reprint ed. Arno Press Inc., 1970. Original title, *American Imperialism: Viewpoints of U.S. Foreign Policy, 1898-1941.* Arno Press and *The New York Times.*

Gillan, Donald G. *Warlord: Yen Hsi-shan in Shansi Province 1911-1949.* Princeton, NJ: Princeton University Press, 1967.

Grun, Bernard. *The Timetables of History: A Horizontal Linkage of People and Events* (based upon Werner Stein's *Kulturfahrplan*) New York: Simon & Schuster, Inc. First Touchstone Edition, 1982.

Hinton, William. *Fanshen: A Documentary of Revolution in a Chinese Village.* Random House, 1968.

Horowitz, David. *Radical Son: A Generational Odyssey.* New York: Simon & Schuster, 1997.

Howard, Dr. and Mrs. *Hudson Taylor's Spiritual Secret.* London: China Inland Mission, 1955.

Hsu, Francis L. K. *Under the Ancestors' Shadow: Kinship, Personality, and Social Mobility in Village China.* Garden City, NY: Anchor Books, Doubleday & Co., 1967.

Johnson, Paul. *Modern Times: The World From the Twenties to the Nineties.* 2nd ed. New York: Harper Collins Publishers, Inc. 1983.

Kartozian, Annie. *God Has a Green Thumb: A veteran missionary recounts her years in China and Taiwan.* Greenwood, IN: OMS International, Inc., 1987.

Kingston, Maxine Hong. *China Men.* New York: Alfred A. Knopf, 1980.

Kingston, Maxine Hong. *The Woman Warrior: Memoirs of a Girlhood Among Ghosts.* New York: Random House, 1975.

Kinnear, Angus I. *Against the Tide: The Story of Watchman Nee.* Ft. Washington, PA: Christian Literature Crusade.

Lawrence, Carl. *The Church in China: How it Survives & Prospers Under Communism.* Minneapolis, MN: Bethany House Publishers, 1985.

Leynse, James P. *Beauty for Ashes.* Westchester, IL: Good News Publishers, 1971.

Li, Lincoln. *The Japanese Army in North China* 1937-1941. Oxford University Press, 1975.

Lord, Bette Bao. *Legacies: A Chinese Mosaic.* New York: Fawcett Columbine, 1991.

Lord, Bette Bao. *Spring Moon.* New York: Avon Books, 1981.

Margolis, M.D., Ph.D., Simeon. *Johns Hopkins Symptoms and Remedies: The Complete Home*

Medical Reference. New York: REBUS, 1995.

Marshall, Catherine. *Something More: In Search of a Deeper Faith.* Carmel, NY: Guideposts Associates, Inc. by arrangement with McGraw-Hill Book Co., Inc., 1974.

McGrath, Alister. *Evangelicalism & the Future of Christianity.* InterVarsity Press. Downers Grove, IL, 1995.

Miller, Basil. *George Müller: Man of Faith and Miracles.* Bethany House Publishers. Minneapolis, MN, 1941.

National Geographic Society. *Journey into China.* Washington, D.C.: National Geographic Society, 1982.

Palmer, R. R. and Colton, Joel. *A History of the Modern World.* New York: Alfred A. Knopf, 1965.

Pollock, J. C. *Hudson Taylor and Maria: Pioneers in China.* McGraw-Hill Book Company, Inc., 1962.

Pye, Lucian W. *Warlord Politics: Conflict and Coalition in the Modernization of Republican China.* Praeger Publishers, 1971.

Rees, Dr. D. Vaughan. *The "Jesus Family" in Communist China.* Chicago: Moody Press, 1956.

Rozman, Gilbert, ed. *The Modernization of China.* New York: The Free Press, a division of MacMillan Publishing Co., 1981.

Sowell, Thomas. *Marxism: Philosophy and Economics.* New York: William Morrow & Co., Inc., 1985.

Spence, Jonathan D. *The Gate of Heavenly Peace: The Chinese and Their Revolution,* 1895-1980. New York: The Viking Press, 1981.

Timperley, H. J., ed. *Japanese Terror in China.* Modern Age Books, Inc., 1938.

Toliver, Ralph. *Gold Fears No Fire: A Family Saga from China.* Overseas Missionary Fellowship, 1986.

Wesley, Luke. *Stories from China: Fried Rice for the Soul.* Atlanta, London, and Hyderabad: Authentic Media, 2005.

Willis, G. Christopher. *I Was Among the Captives.* Hong Kong: Bible Light Publishers, Ltd. No copyright date listed.

Wong, Ming Dao, translated by Arthur Reynolds. *A Stone Made Smooth,* 2nd ed. Hants, Great Britain: Mayflower Christian Books, 1984.

Yue Daiyun and Wakeman, Carolyn. *To the Storm: The Odyssey of a Revolutionary Chinese Woman.* Berkeley and Los Angeles: University of California Press, 1985.

ARTICLES, PAMPHLETS

Hinton, Keith W. "In Singapore, Christians Witness Through Kinship Networks," in *Together: A Journal of WV Internaional, July-Sept.* 1985.

Logan, Florence, *Now It May Be Told* (ten-page pamphlet describing the situation and history of Canaan Home orphanage, written the Summer of 1941) and two letters in *War Letters* published by the Board of Foreign Missions of the Presbyterian Church of the USA, 1941.

Lowrie, J. Walter. "The Tragedy of Paotingfu," from *The Mission Crisis in China*. Philadelphia: Board of Foreign Missions of the Presbyterian Church in the U.S.A.

Putman, John J. "China's Opening Door," *National Geographic*, July 1983.

Rodriguez, Roberto and Gonzales, Patrisia, "Relating history important to Chinese-Americans" in the *El Paso Times*, undated.

The Sidney Daily News, Sidney, Ohio. "Proof of Power of Prayer is Found in Story of Mission Home in China for Orphaned Children," 1952.

U.S. News & World Report, Apr. 30, 2001. "China's Christian Underground."

Endnotes

Forbidden Orphanage Outside the Forbidden City is an account of the life of Laura May Richards based on letters, memoirs, journal entries, interviews, news accounts, historical and sociological research, as well as educated guesswork. It is biography: the events related here actually happened. But it is creative, using the strategies of novel writing. In order to make the storyline flow, I reconstructed scenes and conversations imaginatively—always trying to base this reconstruction on what seemed likely or plausible given the research data and the personalities of the people involved. All answers to prayer in this account are documented in eyewitness reports, either written or spoken. Many answers to prayer had to be left out in order to keep the narrative flowing.

Quotations from primary sources are inserted in the Album Section between chapters in order to present other people's viewpoints and/or additional material that could not be easily fitted into the basic storyline. For the sake of smooth reading flow, I removed the ellipses marking gaps in these quoted portions and then rearranged punctuation. Author's explanatory material is in parentheses.

Detailed endnotes that document sources and explain decisions made during the imaginative reconstruction process can be found at **www.beckypowers.com.**

Chinese Translations

Forbidden Orphanage Outside the Forbidden City has been translated into Chinese and is available in simplified Chinese characters.

- *Faith Journey: Laura Richards and the Orphans of Canaan Home in China* (simplified Chinese) ISBN 978-0-9672134-4-6

More information about this book can be found at **www.beckypowers.com.**

www.ingramcontent.com/pod-product-compliance
Lightning Source LLC
Jackson TN
JSHW020343230126
97041JS00001B/1